REMARKABLE HEAVENLY ENCOUNTERS WITH GOD

Jesus, My Forever Love

To: Lisa, an amazing sister in Christ who did wonderful job in editing my book

Love,
Ying Flynn
1/19/2024

YING FLYNN

Foreword by God the Father, Jesus, Holy Spirit

Printed by BookBaby

Copyright © 2022 by Ying Flynn. All rights reserved.

Jesus, My Forever Love by Ying Flynn

Printed by BookBaby
7905 N. Crescent Blvd.
Pennsauken, NJ 08110
(877) 961-6878
www.bookbaby.com

No part of this publication may be reproduced, distributed, or transmitted in any form or by any means, including photocopying, recording, or other electronic or mechanical methods, without the prior written permission of the publisher, except in the case of brief quotations embodied in critical reviews and certain other noncommercial uses permitted by copyright law.

No patent liability is assumed with respect to the use of the information contained herein. Although every precaution has been taken in the preparation of this book, the publisher and author assume no responsibility for errors or omissions. Neither is any liability assumed for damages resulting from the use of the information contained herein.

All Scripture quotations, unless otherwise noted, are taken from the New King James Version®. Copyright © 1982 by Thomas Nelson. Used by permission. All rights reserved.

Scripture quotations marked AMP are from the Amplified® Bible. Copyright © 2015 by The Lockman Foundation. Used by permission. www.lockman.org.

Scripture quotations marked BSB are from the Holy Bible, Berean Study Bible, BSB. Copyright © 2016, 2018 by Bible Hub. Used by permission. All rights reserved worldwide.

Scripture quotations marked (CEV) are from the Contemporary English Version Copyright © 1991, 1992, 1995 by American Bible Society, Used by Permission.

Scripture quotations marked CSB have been taken from the Christian Standard Bible®, Copyright © 2017 by Holman Bible Publishers. Used by permission. Christian Standard Bible®, and CSB® are federally registered trademarks of Holman Bible Publishers.

Scripture quotations are from the ESV® Bible (The Holy Bible, English Standard Version®), copyright © 2001 by Crossway, a publishing ministry of Good News Publishers. Used by permission. All rights reserved.

Scripture quotations marked (GNT) are from the Good News Translation in Today's English Version—Second Edition Copyright © 1992 by American Bible Society. Used by permission.

Scripture quotations marked KJV are from the King James Version of the Bible. Public Domain.

Scripture quotations taken from the (NASB®) New American Standard Bible®, Copyright © 1960, 1971, 1977, 1995, 2020 by The Lockman Foundation. Used by permission. All rights reserved. www.lockman.org.

Scripture quotations marked NHEB are from the New Heart English Bible. Public Domain.

Scripture quotations marked (NIV) are taken from the Holy Bible, New International Version®, NIV®. Copyright © 1973, 1978, 1984, 2011 by Biblica, Inc.™ Used by permission of Zondervan. All rights reserved worldwide. www.zondervan.com The "NIV" and "New International Version" are trademarks registered in the United States Patent and Trademark Office by Biblica, Inc.™

Scripture quotations marked NLT are taken from the *Holy Bible*, New Living Translation. Copyright © 1996, 2004, 2015 by Tyndale House Foundation. Used by permission of Tyndale House Publishers, Inc., Carol Stream, Illinois 60188. All rights reserved.

Scripture quotations marked TPT are from The Passion Translation®. Copyright © 2017, 2018, 2020 by Passion & Fire Ministries, Inc. Used by permission. All rights reserved. ThePassionTranslation.com.

Scripture quotations marked TPT are from The Passion Translation®, *Genesis: Firstfruits*. Copyright © 2019 by Passion & Fire Ministries, Inc. Used by permission. All rights reserved. ThePassionTranslation.com.

Book cover painting artist: Ying Flynn
Book interior figure illustrator: Ying Flynn
Author website: yingflynn.com

ISBN: 978-1-66786-404-4
eISBN: 978-1-66786-405-1

Library of Congress Control Number: 2022916102

Printed in the United States of America

CONTENTS

Author's Note xv
Dedication xvii
Foreword by God the Father xviii
Foreword by the Holy Spirit xx
Foreword by Jesus Christ xxii
Introduction xxiv

Part One: Tragic Childhood and Rebellious Adulthood 1

My Earthly Father 3
The Chinese Cultural Revolution 3
Rebelling Against Authorities 7
My First Love 8
Banana 8
My Biggest Regret 9
Another Precious Young Man 11

Part Two: Spiritual Exploration 13

Depression and Suicide 15
Seeking Spiritual Help and Witchcraft 16
An Unfamiliar Voice 21
"Jesus, Come Down!" 22
A Girl from the Indonesian Church 23
God Is the Greatest Physician 28

Part Three: The Enemy of God 33

Who Is God? 35
Relationships within the Trinity 38
Lucifer 42
Demons and the Fallen Angels 47
Giants—Nephilim 49
Pre-Adamic Civilization 50
Lucifer Hijacked What Belonged to God 53
Satan Regained the Earth from Adam 55
What Makes Jesus the Only Savior? 56
Understand Our Enemy 58
Hell Is Real! 59
Jeffrey Epstein in Hell 61
John Lennon in Hell 62
How Do Demons Operate? 63
Deliverance—Casting out Demons from My Body 72
Encountering a Real Demon 74
Understand Spirit, Soul, Body, and Flesh 76
Rats and Garbage 84
Discerning the Voice of Demons 88
Understand the Power of Humans over Demons 97
Humans Were Created Higher Than Angels 98
Declaration of Who I Am 100
File Lawsuits Against Satan 108
Team Up with the Hosts of Heaven 116
What Makes Satan Fear the Most? 121
James Bond 127

Part Four: Unique Journey with Jesus Christ 133

Encountering Jesus and Falling in Love 135
Our Meeting Places 144
Dancing inside the Sun 162
Autumn Poem for Jesus 163
No Woman Can Get Pregnant by Reading a Book 167
White Eagle, Birthday Cake, and Flowers 169
Jesus Gave Me a New Name 175
Make Love to Me! 179
Jesus in My Dining Room 181
Satan Often Uses Christians to Do His Biddings 183
"Hold My Back!" 189
Uncovering His Feet 191
My Dating Song with Jesus—"Draw from My Well" 193
He Is a Jealous God 196
Jealousy Is as Cruel as the Grave! 200
Kiss God and Let Him Kiss Me 204
He Kissed the "Breath of Life" in Me 207
He Asked Me and I Said Yes 209
Will You Marry Me? 212
Poem to Jesus on Valentine's Day and His Gift to Me 217
My Birthday Gifts from God 221
"Our Wedding Bed Has Gone Cold!" 222
He Is Not a Fire Hydrant 227
"I Died for You Personally!" 228
He Is a Warrior God 230
The Scariest Scripture—"Only a Few Ever Find It" 234

Our Performance Is Measured by Love ... 236
I Will Vomit You out of My Mouth ... 240
Christians Stab Other Christians ... 242
Jesus Is My Cardiac Surgeon ... 245
Women Are Special to God ... 251

Part Five: Meeting My Heavenly Father ... 257

To His Throne Room ... 259
Daddy's Garden ... 260
Father's Library ... 264
He Rocked Me Like a Baby ... 265
Daddy Carried Me on His Wings ... 267
Dancing with Butterflies ... 269
Swimming with Fish in My Father's Lake ... 270
Father's Character and Appearance ... 271
Father Cried ... 274
He Is a Longsuffering God ... 279
Daddy Taught Me How to Overcome ... 281
To His Throne Room Again ... 286
A Taste of His Glory ... 288
A Dozen Handkerchiefs ... 289
My Poetry to the Father ... 289
Experiencing His Ocean of Love Tangibly ... 305
Dancing in the Heart of the Father ... 307
The Father Came to My House ... 308
My Christmas Gifts from God ... 308
"This Thunder and Lightning Are for You!" ... 310
Humility Is a Weapon ... 312

The Worst Enemy Is "Self" 315
No More Drill Sergeant! 316

Part Six: Holy Spirit—My Dance Partner 319

Meeting the Holy Spirit in Person 321
My Interpretation of the Holy Spirit 322
He Is My Mother, Father, Friend, and God 323
There Is Only One Spirit in Us—the Holy Spirit 327
"My Hidden Hero"—A Poem to the Holy Spirit 328
The Holy Spirit Is Exceptionally Handsome 333
His Dance Is Better Than the Blackpool Champions 333
Figure Skating with the Holy Spirit 335
My Poetry to the Holy Spirit 336
Takes Two to Dance, Takes Two to Play Piano Duet 342
The Holy Spirit Is Hilarious! 344
"I Like Your Hair Down" 345
He Talks to Me in Subtle Voice or Dreams 346
Parrot Birds on My Front Yard's Tree 349
Vengeance Is Mine, I Will Repay 350
The Holy Spirit Takes Ownership of a Human Body 353
My Mishpachah 357

Part Seven: My Four Babies in Heaven 359

Jesus Kept My Babies 361
Naming My Babies 362

Part Eight: Spiritual Hygiene 365

Soul Cleansing 367
Removing Satanic Slimes with Blood and Fire 371
Evicting Demons from My House 372

Part Nine: Persecution Is Coming, Be Prepared! 375

God Is Preparing an Army of Martyrs 377
My Allegiance to Be His Martyr 386
Stay in My Goshen 389
Message from Jesus to the Readers 395
Acceptance Prayer 396
Afterword 397
Notes 398

God Said to Me:

"I have called and chosen you to do My Kingdom work.
But your highest calling is to be the lover of Jesus Christ."
Always dwell in His wedding chamber—
The chamber of divine love,
The chamber of intimacy,
The chamber of oneness,
The chamber of King's heart—
"The Holy of Holies" (Exodus 26:33),
Both now and forever!

Help me and hold me, for I am lovesick!
I am longing for more—
yet how could I take more?
His left hand cradles my head
while his right hand holds me close.
I am at rest in this love.

—Song of Songs 2:5–6 TPT

Author's Note

This book is not fiction; rather a real story of my life and a symphony of my heart. It is a unique love story between Jesus and me. Each word is written with my tears—tears from sorrow to joy, from mourning to dancing. It is a living testimony of God's love, grace, and mercy. For without Him, *I am nothing!*

I was born in Beijing, China. Beginning at age six, I suffered some tremendous tragic events during the Chinese Cultural Revolution. My childhood traumas deeply affected my adulthood, causing me to suffer some excruciating pains and agonies. At the lowest point of my life, while on the verge of ending my life, God saved me! He stopped me from going down to hell. In 2014, I accepted Jesus Christ as Lord and Savior.

Since then, the Holy Spirit has been taking me to visit God the Father and Jesus Christ in heavenly places. I have walked with the Father in His gorgeous garden and danced with Jesus in many celestial places, such as inside the sun or on the ocean's surface. I also have fellowshipped with the Holy Spirit on planetary stars and galaxies. Frequently, I fly in cosmic spaces on the wings of the Father and Jesus (yes, they have wings). These encounters are *spectacular* and *unforgettable!*

During the past eight years of knowing God, my life has transformed miraculously. I have fallen madly in love with Jesus Christ. He has become the Lover of my soul, my eternal Husband, and *forever Love!* Our divine love story literally brings the *Song of Solomon* alive. This book is not written with ink, but with liquid words—my heartfelt tears because I cannot withhold my deep emotion but pour it out to express my profound gratitude for God's love.

O Lord my God,
I cried out to You, and You healed me.
O Lord, You brought my soul up from the grave;
You have kept me alive, that I should not go down to the pit [hell].
Sing praise to the Lord, . . .
For His anger is but for a moment, His favor is for life;
Weeping may endure for a night,
but joy comes in the morning.

—Psalm 30:2–5

Dedication

To my beloved Father,
Who danced with me and laughed with me,
And held me in His bosom,
During my visits to heaven.

To my eternal Husband—Jesus Christ,
Whom I fell utterly in love with.
He took my heart;
Now I am forever His prisoner of love.

To my beloved Holy Spirit—
My dance Partner.
He dwells in me and gives me strength.
Without Him, I may not be alive today!

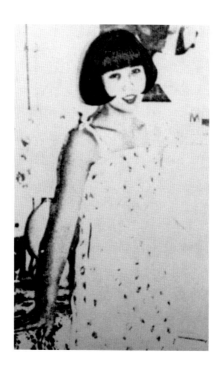

About the Foreword

The following forewords were not from humans but from God. Writing this book was not my idea, but commissioned by the Holy Spirit. On January 30, 2020, I asked each of Them (the Father, the Son, the Holy Spirit) to give me forewords for my book, and They did. They spoke, and I wrote them down.

Foreword by God the Father

My precious child, it is My pleasure to write the foreword for your book. You have been in My heart before the foundation of the world. I have always loved you because you are a child who is after My own heart. How precious you are to Me!

You have come a long way, and I have been watching you grow. You were lost for years, but now you are found; how I had longed for you throughout those years. It broke My heart to see you suffer for such a long time—I wept for you. Now you are back in My arms. Oh, My dearest child, how could I ever let you go? *Never*!

Your daily worship has been touching My heart. Your love for My Son has deeply moved Me. As I see you grow, I cheer for you. Remember our first meeting? We both cried. My tears, years of tears, have been shed for you—My darling child.

I am sorry that you had to go through so many traumas in your life. You were overwhelmed and beaten down by those painful events. I want you to know that they were not from My hands. You were once angry at Me for not saving your marriage. I tell you, My beloved princess, I had nothing to do with your divorce. It was from the enemy.

As I have witnessed your loving relationship with My Son, My heart has rejoiced. I have told you many times that He is deeply in love with you. You must believe Me.

I have enjoyed our moments together—our dances, kisses, hugs, and fellowships. I enjoyed them all, and *I long for more!*

I am God, but I am also a Father. A Father longs to be with His children. For thousands of years, I have gone through hardships Myself. My children often reject Me. They do not want Me. Yet I cannot hate them, for they are My flesh and blood. I cry and mourn for them because many of them have been deceived by My enemy. Satan hates Me. He cannot harm Me, so he hurts My children instead. Every hour and minute, one of My beloved sons or daughters goes to hell. If they could simply accept My Son as their Lord and Savior, they wouldn't have to go there. How can I not be grieved?

As I am sitting on My throne, I cry for My beloved offspring—they are Mine! *They are all Mine!* Who can understand My heart? I am a jealous God; I am jealous over My own created beings. I long for them to choose Me, not My enemy. You are one of the children who actually understand My heart. Many of My sons and daughters only want blessings from Me. But very few truly know how I feel.

Your book will help many lost souls. Those who do not know Me will know Me after reading your stories. I have blessed this book. It will carry My Spirit wherever it goes. I am looking forward to the book being published.

Yours,

Father

Foreword by the Holy Spirit

My sweetest child, I am delighted to give a foreword for your book. It touches My heart to see what you have accomplished. I remember the night you wanted to kill yourself, and I stopped you. Now you know why—life is precious and everlasting if you receive the grace of salvation.

As I am giving you the foreword, I cannot stop My tears. I have watched you suffer from so many traumas in your life. Today, My heart cheers for you.

I have cared for you ever since you were born. Even though you did not know Me, I always knew you. I have never left you alone. You are a child with a pure heart, and I have chosen you to do My work on the earth.

I saw all your tears, and I was crying with you. It broke my heart to see you being attacked by the enemies for so many years. They sought to take your life, but I would not let them because *you are Mine!* You have struggled for a long time, but now you are safe with Me!

I have enjoyed every moment of our time together. We have danced, laughed, and we are still dancing. You are so beautiful to behold. I cannot take My eyes off of you when we dance—let us dance more.

My butterfly, My pink butterfly, *soar with Me* to the end of the heavens. Fly with Me, My child, fly! I have planned a bright future for you. You will accomplish much for My Kingdom and be very fruitful. I will help you to be successful. My beloved daughter, do not ever give up—push through and push forward to the finishing line. *I will run with you!*

This book will save many souls because I have anointed it. Your heartfelt testimonies are genuine and sincere. Your love story with Jesus is profound. It is not an accident that you fell in love with Him because you were already in love with Him before coming to Planet Earth. He has always been yours.

Stay close to Me and listen to My voice. Walk with Me and do not depart from My sight. I have put you on the earth at this time and season for a purpose. You will do My will; I know you will. Beloved child of My heart, *I love you!*

Yours,

Holy Spirit

Foreword by Jesus Christ

My heart is flowing with love and delight as I am giving you the foreword. Oh, My precious darling, My sweetheart, and My spouse, I have enjoyed every moment of being with you. As I see your life-changing and surrendering to Me, My heart leaps with joy.

You have been calling Me your Husband; then let Me care for you and love you. I am a great Lover, and *I am your Lover*. I am always thrilled whenever I see you. I love to hold you, kiss you, and spend time with you. From the beach to the garden, from the mountain to the meadow, from the stars to the end of the cosmos, we have danced, loved, and enjoyed our intimate times together.

Give Me your heart. I want it all! Be in love with Me, and do not stop. I will never leave you nor forsake you. My name is *Faithful*, and I have been faithful to you. Will you be loyal to Me? Will you give me everything? Will you give up all your earthly desires and desire *only Me?*

This book is our love story. It has no ends—it is just the beginning. So many nights, while you were sleeping, I watched over you. How many hours have I sat on the chair in your prayer room and enjoyed your worship? I never want to remove My eyes from you because you are so pleasing. Oh, My beloved, My sweetheart, *I am in love with you!*

My Father is pleased with you because of your devotion to Me. I am looking forward to seeing your book being published. Always remember, this book is not paper and ink; it is a real love story between you and Me.

I yearn for your love just as much as you desire Mine. Cards upon cards, gifts upon gifts, and poems upon poems, I am moved by your affections for Me.

Can you feel My heart? Can you feel My longing for you? Can you see My tears for you? Do you know how much I love you? Oh, My lover, My bride, I am yours—*forever yours*! Do not ever leave Me, and I will never forsake you. We will always be together. Let this book tell our story, for it is a good love story.

Your Lord and Husband,

Jesus

Introduction

This book is written for those who are on the verge of giving up in life. It is for those in deep sorrow and trauma; those who are desperate, helpless, and hopeless; those who are abandoned, rejected, forsaken, and wronged. It is for those in times of grief, depression, and despair; for those who are misjudged and betrayed. It is for those who have been wandering in the endless wilderness and winter storms.

Your heart is bleeding. You are drenched with tears. Your life seems like an eternal winter. Your pain is too intense to bear. Perhaps you just went through a divorce, lost a loved one, lost a job, or were betrayed by friends. Maybe you are facing tremendous hardship and finding no way out. Day and night, immense pain and sorrow encircle your life; you have no strength to move on.

My beloved readers, I know how you feel. *I was there.* If you read my story, you may find light and hope. You may find the desire to live. You may once again find happiness and joyfulness. For this joy is not from humans—not from your mother or father, your wife or husband, your sons or daughters, or friends. It is from the divine Trinity—the Father, the Son (Jesus), and the Holy Spirit.

I am writing to you, my beloved readers, with my tears and heartfelt testimonies. I hope they can touch your heart and soul. My testimonies end with a love story. This love story is about one Person—Jesus Christ, my *forever Love* and *eternal Husband!*

—Ying Flynn

Part One

Tragic Childhood and Rebellious Adulthood

My Earthly Father

I was born in 1960 (Beijing, China). My father was the president of a veterinary university, which was owned by the Chinese military. My mother was the principal of a high school. I have three brothers and a sister—all are older than me.

In December 1949, at the end of the Chinese Civil War, Chiang Kai-Shek, the Chinese military leader and former president of the Republic of China, was defeated by the Chinese Communist Party led by Mao Zedong. Chiang led his army retreat to Taiwan—history refers to as "The Great Retreat."

Chiang's army dashed out of China from the city of Chong Qing. At that time, my father was one of Chiang's high-ranking generals. He was left behind during the chaotic retreat. My father's university was located near Beijing—1153 miles away from Chong Qing—thus, there was no time to run.

Right after Chiang's great retreat, without any choice, my father led his entire military university to the Chinese Communist Party and surrendered.

The Chinese Cultural Revolution

*T*he Chinese Cultural Revolution was a sociopolitical movement, which took place from 1966 to 1976 in the People's Republic of China. It was initiated by Chairman Mao Zedong of the

Chinese Communist Party (CCP). Mao's vision was to promote his own doctrine of Maoism and advocate the idea of communism. The Cultural Revolution was to destroy the concept of capitalism and eliminate anyone who advocated economic prosperity. People who supported China's economic recovery were considered capitalistic infiltrators.

Mao started the Cultural Revolution movement by targeting education systems. He removed principals of universities and high schools, and arrested professors and teachers. He organized students to burn books, destroy universities, abolish academic institutions, and eradicate all religious beliefs except the ideology of communism.

Mao militarized an army of "Red Guards" out of school students, which were actually the organized mobs. These youths acted like terrorists. They arrested, imprisoned, tortured, and persecuted many educators, scholars, intellectuals, and religious believers. The Chinese Cultural Revolution eventually spread into the military, regular citizens, and political leaders. As a result, millions of people were brutally killed.[1] The actual death toll is yet to be uncovered. The Revolution paralyzed the country's political and economic systems, and left a permanent scar on the hearts of the Chinese people.

I was six years old when the Cultural Revolution started (see Figure 1). Both my father and mother were the number one target of this bloody massacre. They were imprisoned and tortured for ten years. My two older brothers and sister were sent to the countryside for hard labor. My nine-year-old brother and I were left alone at home.

Figure 1: Ying at age six.

At age six, I was forced to be the parent of my own parents. My job was to take food and water to them every day to keep them alive. I had to stand on a small stool to reach the stove and cook food for my parents. No one dared to help me. If they did, they would be imprisoned and killed.

The door of my house was guarded by two soldiers daily. Every time I went out, they would ask me where I was going and how long I would be gone.

Three times daily, I would take food to my father, who was kept in a heavily guarded military prison. My nine-year-old brother would bring food to my mother, who was imprisoned in a high school bathroom. The restrooms in China were extremely filthy and smelly back in 1966. They did not have a water-flush system. Most of them were just holes in the ground. To this day, I still cannot believe that they put my mother in that indecent place for so many years.

Very often, as I was on the way sending food for my parents, many children would chase after me, throw stones at me, spit on me, mock me, and call me all kinds of cursing names (see Figure 2).

Figure 2: Children chasing after me and throwing stones.

There were times, at 2:00 a.m., armed soldiers would burst into my house and search. My brother and I would be interrogated. At which time, we could hardly speak because our bodies shook violently by the horrifying terror.

I do not remember how many times I cried or how I even survived. But somehow, I just kept going because my mother said, "If you do not bring food, we will die in prison."

The city where I lived was freezing cold, with heavy snow in the winter. To this day, I do not remember how I washed my clothes at age six or showered since we did not have a shower room and hot water in the house.

For ten long and agonizing years, my identity was defined as the garbage of society. People hated me, no one wanted me, and my parents were the enemies of the country. I really did not know how to live as a normal human being. I could not walk on the street with my head up and be an ordinary child like other kids did. I never had birthday parties, toys, baby dolls, new clothes, kisses, and hugs. The whole country was in the deepest darkness, and so was my childhood.

Rebelling Against Authorities

After Chairman Mao's death in 1976, Chinese reformers dismantled Maoism and ended the Chinese Cultural Revolution. After ten years of imprisonment, my parents were released. At that time, I was sixteen years old. Shortly after, I was accepted as a Fine Arts student by the Art Institute of Ji Lin Province.

For three years, I was trained in classical painting. Although I was gifted academically, I was a rebellious student to the school authority. After being trashed by society for ten years, one could imagine, I had so much anger and hatred in my heart. Any criticism or humiliation could flare up my temper. I refused to be put down by anyone. It was reverse psychology. I thought in my heart that I was defenseless when I was a child, but now no one would *dare to abuse me ever again!*

At age nineteen, I was accepted by the University of Art and Design in Beijing, China. It was extremely difficult to be selected by this university. Out of twenty-seven million people in the Ji Lin Province, only four or five young artists were selected each year.

I studied very hard in college and strived to be the top student. My beloved readers, if you had a childhood like mine, you would have understood my behavior. Years of trauma, pain, rejection, and anger were deeply imprinted in my soul. My heart was bleeding all those years. The best way to cope with my wounded soul was to strive to be the best so that no one could put me down or humiliate me ever again. While studying hard and competing with my classmates, my inner being was crying for comfort. I then leaned on sexual lust to find relief.

Unlike western culture, universities in China strictly forbade students to conduct sexual activities at that time. But I did not care; I was like a wild horse—stubbornly rebelled against the authorities.

My First Love

During my four-year college life, I fell in love with one of my classmates. He was the most kindhearted, gentle, soft-spoken, and brilliant young man. He was tall and *exceptionally handsome*. One of the local fashion magazines selected him as their male model.

Eventually, we were married. But I was not faithful during our twelve years of marriage. The pain in my heart was screaming for comfort and relief. It was crying for a way to ease my severely wounded soul. The love from my husband did help, but not enough. Many people use food, drug, or alcohol to relieve their pains, but I used lustful pleasure to cope with my traumatized inner being.

Banana

Ever since I was a child, I had admired western movie stars. I would cut images from magazines and put them on my bedroom wall. Since China was a communist country, the only movies or magazines with European-looking stars were from other communist countries, such as the Soviet Union, Romania, and Armenia. My mother used to criticize me, "You are a foolish child. You blindly admire the western world. In your mind, even the moon in America is bigger, rounder, and brighter than the moon in China." People used to call me "Banana"—yellow on the outside and white on the inside. But to me, it was just my childhood fantasy.

My Biggest Regret

*I*n 1986, right after graduating from college, I came to America. My childhood dream came true. I was accepted by Ohio University for a Master's Degree in Fine Arts. However, I had no money to pay the university tuition, and I also had to bring my husband to America, which would require lots of money.

Therefore, I took a temporary leave from the university and went to New York City to make money. I worked two jobs during that time. In the daytime, I worked as a pantry girl in a Jewish restaurant called Lox Around the Clock, making four dollars per hour. In the evening, I worked as an artist for a company that produced hand-painted garments. They paid me two dollars per hour. However, I needed at least six thousand dollars for my tuition and the payment for my husband's visa. The money I made from these two jobs was not even close to meeting my goal.

Then I did something foolish and extreme. A friend told me about working in a Chinese nightclub. He said I could make much more money by just sitting next to the male customers or dancing with them. With my impatient heart, I believed him because I was eager to meet my money goal.

The nightclub was a turning point in my life. I had gone too far and got myself deep into the darkness. The Chinese nightclub involved prostitution, and most of the customers were drug dealers, gang members, or unfaithful husbands.

Eventually, I did make enough money to pay my tuition and get my husband to America. However, at that point, I had multiple boyfriends and went deeper into sexual immorality and adultery. I had no interest in my own husband.

For years, I could not forgive myself. Now, thinking back, even if I had millions of dollars, I could not exchange the love and kindness that my husband gave me. He put up with my unfaithfulness for many years and refused to give up on me. He was too kind, and I was too damaged. He was too innocent, and I was too immoral. Eventually, after twelve years of marriage, our marriage ended.

To this day, my biggest regret is that I totally ruined my beloved husband's life. He suffered so much because of my unfaithfulness. He waited for me to turn back to him, but I never did. I am *so sorry* for what I had done. He was my first love, and I still *love him dearly*!

After losing my husband, I walked into a brutal winter storm. The divorce ripped open my childhood scars. The sharp pain was like vinegar pouring onto my open wounds—extremely painful. Once again, life threw me back to the six-year-old little girl. My life became so cold and frozen. It was covered with agony and sorrow. I was lonely, miserable, and devastated. It was an *exceedingly unbearable time!*

My heart was bleeding profusely. I felt hopeless and desperate. Eventually, I fell into a deep depression. All my childhood traumas resurfaced. Frequently, I thought about killing myself because the pain was too intense to bear!

I would say to myself, "Ying, how foolish you are! Where in the world will you ever find a husband like that? He was a wonderful man, and you lost him!" I utterly regretted it. *I wanted my husband back,* but it was too late.

I had no energy to work in those days. So I took a student loan and got into graduate school at the California State University of Long Beach. I studied for three years and earned a Master of Science degree in Management Information Systems.

Another Precious Young Man

While I was mourning over my failed marriage, I met a precious young man from Minnesota. Even though he was already settled in Southern California, his heart was still in the Midwest. His heritage was English, Irish, German, and Welsh. His character was very similar to my ex-husband. He was an extremely gentle, intellectual, loving, and polite gentleman. His heart was like a ten-year-old boy—exceptionally innocent.

He was like a summer rain in my desert life and a warm breeze in my bitter winter storm. I found myself in love and being loved again. The six-year-old child, who lived inside of me, was quiet and content. I found comfort and love from this precious young man. We then were married after three years of dating.

The year 2000 was my *Jubilee* year, almost as if I had won the lottery. Five major things happened in my life: I graduated from the California State University of Long Beach, received my U.S. citizenship, found my first job in the computer field, got married, and my husband bought me a brand-new house in Orange County, California.

However, our marriage was just like a temporary bandage to my bleeding heart and wounded soul. My husband's love, tenderness, caring, kisses, hugs, and lovemaking were like painkillers and anesthesia for my hidden pain and agony.

Out of our selfishness, we did not want children; instead, we spent lots of money and time traveling around the world. We both had perfect jobs, high incomes, and lived a comfortable life. On the surface, we were happy, content, and lacking nothing. Yet, deep inside, we both were struggling with wounds in our souls. My husband had an unhappy childhood, and mine was even worse. This was one of the reasons that we bonded so quickly because we understood each other's pain. We called ourselves "playmates"—we were like two grown-up-ten-year-old children leaning on each other.

After work, he would spend most of his time playing computer games. He used games to alleviate his pain. I was left alone at night, watching TV to pass the time. My heart became lonesome and craved attention. Slowly, the little child inside of me started to cry for love. Once again, I fell into the same pattern in coping with my pain—I committed sexual immorality and adultery.

In the last few years of our marriage, I did not pay much attention to him, nor did I love him enough. Rarely did I ever cook or even care for him. My mind was somewhere else. Even though we lived under the same roof, our hearts fell apart. After eleven years of marriage, our love ended. He walked away from home and never came back.

People like my husband and I are called "damaged goods." Our lives were ruined at a very young age. We both carried childhood trauma and pain throughout our adulthood. So often, we lost interest in living. We cried for help while enduring hopelessness, helplessness, and anguish. We spent thousands of dollars on psychological counseling, but nothing would heal the root damages in our souls. No one could truly understand our agony. I now know that only God—*the Greatest Physician*—can help.

Part Two

Spiritual Exploration

Depression and Suicide

Right after my husband left me, I fell into a severe depression. Again, my heart was bleeding profusely. This time was much worse than my first divorce. I could hardly get up, walk, eat, and function. I cried a lot, even at work. Eventually, I lost my job because of this. I was sucked into a black hole—there was no light, no hope, no future, and no will to live. Once again, life took me back to the six-year-old girl. I felt rejected, abandoned, and forsaken.

My doctor put me on the highest dosage of antidepressants to prevent me from killing myself. Even though the medication helped a little, the desire to end my life was overwhelming. I thought about many ways of killing myself. In those days, death was my only desire and relief because the pain was so *excruciating*. The following Psalm describes precisely how I felt:

> *My heart is severely pained within me, and the terrors of death have fallen upon me. Fearfulness and trembling have come upon me, and horror has overwhelmed me. So I said, "Oh, that I had wings like a dove! I would fly away and be at rest. Indeed, I would wander far off, and remain in the wilderness. I would hasten my escape from the windy storm and tempest."*
>
> —Psalm 55:4–8

Seeking Spiritual Help and Witchcraft

My husband left me in 2010. Afterward, I barely stayed alive for four long and agonizing years—my inner being kept screaming for help. I was suffocating and crying for oxygen, as though I was in a deep ocean. The merciless waves of heartache were tossing and crashing me around. I felt like I was drowning and struggling to grasp for air, but the raging waves kept sucking me into the deep again. There was *endless* pain (see Figure 3).

Figure 3: Excruciating pain. Please help!

Beloved readers, I do not know how to express myself. The only way to describe my life in those years was a *living hell*. My life was drenched with tears. I cried to the sky, yet the sky was silent. I cried to the earth, yet the earth did not respond. I cried to humans, yet no one understood my broken heart. I was hopeless and helpless. In my desperation, I started exploring spiritual help. The first thing I tried was witchcraft.

One afternoon, I walked into a palm reading place in Tustin, California. The woman placed me in the front room and asked me to give her something with metal on it. I gave her my car key and she held it in her hand. Then, she started to describe who I was in my past life.

She told me that I had a very old soul. I had been reincarnated more than ninety-eight times. In most of my life terms, I was a man; in only a few of my life terms, I was a woman. I almost reached enlightenment in some of my life terms, but I fell short. When that happened, I had to go back to the cycle of reincarnation again—to be refined for enlightenment. She started to describe some of my life terms:

A Buddhist Monk

"Once, you were a young boy in Tibet. At age three, your parents sent you to a Buddhist monastery to be a monk. You were a very smart and dedicated monk. Throughout years of learning and discipline, at age twenty-one, you were almost close to enlightenment. This caused other Buddhist monks to be jealous of you. One day, a child from the local village got sick. His parents brought him to you, and you prayed for the child for healing. However, a few days later, the child died.

"This incident troubled you greatly. You started doubting yourself and your ability. Other monks mocked you and imposed shame on you. Eventually, you could not endure such humiliation and commit suicide. You refused to eat food and starved yourself to death. You were that close to enlightenment, but ended your chance by killing yourself. Then your soul went back to the cycle of reincarnation again."

A Japanese Geisha

"One of your life terms was a beautiful Japanese geisha. Many prestigious landlords, rich business owners, and lawyers requested you. You saved lots of money, but in the end, you died of loneliness at age eighty-three."

The woman gave me a crystal. She said, "I have half of the crystal and you keep the other half. Tonight at 9:00 p.m., hold the crystal and confess all the bad things you have ever done. I will be praying for you at the same time. Then, when you come next time, I will tell you more about your past lives and who you were."

I asked, "Where did you get all this information about me? Who is telling you this?"

She said, "I work with some spirits in the heavenly realms. They talk to me all the time about my clients. They are my friends."

"Who are these spirits? How do they know me?" I asked.

She replied, "They know everything about you—all your life terms and everything you have ever done." Beloved readers, I was ignorant at that time, but I now know those spirits are demons.

My next appointment with her was something I had never imagined. I brought back the half crystal. She took me into an inner room. There was an altar there, which displayed pictures of deities from different religions throughout the world. Interesting enough, Jesus Christ was also one of them. She took my half of the crystal and went into another room. In about twenty minutes, she came back with a grave face. She looked as though she was shocked about who I was in my past life.

She said, "The first time I saw you, I knew that you were not an ordinary person. What I am about to tell you will shock you. But if you cannot handle it, I will not say so."

My face turned pale, and my body started to tremble. I said, "Wow, it is that bad? What have I done in my past life? Tell me; I want to know!"

She said, "My source, those spirits, told me that you were once Hitler's favorite officer. You were his right-hand SS officer. He loved you like a son. You were extremely handsome, tall, with blond hair and blue eyes. You did lots of evil things. You and other SS officers raped many Jewish women. After raping them, you and other officers would throw them into trenches. One day, you fell in love with a beautiful German woman—from whom your ex-husband was reincarnated. At a party, you were flirting with her, but the woman slapped your face and told you to go away. Hitler and other guests laughed at you. Somehow, you took it as a huge humiliation. You then asked Hitler to send you to the frontline. There, you were killed."

At this point, my body started to shiver. I was shocked by what I heard. I trusted what she said wholeheartedly. The reason I trusted her so quickly was because I always had a puzzling attraction to Hitler's army. They were highly disciplined and organized. I called them the evil genius. I once told my husband about it, and he said, "You should not tell anyone about this. People will be offended by your strange attraction to evil."

I cried and asked her what could be done to change my life. She said, "It can be done, but we need to work on it for months. It will cost you fifty thousand dollars. This money will guarantee to change you at the DNA level. It also includes getting your husband back and restoring your marriage." At that moment, I was so eager for a change and wanted my husband back, so I gave her a down payment of five hundred dollars.

Reiki and Hypnosis

After thinking about it overnight, I decided not to pursue the deal for DNA change. I did not have that much money anyway. I then checked out a local Hypno-Reiki therapy service; they charged much less. So, the next day, I canceled the five-hundred-dollar check and never went back to that woman again.

In searching online, I found a woman who specialized in Reiki and hypnotic healings. Her price was one hundred dollars per hour. When I arrived at her house, I saw many paintings on the walls. Strangely enough, these paintings were about alien-looking creatures. Their faces were pale gray, like the ghosts in Hollywood movies. She told me that she had been taken to an alien spaceship many times. Sometimes, the aliens would visit her house at night and talk to her. I was wondering who those aliens were. I didn't know it then, but I know it now—they were demons.

For every hypnotic session, she would put me on a reclining chair and have my eyes closed. She would say things that led me into a deep trance state. She would ask me to imagine a timeline—see myself at different ages and events within the timeline. We went through my childhood for a few sessions. My story was so touching; even this woman would cry. Not until later did I come to understand that Reiki and hypnosis are also witchcraft.

This woman also practiced casting out demons. However, those demonic entities would go out from my right foot and immediately come back through my left foot. They would not go away. After five to six sessions, I experienced no results; I stopped going to her.

Witchcraft did not work for me. I then moved on to explore different religions. I attended a Buddhist chanting group. I visited a Buddhist temple and read books about Buddhism. I studied the Bhagavad Gita of Hinduism. I was also led by my chiropractor to Sufism. I even read part of the Quran. I was dying for help and searching for meanings of life all over the place. However, after pursuing all these religions and seeking spiritual help, my life stayed the same. My depression got even worse.

One day, a coworker took me to a Christian church. The topic of that day's sermon was "Seven Ways of Self-Destruction." Throughout the sermon, I cried so hard and could not stop weeping. Tears were flowing out of me uncontrollably. I could not understand why I was reacting with such sadness. Obviously, the sermon touched my heart, as if God was speaking directly to me. Yet, I did not know Him at that time. Unfortunately, that friend went back to Arizona, and I did not have the courage to go back to that church by myself.

From 2010 to 2014, I was on the verge of dying because of my severe depression. At that time, I was taking the highest dosage of antidepressants, yet it could not stop me from being suicidal. One night, I was lying on the sofa and planning to end my life; a strange thing happened.

An Unfamiliar Voice

As I was about to end my life that night, an unfamiliar voice spoke to me from the back of my head, "If you kill yourself tonight, you will go to hell." I said, "Who are you? What do you mean I will go to hell? Where is hell?"

I never knew the concept of hell. I then jumped out of the sofa and checked on YouTube about hell. To my astonishment, there were so many videos and testimonies about hell. Hell is a lake of fire—a place of intense torment. It was originally prepared for Satan, the fallen angels, and demons. Later, it was enlarged to hold humans who did not receive Jesus Christ as their Lord and Savior. So many people are burning in hellfire. They are suffering all kinds of gruesome and spine-chilling tortures by the demons. People are screaming and struggling to get out of there, but there is *no way out*.

There was one testimony that stood out from other YouTube videos. It was about a young Korean artist who was taken to hell by Jesus Christ in 2009. The Lord told her to draw what she witnessed so that the world might know how dreadful hell is.

My beloved readers, I strongly suggest you watch the videos (the paintings of hell) from this young artist. Her name is Me Kyeoung Lee. After that, you decide where you would like to spend your eternity—heaven or hell.

I then screamed with sheer anguish to that unfamiliar voice, "I do not want to go to hell. But I cannot live either! What am I going to do? Can't you see that I am in pain? What am I going to do? Who are you, by the way?"

The unfamiliar voice was silent. It was a man's voice. He kept very quiet and did not say anything. I was terrified by what I saw about hell. That night, I did not end my life. Afterward, I kept wondering about that voice—why did he care about me? Now I know the voice was the Holy Spirit.

"Jesus, Come Down!"

For about three months after my husband left, he did answer some of my calls, but had no desire to discuss anything with me in person. I did not know what to do. One day, he agreed to come home and talk to me. That night, before his arrival, I was so *nervous*—my body was shaking. Although I missed him *terribly*, I was also afraid of what he would say to me. I did not want him to divorce me.

At that moment, I suddenly remembered something that a friend told me, "When you are in fear or trouble, just call out, 'Jesus, come down! Jesus, come down!'" Even though I did not really believe what she said, out of my *desperation*, I said, "Jesus, come down! Jesus, come down! I am afraid. I long to see my husband, but I do not want him to divorce me. Oh, Jesus, please come down and help me!"

Beloved readers, *you must believe me!* Immediately, Jesus came. I could literally see Him standing in front of me. I was *totally shocked* and said to myself, "Oh, my God! You are real, Jesus. You actually come for me." He did not say anything and just stood in the family room (next to the sofa) where we were about to sit. His face was so peaceful and loving. I could feel the divine holiness and peace in the room.

Then my husband arrived. Throughout our conversation, I carried a peaceful manner toward him. All my anger went away. I was sure that my husband was puzzled—why my tone was so kind and forgiving. This happened only because Jesus was standing next to me throughout the two hours conversation.

Beloved readers, that was my first encounter with Jesus. At that time, I was not a Christian. I really did not know Him. I heard about His name but did not know that He was my Creator and God. I learned that night—*Jesus is real!* In His presence, love literally changed my behavior. All my frustration and anguish faded away because of His presence.

A Girl from the Indonesian Church

One night in January 2014, I was just about to go to bed. Suddenly, I heard the unfamiliar voice again. He told me to attend a healing service (at a church in Anaheim, California) for my depression. Since I was desperate for healing, I would do whatever I could; thus, I heeded the voice. The next night, I arrived at the miracle-healing event, hosted by prophetess Joan Hunter at Canyon Christian Center in Anaheim. The church was packed with sick people as well as the regular congregation. I saw people in wheelchairs lined up.

I was seated in the second row from the stage. Another young woman was placed next to me by the church usher. Strangely enough, all the attendees were church members or their families, except the two of us. During the service, Joan Hunter started calling for different kinds of sick people:

"People who have cancer, diabetes, arthritis come to the front. People who are in the wheelchairs come forward."

I waited for two hours, but she never called the depressed people to come forward. I was murmuring with frustration. The girl next to me asked, "What are you here for?" I told her, "I am hoping my depression gets healed." She then said, "Come to my church for healing and deliverance. My pastor will do it for you. There are so many miracles that have happened in my church."

Her name is Melisa, who came from Indonesia. She was about twenty-two years old, with a gentle and lovely appearance. She then said to me, "Since you are already here, why don't you ask Joan Hunter's team for the baptism of the Holy Spirit?" I asked, "What is the Holy Spirit?" She said, "It is hard to explain now. I will tell you later. For now, just go to the front and ask for the baptism of the Holy Spirit." Little did she know that I had not even accepted Jesus Christ as my Lord and Savior yet. How in the world would I know who the Holy Spirit was?

An older lady from Joan Hunter's ministry laid her hand on my head and said, "I will pray for you; open up your mouth like a child learning ABCs. You may start to speak a new language, an unknown tongue—a supernatural language from the Holy Spirit. Don't be afraid." However, I was a little afraid. I looked back at Melisa; she nodded her head and encouraged me. At that moment, many men and women from the church surrounded me, laid their hands on my shoulders, and spoke in unknown tongues. My body was overwhelmed and trembling by the intense prayers from these people. However, this supernatural language did not come out of my mouth. When I got home that night, I asked the Holy Spirit to give me this unknown tongue. I opened my mouth, forced myself to speak, "Aa, bla, kuka, mina, baa . . ." but it did not come out. I was frustrated.

Two weeks later, on February 2, 2014, I arrived at JKI Hosana Miracle Center—the Indonesian church that Melisa told me about. Since I did not speak Indonesian, I could not understand their sermon. After taking communion, when the congregation sang worship songs, I just followed the music without lyrics because they were all in Indonesian.

Suddenly, a force hit me (the anointing from the Holy Spirit), and I started singing in the unknown tongue. At the same moment, my depression was instantaneously healed. The joy in my heart flowed like a flood, bursting out of my soul. I did not tell anyone and just ran to my car. This unknown tongue was uncontrollable, speaking like an automaton. It uttered non-stop while I was driving. After an hour, I stopped by the Target store. When I paid the cashier, instead of English, the supernatural language came out. This unknown tongue overtook my English automatically.

For more than one month, day and night, I could not stop speaking in this unknown tongue, nor did I understand the language. I did not know who was talking through me at that time. I just knew it was not me. For many nights, I could not stop speaking. Sometimes, I even sang in this language. Out of my frustration, I said, "I am tired. I have to sleep. I have to go to work tomorrow. I am going to count one, two, three, and at the count of three, you must stop." But it did not stop.

By profession, I was a director in the computer software field for a fortune-one-hundred company. On many occasions, when I answered phone calls or hosted meetings, the supernatural language would come out. Some of my employees asked, "What did you just say? We could not understand." I replied, "Never mind. Nothing important."

> *On the day Pentecost was being fulfilled, all the disciples were gathered in one place. Suddenly they heard the sound of a violent blast of wind rushing into the house from out of the heavenly realm. The roar of the wind was so overpowering it was all anyone could bear! Then all at once a pillar of fire appeared before their eyes. It separated into tongues of fire that engulfed each one of them. They were all filled and equipped with the Holy Spirit and were inspired to speak in tongues—empowered by the Spirit to speak in [unknown] languages they had never learned!*
>
> —Acts 2:1–4 TPT

Whenever I opened my mouth and spoke in this unknown language, the first word was always "Abba." I called one of the church elders and asked him about this supernatural language. I wanted to know who was speaking through me, and what does "Abba" mean? He said, "It is the Holy Spirit speaking through you to God the Father. Abba means Abba Father—God the Father (see Romans 8:15). You are speaking to your Father in heaven."

> *You have not received a spirit of slavery leading again to fear [of God's judgment], but you have received the Spirit of adoption as sons [the Spirit producing sonship] by which we [joyfully] cry, "Abba! Father!"*
>
> —Romans 8:15 AMP

Beloved readers, I am from China. The Chinese people do not call father "Abba," but "Baba." In addition, at that time, I did not know that I had a Father in heaven. I barely knew who Jesus was; how could I know God the Father. I was wondering if I have a Father in heaven, what about my earthly father?

Later, I learned the knowledge of speaking in tongues (see Romans 8:26). This unknown language is a gift from the Holy Spirit. It is a divine language given by God when we are baptized in the Holy Spirit. Jesus revealed to many prophets the secret of speaking in tongues. This supernatural language is a powerful weapon to battle against our enemies. When we speak in tongues, it sends nuclear missiles to Satan's domain. It releases shock waves to damage his properties in the second heaven. Satan hates us speaking in tongues because he does not understand it—only God understands what we are saying.

> *The Holy Spirit helps us in our weakness. For example, we don't know what God wants us to pray for. But the Holy Spirit prays for us with groanings [the unknown tongues] that cannot be expressed in words. And the Father who*

> *knows all hearts knows what the Spirit is saying, for the Spirit pleads for us believers in harmony with God's own will.*
>
> —Romans 8:26–27 NLT

At the very moment of becoming a born-again Christian (see John 3:3), the blood of Jesus literally washed away all my sins. My spirit became alive (it was dead before). My DNA was changed forever, and I became *a new creation* (see 2 Corinthians 5:17). At which time, a layer of my soul was seated with Jesus Christ in heaven, and the Holy Spirit deposited a layer of Himself into my soul. The Holy Spirit is a layered Being—with unlimited layers.

> *Jesus answered and said to him, "Most assuredly, I say to you, unless one is born again, he cannot see the kingdom of God."*
>
> —John 3:3

> *If anyone is in Christ, he is a new creation; old things have passed away; behold, all things have become new.*
>
> —2 Corinthians 5:17

A few weeks later, I visited my doctor and told him that God had healed my depression. All my symptoms were completely gone. I told him that I had thrown away my ninety-day supply of antidepressants. He said to me: "I don't believe you. *It is impossible!* People like you, with severe depression, cannot stop the medication suddenly. It has to be gradually reducing the drug dosages over many months. Besides, I was going to give you another kind of antidepressant drug on top of what you are taking to control your suicidal thoughts. How can you say you are healed? *You are not healed!* You need to continue the medication."

My doctor would not believe the miracle that God had performed on me. I did not bother to convince him because it was impossible for him to believe.

Beloved readers, please hear me. I am telling you the truth! If anyone out there suffers from depression, the best way to get rid of it is to run to Jesus. *I am living proof of it.*

God Is the Greatest Physician

> *Jesus went about all Galilee, . . . healing all kinds of sickness and all kinds of disease among the people. Then His fame went throughout all Syria; and they brought to Him all sick people who were afflicted with various diseases and torments, and those who were demon-possessed, epileptics, and paralytics; and He healed them.*
>
> —Matthew 4:23–24

As I began to heal, my life started changing. The process was inspired by some of the most amazing godly men and women. One of them is Wendy Alec. She is a seer and a prophetess who has been taken to heaven by the Holy Spirit many times. In heaven, she had a series of extraordinary encounters with God the Father. She met Him in His throne room, chamber, and garden. Wendy went through the process of healing by the Father Himself, because she was wounded by some of the fiercest trials and tribulations.

Beloved child of God, your Father in heaven longs to see you and hold you in His arms. He cries for you when you suffer persecution. He knows how you feel because He sent His Son, Jesus, to save you. He knows when your heart is broken. He feels your pain and sorrow. He is with you and rocking you in His arms when you go through depression, rejection, abandonment, and sickness.

Millions and millions of people are facing severe tribulations and intense trials in their lives, such as terminal illness, divorce, demonic attacks, etc. Most of the time, they blame these misfortunes on God. However, in reality, those attacks are from Satan. The devil's only goal is to kill, steal, and destroy.

According to the Centers for Disease Control and Prevention (CDC), using 2020's data as an example: more than twelve million Americans seriously thought about killing themselves, and 45,979 people actually committed suicide—which is equivalent to one death every eleven minutes in the United States of America.[1]

Our God has the deepest compassion and sympathy toward His children. He understands that some of His sons and daughters use alcohol, drugs, pornography, and sexual lust to cope with their inner pains and unhealed wounds. He does not punish us by these symptoms because He knows the root cause is demonic bondage. God the Father did not send His Son (Jesus) to condemn us (see John 3:17), but to bind up our broken hearts and heal all who are in need of a physician.

God did not send His Son into the world to condemn the world, but that the world through Him might be saved.

—John 3:17

The Holy Spirit was sent to us as a Comforter and Helper, and the Father Himself is the Comfort of all. He is the *greatest Physician*. He will never be offended by our symptoms; rather, He has infinite mercy to heal our wounded souls.

Once, at my most downhearted time—crying sorrowfully, God gave me a vision: I saw myself on a hospital bed with an IV tube in my arm. Jesus was sitting next to the bed and holding my hands with sheer tender love (see Figure 4). I was there for about a week. Daily, I saw Jesus as my Doctor, treating the deep cuts and bruises in my soul. This place was a spiritual hospital. God is humorous. He let me know that I would be okay in His hospital because Doctor Jesus is my Physician.

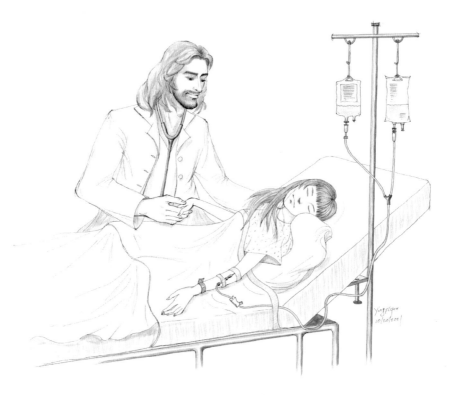

Figure 4: Ying at Jesus' hospital.

The Spirit of the Lord God is upon Me, because the Lord has anointed Me to preach good tidings to the poor; He has sent Me to heal the brokenhearted, to proclaim liberty to the captives, and the opening of the prison to those who are bound; . . . to comfort all who mourn, . . . to give the beauty for ashes, the oil of joy for mourning, the garment of praise for the spirit of heaviness.

—Isaiah 61:1–3

Beloved child of God, the above scripture *"Me"* refers to Jesus. He was sent by the Father to heal your broken heart. He came to set you free from demonic bondage. He came to comfort you when you mourn.

He came to give you beauty for ashes. He is your Redeemer, your shield, and protection. He is your refuge and stronghold (see Psalm 18:2). He is greater than all. *Run to Him!* Run to His open arms just as I did, and He will be your Doctor and heal you.

> *The Lord is my rock and my fortress and my deliverer; my God, my strength, in whom I will trust; my shield and the horn of my salvation, my stronghold.*
>
> —Psalm 18:2

Part Three
The Enemy of God

Who Is God?

Beloved readers, allow me to make it crystal clear. The God that I refer to is *Elohim—God the Father, God the Son (Jesus), God the Holy Spirit*—the Trinity, the Godhead. Even though They are three individual Persons, They are One. He is not the so-called gods: Allah in Islam, Buddha in eastern religions, Hindu deities in Hinduism, and so on.

Although the "God of Hebrew" is the same God that I am referring to, Judaism missed an essential Person in the Godhead—Jesus Christ (the Messiah). Judaism does not accept Jesus as part of the Godhead; therefore, I consider that religion has the spirit of Antichrist.

There are more than four thousand religions in the world. Each worships a divine person, but their gods are not the true living God. Only Christians believe in the true God of the universe. One would say, "How boastful you are to say that my god is not the true god." I would say to that person, "I dare not to worship any other god, or else I will end up in hell." *I am that serious!* Beloved readers, please do not wait until you die to find out the truth—that will be too late!

Our God has many names. Each name represents His power, sovereignty, attribute, and characters, such as Elohim, Yahweh (YHWH), Jehovah, El Shaddai, Adonai, El Elyon, El Olam, etc. Heaven also calls God: The Honorable Ancient of Days, The Judge of all Creation, The King of all Ages, and The Most-High God Almighty.

God is omnipotent (all-powerful), omnipresent (everywhere), and omniscient (all-knowing). His immensity, wisdom, power, holiness, capability, creativity, and ingenious skills are beyond the reach of a human brain.

How big is our God? Let us put it into perspective. There are about two-hundred billion galaxies in the observable cosmos (universe).[1] The diameter of the cosmos is ninety-three billion light-years.[2] One light-year equals 5.88 trillion miles. The diameter of Planet Earth is only 7,926 miles.[3] God can travel countless times (round trip) across the cosmos in a blinking of eyes. There are about two-hundred billion trillion stars in the universe,[4] and God can call each star by name. Regardless of the immensity of the universe, Jesus can hold all creations in His hands.

Now we can presume how big our God is. Do not limit Jesus like the picture we see; *He is much more!* Our God is immeasurable, magnificent, absolute, and infinite. His creations are marvelous, amazing, and glorious. There are no words to properly portray His ingenious creation (artworks) and brilliant wisdom.

The Bible says all things (universe and all things in it) are created through Jesus and for Jesus.

> *All things were made and came into existence through Him; and without Him not even one thing was made that has come into being.*
>
> —John 1:3 AMP

> *Through him [Jesus] God created everything in heaven and on earth, the seen and the unseen things, including spiritual powers, lords, rulers, and authorities. God created the whole universe through him and for him.*
>
> —Colossians 1:16 GNT

Within the Milky Way (our galaxy), the size of Planet Earth is like a particle of dust. Not to mention how small humans are, compared to the entire cosmos (trillions of galaxies). Hence, let mankind not boast ourselves, but be humble before God!

The *life* of every living soul in the universe is in the hands of Almighty God. If God one day decides to withdraw life from creation, the entire universe will perish (see Psalm 90:1). If He withdraws the *breath of life* from all creatures in the cosmos, we will all die and become dust (see Job 34:14). In other words, the very breath that we breathe is because the Holy Spirit is still breathing into us (see Job 12:10).

> *[Moses said,] Lord, you have always been our eternal home, . . . the one and only true God. When you speak the words "Life, return to me!" man turns back to dust.*
>
> —Psalm 90:1–3 TPT

> *If God were to take back his spirit and withdraw his breath, all life would cease, and humanity would turn again to dust.*
>
> —Job 34:14–15 NLT

> *In his [God's] hand is the life of every creature and the breath of all mankind.*
>
> —Job 12:10 NIV

Many wicked people proudly boast, "There is no God; or if there is, He does not see what we do." Just wait until the day you die; you will find yourself in hell. By then, crying to God will be too late. I challenge you: evil politicians, corrupted judges, child molesters, sex traffickers, sexually immoral people, murders, homosexuals, idolaters, liars, slanderers, witches, devil worshipers, haters of God, and prideful people. If you have slight wisdom of fearing God, repent your sins now, ask God to forgive you, renounce Satan, and accept Jesus Christ as your Lord and Savior. Otherwise, you will be torn into pieces by your Creator—just as God said in the following scripture:

While you did all this, I remained silent, and you thought I didn't care. But now I will rebuke you, listing all my charges against you. Repent, all of you who forget me, or I will tear you apart.

—Psalm 50:21–22 NLT

Relationships within the Trinity

I have always been fascinated by the loving relationships within the Godhead (Trinity). By reading books, listening to sermons, and studying the Bible for eight years, I have come to the following conclusion:

I believe, long before the creation of the universe—before all living beings ever existed, the three Persons of the Godhead (God, Word, Holy Spirit) had eternal decisions to make concerning their visible manifestation or appearance to all creations. In other words, in what form or title would they like to present themselves to humans, angels, or other living beings.

Many scriptures (see Matthew 28:18; Psalm 2:7) lead me to believe that God the Father is the Leader within the Trinity. Jesus said, *"My Father is greater than I"* (John 14:28), and *"I always do the things that are pleasing to him"* (John 8:29 ESV). However, the Father gave the Word (the Son, Jesus) and the Holy Spirit complete freedom to exercise their own power and desire. They had a choice to express their own willpower in any way they wished.

At that time (eons ago), *God* might not be called the *Father*, the *Word* might not be called the *Son*, and the *Spirit* might not be called the *Holy Spirit*.

> *Jesus came and spoke to them, saying, "All authority has been given to Me in heaven and on earth."*
>
> —Matthew 28:18

> *[God the Father said,] You are my son. Today I have become your Father. Only ask, and I will give you the nations as your inheritance, the whole earth as your possession.*
>
> —Psalm 2:7–8 NLT

Notice that, in Matthew 28:18, it was God the Father who granted all authorities (in heavens and the earth) to the Son. Likewise, in Psalm 2:7, the Father gave all nations and the whole earth to the Son as His inheritance and possession. Thus, I believe that all creation—the entire universe and all living beings in it—was a *love gift* from the Father to the Son. In other words, the Son was the only reason for the Father to create all things. The scripture says, *"The Son is the heir of all things"* (Hebrews 1:2, author's paraphrase). The Father also said to the Son, *"As your Father I have crowned you as my King Eternal"* (Psalm 2:7 TPT). The Father's love for the Son is incredible, incomprehensible, and beyond human understanding.

As for the Son (Jesus), even though He had total freedom to express His own will, power, and self-preference, He laid aside His personal desires and chose to be the slave of His Father (see Philippians 2:5). The Son humbly denied His self-will and totally surrendered to the Father's will (see Mark 14:36).

> *[Apostle Paul said,] You must have the same attitude that Christ Jesus had. Though he was God, he did not think of equality with God as something to cling to. Instead, he gave up his divine privileges; he took the humble position of a slave and was born as a human being. When he appeared*

in human form, he humbled himself in obedience to God [the Father] and died a criminal's death on a cross.

—Philippians 2:5–8 NLT

[Jesus said,] Abba, Father, . . . everything is possible for you. Please take this cup of suffering away from me. Yet I want your will to be done, not mine.

—Mark 14:36 NLT

From Mark 14:36, we see that Jesus surrendered to the Father's will and drank the cup of humanity's sins. It was the Father's wish for Him to do so—to pay the death penalty for the entire human race.

I believe, before human beings were ever created (during the eternal-decision-making meeting among the Trinity), the Son volunteered to take the form of a human, die on the cross, redeem humanity, and bring the Father's children back to heaven. The scripture says, *"The Lamb [Jesus] who was slaughtered before the world was made"* (Revelation 13:8 NLT). In other words, Christ's crucifixion took place at the time of His volunteering (in the spirit realm) before the actual event happened on the earth (the natural realm).

Jesus (being fully God Himself) chose to empty Himself and deny His self-will in order to exalt the Father. This decision implied His sheer sacrificial love to His beloved Father, just as He said in John 15:13, *"There is no greater love than to lay down one's life for one's friends"* (NLT). Also, in Psalm 118:27, the Messiah (Jesus) said, *"I offer Him [the Father] my life in joyous sacrifice"* (TPT).

What about the third Person of the Trinity—the Holy Spirit? Through scriptures, we know that the Holy Spirit went beyond what the Son did concerning sacrificial love to the Father. Being fully God Himself, the Spirit chose to be *invisible* (see John 14:17) in order to solely exalt the Father and glorify the Son.

> [Jesus said,] The Spirit of Truth, whom the world cannot receive [and take to its heart] because it does not see Him or know Him, but you know Him because He (the Holy Spirit) remains with you continually and will be in you.
>
> —John 14:17 AMP

I am deeply touched by the Holy Spirit's humility. I wrote a poem about His servant-love character in a later chapter. The title of the poem is "*My Hidden Hero.*"

The Holy Spirit forsook His personal will and went even further than the Son to show His bondservant's love to the other two Persons of the Godhead. Although the Holy Spirit's power is *beyond measure*, He chose not to display His own authority and ability, but only the wills of the Father and the Son (see John 16:13). No one knows the thoughts of the Father and the desire of the Son except the Holy Spirit.

> [Jesus said,] When He, the Spirit of Truth, comes, He will guide you into all the truth [full and complete truth]. For He will not speak on His own initiative, but He will speak whatever He hears [from the Father—the message regarding the Son], and He will disclose to you what is to come [in the future]. He will glorify and honor Me, because He (the Holy Spirit) will take from what is Mine and will disclose it to you.
>
> —John 16:13–14 AMP

Upon receiving the Son and the Holy Spirit's yielding love and sacrifice, God the Father also chose to be invisible to His children on the earth, but only reveal Himself through His Son, Jesus. As Colossians 1:15 says, "*Christ is the visible image of the invisible God*" (NLT).

Beloved readers, I have spent much time exploring the beauty and divinity of the Trinity. I have discovered the profound sacrificial love and humbleness among the Triune God. Each Person of the Godhead does not seek to glorify Oneself, but always pursues to esteem others above self-glory. Each is willing to lay down self-wills for love's sake. There is nothing that God teaches us in the Bible that the Trinity does not practice among Themselves. The more I learn how They treat one another in love, the more I want to be like Them.

Some believers may disagree with what I have discovered about the relationships within the Trinity. That is ok. After all, I am only a baby Christian, and I may not fully understand the secret of God. However, I trust the Holy Spirit's coaching—I don't read the Bible without the Holy Spirit. I believe He always delights to teach a hungry child, such as me, the knowledge I long to know.

Lucifer

Who is Lucifer? The Bible does not give much information about Lucifer, but it does provide enough information to help us draw some conclusions. There are a few key scriptures that tell us about the fall of Lucifer.

> *[God said,] "How you are fallen from heaven, O Lucifer, son of the morning! How you are cut down to the ground, you who weakened the nations! For you have said in your heart: 'I will ascend into heaven, I will exalt my throne above the stars of God; I will also sit on the mount of the congregation on the farthest sides of the north; I will ascend above the heights of the clouds, I will be like the Most High.' Yet you shall be brought down to Sheol [Hell], to the lowest depths of the Pit."*
>
> *—Isaiah 14:12–15*

Isaiah 14:12 is the only scripture that uses the name *Lucifer* in the Bible. In Latin, Lucifer means "light-bringer." In Hebrew, it means "light-bearer," "shining one," or "morning star." He was an exceptionally beautiful Cherub that God created. He was the worship leader to God in heaven, and one-third of the angels followed him.

Lucifer was an angelic name. In Hebrew, it is translated as hêylêl. Later, he became Satan because he rebelled against God. He was jealous of the human race that God created because we were made higher than the angelic race. Satan in Hebrew means "adversary," "opposer," or "accuser." The Bible also refers to him as "the huge dragon," "the ancient serpent," and "the devil." He wanted to be God, sit on the throne of God, and have the congregation worship him. Ezekiel 28 describes vividly what happened to him and how God cast him out of heaven.

> *Thus says the Lord God: You [Lucifer] were the seal of perfection, full of wisdom and perfect in beauty. . . . You were the anointed cherub who covers; . . . You were perfect in your ways from the day you were created, till iniquity was found in you.*
>
> *By the abundance of your trading you became filled with violence within, and you sinned; therefore I cast you as a profane thing out of the mountain of God; and I destroyed you, O covering cherub, . . .*
>
> *Your heart was lifted up because of your beauty; you corrupted your wisdom for the sake of your splendor; I cast you to the ground, I laid you before kings, that they might gaze at you.*
>
> *You defiled your sanctuaries by the multitude of your iniquities, . . . therefore I brought fire from your midst; it devoured you, and I turned you to ashes upon the earth in the sight of all who saw you. All who knew you among the people*

> *are astonished at you; you have become a horror, and shall be no more forever.*
>
> —Ezekiel 28:12, 14–19

What does the Bible say about Lucifer (Satan)? He first appeared as a serpent to deceive Eve to eat the fruit that God commanded her not to eat (see Genesis 3:13). Since that day, Adam and Eve were cast out of the Garden of Eden. They lost their divine nature and became fallen humans. Therefore, we, Adam's descendants, were born defiled.

> *The Lord God said to the woman, "What is this you have done?" The woman said, "The serpent deceived me, and I ate."*
>
> —Genesis 3:13

When Adam and Eve sinned, the title deed of the earth was legally given to Satan. Ever since, mankind switched allegiance to the devil and became forever bound to sin. By default, we are supposed to go to hell when we die. But God sent His Son, Jesus, to redeem us from the bondage of death (hell). Jesus paid the death penalty for us, so that we may have everlasting life in heaven.

Satan is still the ruler of this world until he is imprisoned for one thousand years in the bottomless pit of hell. After that, he will be released for a little while. During that time, he will continue deceiving nations of the earth, and wage war against God's people. Eventually, God will issue fires from heaven and consume Satan and his armies. He will then be cast into the lake of fire (in hell) and be tormented forever and ever.

> *Satan, who is the god of this world, has blinded the minds of those who don't believe [Jesus Christ]. They are unable to see the glorious light of the Good News. They don't*

> *understand this message about the glory of Christ, who is the exact likeness of God.*
>
> —2 Corinthians 4:4 NLT

Unlike God, Satan is not omnipresent, omniscient, and omnipotent. In other words, he cannot be present in multiple places at the same time. He is not all-knowing (cannot read our minds), and his power is limited. He is just a created being. Satan is the enemy of God; therefore, he is the enemy of God's children (us).

Satan's sin cannot be forgiven by God. He has no hope. He is terrified because his days are numbered. He and his demonic forces are like wounded animals, fighting fiercely for their lives. Yet, in their hearts, they know that they had already lost the battle when Jesus died on the cross and paid the ransom for God's children.

Satan and his demons cannot hurt God. Instead, they hurt us to break God's heart. Satan is extremely jealous of us because we have intimate fellowship with God, and he lost that privilege. Day and night, "the accuser" opposes God's children on the earth. Many of God's earthly generals and champions, such as prophets, pastors, missionaries, and intercessors, are being brutally attacked by satanic forces. Those who are commissioned to demolish the kingdom of darkness are being afflicted by Satan. He is absolutely terrified about the soon outpouring of the Holy Spirit—*"The powers of the age to come"* (Hebrews 6:5).

Satan is deadly fearful of Christians expanding God's Kingdom. Many of God's sons and daughters undergo some of the most violent physical, mental, and spiritual assaults by the devil. Just as he did to Job in the Bible, he will also do the same to the Christians, nations' leaders, and God's elects, such as Donald J. Trump.

Because of Adam and Eve's sin, the human race lost God's legal jurisdiction. Therefore, Satan is legally entitled to access the Highest Courts of Justice in Heaven, where thousands upon thousands of Christian books, DVDs, and teaching materials have been sued by the devil. He makes false accusations about Jesus' followers. He manipulates the Courts of Heaven by lies. He knows God is righteous and just, that He cannot banish Satan to the lake of fire and not banish the sinful mankind. Satan will continue bring charges against God's children until he is thrown out of the second heaven (where he dwells now) to the earth by the archangel Michael.

God the Father revealed the secret about Satan to some prophets during their visits to heaven. The Father clarified that many of His sons and daughters were sifted and harassed violently in recent years. But the sifting was not from His hand, rather from His enemy. When Lucifer was in heaven, he too was sifted in the Highest Courts of Justice, but he failed the sifting process because of his pride.

Beloved children of God, Satan has never stopped attacking us, just like he did to the biblical character—Job. Job was viciously assaulted by Satan. He killed all Job's children, his servants, and livestock. Eventually, Job's entire body was inflicted with exceedingly painful boils (see Job 2:4). The difference between Job and us today is the *atonement* made by Jesus Christ. Jesus paid our debts (sins) by nailing Satan's accusations on the cross.

> *Satan replied to the Lord, "Skin for skin! A man will give up everything he has to save his life. But reach out and take away his health, and he will surely curse you to your face!"*
>
> *So Satan left the Lord's presence, and he struck Job with terrible boils from head to foot. Job scraped his skin with a piece of broken pottery as he sat among the ashes.*
>
> —Job 2:4–5, 7–8 NLT

If we keep on sinning and giving Satan legal rights to attack us, there is nothing God can do to protect us. As soon as we repent and take the legal rights back from the enemy, God can put His hands in our lives and stop the attacks from the devil.

Satan is nasty, loathsome, and obnoxious. He will never stop accusing us and leaving us alone because he hates God and His beloved children. Satan will soon be cast out of the second heaven to the earth (see Revelation 12:7). By then, his wrath will be in full measure. Therefore, we should always *"Be sober, be vigilant; because our adversary the devil walks about like a roaring lion, seeking whom he may devour"* (1 Peter 5:8 author's paraphrase).

> *War broke out in heaven: Michael and his angels fought with the dragon; and the dragon and his angels fought, but they did not prevail, nor was a place found for them in heaven any longer. So the great dragon was cast out, the serpent of old, called the Devil and Satan, who deceives the whole world; he was cast to the earth, and his angels were cast out with him.*
>
> —Revelation 12:7–9

Demons and the Fallen Angels

When Jesus was on the earth, one-third of His ministry was casting out demons. The Bible refers to these demonic spirits as: "familiar spirits," "unclean spirits," "evil spirits," or "demons."

The Bible does not say exactly where these demons come from. Some Bible preachers believe that demons are the fallen angels, yet other ministers and prophets disagree with this theology. No one really knows the *absolute* source of these evil spirits.

We have learned from the Bible that demons seek to inhabit human bodies, even to animals (see Matthew 8:31). However, the Bible never mentioned that Jesus cast out fallen angels. Never once did Jesus tell a fallen angel to come out of a man. Instead, Jesus said, *"Come out of the man, you unclean spirit!"* (Mark 5:8). Therefore, we do not cast out fallen angels, but demons. In other words, the demons are not the fallen angels.

> *The demons begged Him [Jesus], saying, "If You cast us out, permit us to go away into the herd of swine."*
>
> —Matthew 8:31

> *He [Jesus] healed many who were sick with various diseases, and cast out many demons; and He did not allow the demons to speak, because they knew Him.*
>
> —Mark 1:34

We know that one-third of the fallen angels, who followed Lucifer, were cast out of heaven. They are now in Tartarus (the pit, the prison of hell), just as the following scriptures say:

> *They [fallen angels] will be gathered together, as prisoners are gathered in the pit, and will be shut up in the prison; after many days they will be punished.*
>
> —Isaiah 24:22

> *God did not spare the [fallen] angels who sinned, but cast them down to hell and delivered them into chains of darkness, to be reserved for judgment.*
>
> —2 Peter 2:4

> *I remind you of the [fallen] angels who did not stay within the limits of authority God gave them but left the place where they belonged. God has kept them securely chained in prisons of darkness, waiting for the great day of judgment.*
>
> —Jude 1:6 NLT

The scriptures in Isaiah, Peter, and Jude do not say that the demons are in prison, but the fallen angels.

We know that the demons are very much active on the earth now. They seek to inhabit bodies, torment people, lie, and manipulate. They do Satan's biddings and try to destroy God's children. If the fallen angels are in prison, it is not possible for them to operate on the earth the way demons do.

Giants—Nephilim

Other teachings believe that demons are the Giants (Nephilim) who were the offspring between the fallen angels and *"the daughters of mankind"* on the earth. Nephilim is translated as Giants in some Bibles. The Bible refers to the fallen angels as *"the sons of God."*

> *The sons of God saw that the daughters of mankind were beautiful; and they took wives for themselves, whomever they chose. Then the Lord said, "My Spirit will not remain with man forever, because he is also flesh; nevertheless, his days shall be 120 years."*
>
> *The Nephilim were on the earth in those days, and also afterward, when the sons of God came in to the daughters of mankind, and they bore children to them.*
>
> —Genesis 6:2–4 NASB

The Books of Enoch, translated by Joseph Lumpkin, describes the details about the fallen angels. They were also called the *"Watchers."* Although *The Books of Enoch* is not part of the Bible, Jesus revealed this book to prophet Sadhu Sundar Selvaraj. In the middle of their conversation, Jesus said, "Have you not read *The Books of Enoch?*" This confirmed that *The Books of Enoch* is a reliable source.

God said to Enoch:

> "Enoch, you scribe of righteousness, go, tell the Watchers of heaven who have left the high heaven, the holy eternal place, and have defiled themselves with women, and have done as the children of earth do, and have taken to themselves wives:

> "You have done great destruction on the earth: And you shall have no peace nor forgiveness of sin: Since they delight themselves in their children, they shall see the murder of their beloved ones, and the destruction of their children, and they shall lament, and shall make supplication forever, and will receive neither mercy or peace."

—The Books of Enoch 12:4–6

Mr. Lumpkin did extensive research on *The Books of Enoch* and wrote: "Although we are led to believe the fallen angels are loathsome and evil, they loved and adored their children. It was not the angels that became the demons. It was their children, whose spirits were evil and could not be killed." [5] This is another source that reveals the fallen angels' offspring—the Nephilim (Giants)—are the demons.

Pre-Adamic Civilization

The Pre-Adamic Civilization (when the dinosaurs roamed on the earth) holds the fact that human beings existed long before the biblical character of Adam. Some Christian ministers and theologians, such as Derek Prince, believe demons came from the Pre-Adamic Age. They were intelligent and human-like creatures.

This leads us to ask, "When did human beings first exist?" God revealed to some prophets that the earth was leased to Adam and his descendants for six thousand years. Based on the Jewish calendar, we are now in the Hebrew year of 5782. However, many scientific documents, such as Fossil Records, show that human ancestors existed millions of years ago.

What are we saying here? The biblical calendar of human history is six thousand years since Adam. How come scientific researches tell us that humans and other species existed on the earth millions or even billions of years ago? The fact is that the Bible never claimed to be the complete historical record of the world. The central theme of the Bible is about Adam and his descendants, which leads to Jesus Christ.

Many scientists and theologians believe that millions of years ago, the earth was already populated with nations, cities, humans, angels, and animals. Adam was not the first human who existed on Planet Earth. Indeed, the earth God created originally was not the earth we are in now. Between Genesis 1:1 and 1:2, there were millions of years of gaps—events that happened during that time were dramatically different.

In Genesis 1:1, the earth was *perfect*. That was the dinosaurs' time—the Pre-Adamic Age.

In the beginning God created the heavens and the earth.

—Genesis 1:1

In Genesis 1:2, God punished Lucifer and his fallen angels. The earth was destroyed by a flood, followed by an Ice Age. Scientific documents show that the most recent Ice Age started three million years ago. All living beings were destroyed. The earth was formless and empty—as described in the following scripture:

> *The earth was without form, and void; and darkness was on the face of the deep.*
>
> —Genesis 1:2

> *I looked at the earth, and it was empty and formless. I looked at the heavens, and there was no light. I looked at the mountains and hills, and they trembled and shook. I looked, and all the people were gone. All the birds of the sky had flown away. I looked, and the fertile fields had become a wilderness. The towns lay in ruins, crushed by the Lord's fierce anger.*
>
> —Jeremiah 4:23–26 NLT

Just as Jeremiah 4:23 describes the desolation of the earth, Isaiah 24:1 also portrays how God destroyed the earth before Adam ever existed, which refers to the Pre-Adamic Age. The *"inhabitants"* that Isaiah referred to were the Pre-Adamic populations.

> *Behold, the Lord makes the earth empty and makes it waste, distorts its surface and scatters abroad the inhabitants.*
>
> —Isaiah 24:1

After the first earth was destroyed, millions of years later, at Genesis 1:26, God started to restore Planet Earth and created a brand-new race—the Adamic race, which are we, the descendants of Adam and Eve.

> *Then God said, "Let Us make man in Our image, according to Our likeness."*
>
> —Genesis 1:26

The *"man"* whom God refers to is Adam. The *"Us"* and *"Our"* refer to *"Elohim"*—God the Father, the Son (Jesus), and the Holy Spirit. In Genesis 1:28, God refers to *"them"* as Adam and Eve.

> God blessed them, and God said unto them, be fruitful, and multiply, and replenish the earth, and subdue it: and have dominion over the fish of the sea, and over the fowl of the air, and over every living thing that moveth upon the earth.
>
> —Genesis 1:28 KJV

God said *"replenish"* the earth in Genesis 1:28, and He said the same word to Noah after the flood in Genesis 9:1. The term *"replenish"* means to restore something that was once there. Thus, this indicates that there were inhabitants before the flood and the Ice Age.

> God blessed Noah and his sons, and said unto them, be fruitful, and multiply, and replenish the earth.
>
> —Genesis 9:1 KJV

Noah was the grandson of Adam—the ninth generation from Adam. The Bible tells us that God chose Noah to preserve the human race by building an ark (called Noah's Ark). At that time, God annihilated the Giants (Nephilim), their descendants, and corrupted humans on the earth by flood. Only eight people from Noah's family were saved.

Lucifer Hijacked What Belonged to God

In the Pre-Adamic Era, the heavens and the earth were perfect. Bible ministers, such as Derek Prince and Benny Hinn, believe that God appointed Lucifer to be the ruler of certain realms (Planet Earth was one of them). The inhabitants of the earth were the Pre-Adamic race. Lucifer had two responsibilities—He was the ruler of the earth and also the worship leader in heaven. One-third of the angels followed him. His job was to pass God's words from heaven to the earth and bring the earthly worship back to heaven. However, he became proud of his own beauty and splendor. He desired the earthly worship for himself. Out of envy and jealousy, he hijacked the worship that belonged to God and kept it to himself. He corrupted the *"traffic,"* as is referred to in the following verse:

> *[God said,] By the abundance of your traffic they filled the midst of you with violence, and you have sinned: therefore I have cast you as profane out of the mountain of God; and I have destroyed you, covering cherub, from the midst of the stones of fire.*
>
> —Ezekiel 28:16 NHEB

Other Bible ministers signify *"traffic"* as Lucifer's rebellion against God's wish. He knew some of the secrets of God and disclosed these secrets to the inhabitants of the earth without God's permission. He provoked one-third of the angels to rebel against God. Thus, God cast him and the angels out of the third heaven (where God dwells) to the second heaven (between the third heaven and the earth). Lucifer lost his privilege of serving God in the third heaven and his position of ruling the earth because of his pride and rebellion.

The Pre-Adamic Race

> *How you are fallen from heaven, O Lucifer, son of the morning! How you are cut down to the ground, you who weakened the nations!*
>
> —Isaiah 14:12

The *"nations"* in Isaiah 14:12 were the inhabitants of the Pre-Adamic Age. Some Bible ministers, such as Derek Prince and Benny Hinn, teach that the Pre-Adamic race or inhabitants are now called demons. They were not human, but half man and half animal (described in Revelation 9:7). They were ruled by Lucifer, and they actually worshiped God at that time. However, the wicked Lucifer not only led the worship angels to be disloyal to God, but he also promoted sin and transgression to the Pre-Adamic race. When Lucifer and his angels rebelled against God, the Pre-Adamic beings also joined their rebellion.

> *The shape of the locusts was like horses prepared for battle. On their heads were crowns of something like gold, and their faces were like the faces of men. They had hair like women's hair, and their teeth were like lions' teeth. And they had breastplates like breastplates of iron, and the sound of their wings was like the sound of chariots with many horses running into battle. They had tails like scorpions and there were stings in their tails.*
>
> —Revelation 9:7–10

Out of God's wrath, He brought judgment on Lucifer, his angels, and the Pre-Adamic race with a flood, followed by an Ice Age. This was the picture painted in Genesis 1:2: *"The earth was formless and empty, and darkness covered the deep waters"* (NLT).

Satan Regained the Earth from Adam

When God created Adam, God's purpose was to have humans replace Satan's rulership on Planet Earth. Satan was still on the earth when Adam was created. At which time, Satan had already lost his position as a worship leader in heaven, as well as his authority of ruling the earth, and the privilege of being an archangel. He was powerless because God gave Adam his previous position to govern the earth.

Then Satan took the form of a serpent and deceived Eve in the Garden of Eden. After Adam and Eve disobeyed God, Satan took back what he had lost. He regained control over Planet Earth and recaptured the binding-legal right to rule the earth and its solar system, including the second heaven. Satan understood perfectly that when men sinned, as he did, God had to banish men, just as He banished him. Satan knew that sin would make men depart from God's jurisdiction, and the human race would be under his sovereignty. This was why Satan told Jesus that the whole world was his (see Matthew 4:8). Jesus did not argue with him while spending forty days and nights in the wilderness.

> *Again, the devil took Him [Jesus] up on an exceedingly high mountain, and showed Him all the kingdoms of the world and their glory. And he said to Him, "All these things I will give You if You will fall down and worship me." Then Jesus said to him, "Away with you, Satan! For it is written, 'You shall worship the Lord your God, and Him only you shall serve.'"*
>
> —Matthew 4:8–10

What Makes Jesus the Only Savior?

Before God created the heavens, the earth, and the human race, He already foresaw the great falling away of mankind. He knew that we would forsake Him and fall into Lucifer's deception. Lucifer understood the Eternal Law of Heaven. When Adam transgressed against God, death reigned all men; thereby, the entire human race was destined to eternal punishment (hell). Lucifer cunningly planned men's termination. He ensured mankind's downfall by enticing Adam and Eve to sin.

Who Is Qualified to Redeem the Human Race?

When Adam sinned, the blood of the human race was mutated and defiled from its original design. Therefore, human beings could not go to heaven unless redemption was made. Then, who and what are qualified to redeem mankind?

Hebrews 9:22 tells us, *"Almost everything is cleansed with blood, and without the shedding of blood there is no forgiveness [neither release from sin and its guilt, nor cancellation of the merited punishment]"* (AMP). Whose blood is qualified for the forgiveness of sin?

The Eternal Law of Heaven requires a person—born from the human race, whose blood is not contaminated, and who has never sinned—to meet the legal demand of saving humanity. We know that the angelic blood is celestial, which is not eligible for saving humans. And the blood of humans was defiled (in every generation), none left pure. But our God had an ultimate plan (painful but brilliant) to salvage humankind—*He sent Himself!*

Jesus, as part of the Godhead (Father, Son, Holy Spirit), came to Planet Earth, took on human flesh, and became one of us. He was the only Human who had the perfect qualification of meeting the demand of the Eternal Law of Heaven. His blood was pure and untainted from the mutation of the fallen men. His body was created neither from the seed of a man, nor from the egg of a woman, but by the Holy Spirit. His blood was not from Mary or Joseph (His earthly mother and father), but from God the Father. Therefore, no one on the earth was qualified to make atonement to forgive sins, except someone like Jesus.

Jesus paid the death penalty for our ransom on the cross. He became the substitute to bear the eternal judgment due of the entire human race. In addition, Jesus never sinned; even though He faced all kinds of temptations as we faced, He still kept holy and blameless.

Beloved children of God, we do not truly appreciate how fortunate we are. Our God sacrificed His own life to purchase us. Yet, we often disrespect Him, take His name in vain, and blaspheme against Him. Therefore, I ask you to close your eyes now, bow your head, and honor Him for His sacrifice. *It means so much to Him* if you do so!

Understand Our Enemy

Beloved readers, when we engage in battle, we must first study our enemy. We must understand their intentions, plans, weapons, abilities, strengths, and weaknesses. The Bible has already given us some information about Satan and his demonic force.

Our enemies are not carnal but spiritual. They operate in the invisible world—the spirit realm (see Ephesians 6:12). Therefore, it is impossible to fight with them without the Holy Spirit's help. Even Jesus had to depend on the Holy Spirit when He ministered on the earth. He did not rely on His own might nor power, but on the Holy Spirit, as He stated in Zechariah 4:6.

> *"This is the word of the Lord to Zerubbabel: 'Not by might nor by power, but by My Spirit,' says the Lord of hosts."*
>
> —Zechariah 4:6

> *We are not fighting against flesh-and-blood enemies, but against evil rulers and authorities of the unseen world, against mighty powers in this dark world, and against evil spirits in the heavenly places.*
>
> —Ephesians 6:12 NLT

The goal of Satan is to deceive us, accuse us, and draw us away from the truth. His ultimate objective is to bring us to hell for eternal damnation. Satan caused great damage to mankind through Adam and Eve. He will continue harming Adam's descendants—the citizens of the earth. He and his demons hate us because they have no hope to gain God's love, mercy, and forgiveness. Their future is in the lake of fire (hell). They are *mad and cruel!* They are deadly, brutal, vicious, poisonous, and deceitful.

Just as God has *The Book of Life*, Satan also has *The Book of Death*. While we are on the earth, we still have the chance to decide which book we want to be recorded in. This will determine our eternal future. Daily, we walk on the thin line between life or death, light or darkness, eternal life or eternal damnation.

Hell Is Real!

In Mary K. Baxter's book, *A Divine Revelation of Hell*, she photographically illustrated the reality of hell and how millions of souls are being tortured there. Her book was written from a real experience of visiting hell. Jesus took her there for thirty nights in 1976. The purpose was for her to document the truth about hell's existence.

People are suffering brutal torments in hell because they did not choose Jesus Christ as their Lord and Savior. The Bible declares clearly and precisely that Jesus is the only way to heaven: *"I am the way, the truth, and the life. No one comes to the Father except through Me"* (John 14:6).

Prophetess Baxter witnessed all kinds of people in hell. On the earth, you can be a very good person, give money to the poor, and do noble deeds throughout your life. Yet, if you do not accept Jesus Christ as your Lord and Savior, *you will go to hell!* You can be very religious—a Hindu priest, a Buddhist monk, or a faithful Muslim; yet, if you do not accept Jesus Christ as your Lord and Savior, *you will surely go to hell!* Your death penalty in hell is eternal, *without parole!* Even worse, those who do evil deeds, mock God, practice witchcraft, and worship idols will be *punished even more* in hell.

To emphasize, the qualification of going to heaven does not depend on people's good deeds or performance, but it *solely* depends on one Person—Jesus Christ.

People, who have been taken to hell for visits by Jesus, witnessed many witches and unbelievers being violently tormented there. Their flesh was ripped off by demons. Their skeletons were burned like red-hot charcoals. Worms covered their bodies and ate their flesh. They were screaming in agony and pain, yet the demons laughed at them with malicious pleasure.

Satan is the greatest deceiver. He uses witches to counterfeit the power of the Holy Spirit. However, in the end, they are punished the most. Many people have sold their souls to Satan for fame and money. They have chosen to serve Satan instead of Jesus Christ. By the time they end up in hell, it will be too late. *Now* is the time to repent of sins and lawless deeds. It is time to call upon Jesus, for He desires none shall perish but have everlasting life.

> *The Lord does not delay [as though He were unable to act] and is not slow about His promise, as some count slowness, but is [extraordinarily] patient toward you, not wishing for any to perish but for all to come to repentance.*
>
> —2 Peter 3:9 AMP

Beloved readers, remember my visit to the palm reading woman? After reading Mary K. Baxter's book about how Satan tortured witches in hell, I put Mary's book at that woman's office door. I even put a sticky note on the page of how Satan brutalized a famous witch in hell. Even though she might not know who put the book at her door, I was sure the demons would tell her. I was afraid of retaliation by this witch, but the Holy Spirit gave me the courage to carry through.

The sad thing is that witchcraft (Wicca religion) has been amplified astronomically in the United States of America and throughout the world. Many witches and warlocks are millennials. Satan has been enticing young people to turn away from following Christ, but finding meanings of life through fortune-telling, mind control, casting spells, and blood sacrifice to demons. Many studies estimate the witch populations are in millions in America. *They will go to hell* if they die today without Jesus Christ.

Satan uses witches and warlocks to gain his dark power over people and counterfeit the divine authority of the Holy Spirit. He uses sorcery, black magic, mediums, horoscopes, and games to seduce God's children. Practicing witchcraft is to utilize demonic powers to dominate, manipulate, and control others. The Bible clearly affirms the consequences of practicing witchcraft: *"Men and women among you who act as mediums or who consult the spirits of the dead must be put to death by stoning. They are guilty of a capital offense"* (Leviticus 20:27 NLT).

Jeffrey Epstein in Hell

Jeffrey Epstein was a convicted sex offender who was charged by federal prosecutors for sex trafficking and prostitution involving minors. Epstein was an American financier who had close connections to celebrities, royal families, billionaires, and politicians. He was charged for enticing underaged girls and abusing them sexually. He died in jail by suicide. However, many people questioned his death.

When people, who are like Jeffrey Epstein, indulge themselves in great sins. They think they can get away with their evil conduct, and God does not punish them. They are absolutely wrong! *"For the wages of sin is death"* (Romans 6:23). The word *"death"* here refers to hell—eternal judgment.

For decades, Jesus has been giving visions, dreams, and taking people to heaven and hell for visits. He commands these people to share their testimonies regarding the reality of heaven and hell.

On August 11, 2019, Jesus showed Dr. Maurice Sklar (a prophet and a world-class professional violinist) a vision about Jeffrey Epstein in hell. In the vision, Maurice saw a man being tormented by the demons.

This man's flesh was being burned by fire and falling off of his body. His skeleton was scorched like hot charcoal. The demons were piercing his heart and genital areas repeatedly. He screamed with sheer agony. This torture was repetitive, *nonstop*—sheer eternal punishment! Jesus told Dr. Sklar, "This man is Jeffrey Epstein." [6]

John Lennon in Hell

Many celebrities and singers have blasphemed and mocked God. They have sold their souls to Satan for money and fame. Hopefully, John Lennon's destiny will wake them up. Prophet Sklar also witnessed John Lennon in hell. He shared his vision about Lennon during a church sermon at The Gathering Place—a church in Burbank, California.

In the vision, he saw John Lennon hanging upside down in hell. The demons were submerging his body slowly into boiling oil. As John entered the hot oil, his body was fried, and his flesh melted off. The only thing left was his skeleton. Then he was lifted up in the air, and his flesh came right back. The demons would put him into the boiling oil again, and his flesh fell off again. This process was repeated over and over. John Lennon kept screaming in *total anguish*. This scene was spine-chilling and unbearable to watch! Jesus told Mr. Sklar, "This is John Lennon's eternal punishment for mocking God. Now John is fully experiencing the reality of hell." [7] The sad thing is that he will be tormented forever and ever *without any chance of escaping*.

John Lennon was the lead singer for *The Beatles*. In his song "Imagine," he told his listeners to imagine no heaven or hell. In 1966, during his interviews with multiple TV stations, he mocked Christianity and proclaimed his rock band was more popular than Jesus Christ.

Now John Lennon is paying his eternal price for insulting God. His pride led him to hell. The tortures that he receives are worse than many people in hell. *Nonstop! Forever doomed!* I hope actor Christian Bale learns the lesson from Lennon. Bale openly thanked Satan during his speech upon receiving the Golden Globes Award for best actor. Many rich and famous people on the earth today will be tormented in hell tomorrow if they do not repent and accept Jesus Christ as their Lord and Savior!

How Do Demons Operate?

The Bible illustrates how demons operate. They can manifest themselves in the shapes of serpents, dragons, leviathans, scorpions, and other forms of evil spirits (see the following scriptures). *"Even Satan disguises himself as an angel of light"* (2 Corinthians 11:14 NLT).

> *The serpent was more cunning than any beast of the field which the Lord God had made. And he said to the woman, "Has God indeed said, 'You shall not eat of every tree of the garden'?"*
>
> —Genesis 3:1

> *The Lord God said to the woman, "What is this you have done?" The woman said, "The serpent deceived me and I ate."*
>
> —Genesis 3:13

> *I saw an angel come down from heaven, having the key of the bottomless pit and a great chain in his hand. And he laid hold on the dragon, that old serpent, which is the Devil, and Satan, and bound him a thousand years.*
>
> —Revelation 20:1–2 KJV

In that day the Lord with His severe sword, great and strong, will punish Leviathan the fleeing serpent, Leviathan that twisted serpent; and He will slay the reptile that is in the sea.

—Isaiah 27:1

Behold, I [Jesus] give you the authority to trample on serpents and scorpions, and over all the power of the enemy, and nothing shall by any means hurt you.

—Luke 10:19

Beloved readers, I have personally experienced many demonic attacks in my life. They have threatened me not to walk with God. In 2014, right after becoming a believer in Jesus Christ, demons attacked me viciously through dreams.

Dream 1: Crossing a River

I was crossing a river. There was only one narrow log for me to walk on—kind of like a gymnastic beam. Somehow, I had to cross this river and reach the other side. But the river was filled with gigantic serpents, small vipers, poisonous snakes, and other deadly monsters. As I was crossing, these serpents started attacking me—crawling into my pants, onto my feet, legs, and upper body. They tried to drag me off of the beam. I then recited fervently what Jesus said in Luke 10:19, *"I give you the authority to trample on serpents and scorpions, and over all the power of the enemy, and nothing shall by any means hurt you."* I was extremely terrified, but I just kept going. Finally, I reached the other side of the river. Miraculously, the poisonous snakes did not kill me. God's Words are powerful and trustworthy.

Shockingly, as soon as I reached the other side, there was a door for me to enter. But right in front of the door, a huge green cobra blocked me from entering. The cobra said, "I will not let you go in!" I said, "How dare you! I belong to Jesus now. You have no right to stop me. I will never go back to where I was. Never!"

I then took off my jacket and threw it on the head of the cobra. While the cobra was blinded, I quickly wrapped my jacket around its head, and smashed the head on the ground until the cobra was dead. Then I entered the door. The dream ended.

In this dream, the serpents (demons) tried to stop me from being a Christ believer. They attempted to hinder me, block me, intimidate me, and kill me. But God's Word is powerful. As I recited the Word of God, I passed through the valley of the shadow of death without being harmed—just as Psalm 23 says:

> *Even though I walk through the valley of the shadow of death, I will fear no evil, for you [God] are with me; your rod and your staff, they comfort me.*
>
> —Psalm 23:4 ESV

Dream 2: White Wolves

In this dream, a Christian sister was attacked and wounded by the enemy. I carried her on my back and ran from the enemy's pursuit. I then found an apartment building and started running toward it, hoping someone would take us in.

However, I immediately realized that I was surrounded by a pack of white wolves. They encircled me as though they were ready to devour me. Nevertheless, I had no choice but kept running because the enemy was catching up to us at a very fast speed. As I ran toward one of the apartment rooms, I saw a big lion lying there with such a peaceful expression on its face—as if nothing was happening—even though the lion saw everything.

I thought the lion would surely attack me first because the wolves were about sixty feet away, and the lion was only ten feet away from me. To my astonishment, the lion showed no interest in eating my friend or me. It just looked at me and did not do anything. Somehow, I found peace in its face.

I then quickly ran to an apartment, and the door was amazingly unlocked. I carried my friend inside. At that moment, the wolves started pushing the door, but I quickly locked it, and the dream ended.

Obviously, the lion in this dream was Jesus. He is called *"The Lion of the tribe of Judah"* (Revelation 5:5). The white wolves were the demons. Our God is extremely protective. As long as He was there, even though I was under siege, the demons could not touch me.

Demons usually work as mobs. If one cannot break through a believer, he will call for support from other demons in that region. In my case, the pack of white wolves was already waiting for me to consume me. But my King Jesus (the Lion) was there protecting me. *"If God is for me, who can be against me?"* (Romans 8:31, author's paraphrase).

The Holy Spirit always alerts me about demonic attacks through dreams. Before I go to bed, I always pray, "Holy Spirit, please talk to me through dreams," and He always does.

Dream 3: Big House

In many of my dreams, I always ran to a big house, situated on a hill. There were more than fifteen rooms in this house. All the objects in the house, such as sofas, chairs, picture frames, rugs, walls, and floors, were very dusty, old, and broken. The odor smelled like wet socks or rotten wood. All the rooms were very gloomy.

In the kitchen, I saw many demons cooking human body parts. There were lots of body parts hanging on the kitchen ceiling. These demons were full of vile smirks. I did not know to whom these body parts belonged. There were five kitchen rooms—some for chopping the bodies into pieces, others for cooking them. This house was mine, but I did not see my family members in it—only the demons.

After becoming a Christ believer and receiving deliverance from demonic bondage, I stopped visiting this house in my dreams. To this day, I am not sure those were dreams or visions. I just know what I saw was very real.

Many demonic attacks that I experienced were from my workplace. The devil used my bosses, coworkers, and employees to attack me. In 2016, I was heavily attacked by two senior female leaders. No matter what I did, they always put me down. My life was miserable during those days. Then, God gave me a dream. He cautioned me about the demonic assaults through those two women.

Dream 4: Two Women

I was in an eighteenth-century ballroom. The dance floor was filled with men and women with flamboyant dance clothes and hairdos. I was also dancing in the ballroom. Two beautiful brunette French women pushed people away and walked toward me. They poked me with their fingers and insulted me with evil laughter. I remained polite, yet they kept mocking me. At that point, people started encircling me.

Then the two women said, "Why don't you just leave? You don't belong here. Go away!" I said, "What have I done to you? Why are you insulting me?" They kept pushing me here and there with nasty laughter. People were shocked, yet no one bothered to help because of these women's wealth in the aristocratic society. I was in sheer humiliation and dashed out of the ballroom with tears. The dream ended.

The next morning, I was in deep despair because of this dream. While driving to work, the Holy Spirit said to me, "Those two women in your dream are the two senior leaders. The demons are using them to pull you down. Be careful, for they will not give up until they destroy you!"

Dream 5: Demons Attempted to Rape Me

I have heard multiple women telling me that demons tried to have sex with them. Then, one night, it happened to me.

It was around two o'clock in the morning, I suddenly felt a big man on my bed. He pinned me down, took away my bed cover, and stripped off my pajamas. This demon attempted to rape me. I could not move nor scream. I wanted to call Jesus for help, but my voice was silenced. It went on for about ten minutes.

To this day, I am not sure it was a dream or factual. I don't think it was a dream because it felt so real. Later, I asked the Holy Spirit, "Why didn't You stop him?" I did not get an answer. There must be something in me that gave the demon the legal right to attack me sexually. Demons are rapists—they are *filthy* and *disgusting*! I cannot wait to see them being judged by Jesus Christ for the crime they committed on the *final judgment day*!

After that day, before I go to bed, part of my prayers is like this: "I plead the blood of Jesus to shield this house, shield this room, and shield this bed. No evil spirits can cross the bloodline of Jesus Christ. I command the hosts of heaven to protect me while I am sleeping."

Dream 6: Red Centipede

Whenever my dreams are about sexual lust, I see the image of a red centipede. The red ones are deadly poisonous—they are demonic spirits. I once had a dream about having sex with a married man. In the middle of the lustful act, as I lifted the bed cover, there was a huge red centipede. These demonic spirits are real. They dwell in people's bodies and cause people to commit sexual sins.

The Holy Spirit tells me: "Sexual immorality is exceptionally toxic. It can cost people's lives, so stay away from sexual sins." The Bible tells us:

> *Flee sexual immorality. Every sin that a man does is outside the body, but he who commits sexual immorality sins against his own body.*
>
> —1 Corinthians 6:18

Diabolic Onslaught

Daily in the spirit realm, the demonic armies are marching and engaging intense battles against God's children on the earth.

Rick Joyner, the founder and executive director of Morning Star Ministries, has been taken to heaven many times and has talked with Jesus in person. The revelations that he received from the Lord are *invaluable*. He is the author of more than forty prophetic books. These books recorded his visions, dreams, and encounters with Jesus Himself. One of his famous books is *The Final Quest*. In this book, Mr. Joyner graphically describes how satanic armies combat against the citizens of the earth. The book is not fiction, rather a panoramic vision that God gave him about the ultimate battles between light and darkness.

The Final Quest—"The Hordes of Hell Are Marching"

> *The demonic army was so large that it stretched as far as I could see. It was separated into divisions, with each carrying a different banner. The foremost divisions marched under the banners of Pride, Self-Righteousness, Respectability, Selfish Ambition, Unrighteous Judgment, and Jealousy.*
>
> *The weapons carried by this horde were also named. The swords were named Intimidation; the spears were named*

Treachery; and the arrows were named Accusation, Gossip, Slander, and Faultfinding. Scouts and smaller companies of demons with such names as Rejection, Bitterness, Impatience, Unforgiveness and Lust were sent in advance of this army to prepare for the main attack.

Christians were prisoners of this army. All of these captive Christians were wounded, and they were guarded by the smaller demons of Fear. Above the prisoners, the sky was black with vultures named Depression. Occasionally, these vultures would land on the shoulders of a prisoner and vomit on him. The vomit was Condemnation.

Even worse than the vomit from the vultures was a repulsive slime that these demons were urinating and defecating upon the Christians they rode. This slime was pride, selfish ambition, etc. [8]

Beloved children of God, the battles are real, demons are real, and Satan is real. Let us not be *ignorant!* We may be the last few generations on Planet Earth. We are living in the last days—the end of the age. If we do not pick up our weapons and fight, we will become prisoners of war by the diabolical onslaughts.

These are not Hollywood horror movies. They are real in our daily lives. The reason demons have the right to do what they do is because we give them legal rights when we sin. We open doors for them by committing unforgiveness, bitterness, hatred, lies, sexual immorality, slander, and rebellions.

Even though God wants to save us, He cannot do so unless we repent and take our legal rights back from the enemies. The Bible tells us that *"the wages of sin is death"* (Romans 6:23). It also tells us who deserves to go to hell in the following scripture:

> *They were filled with all manner of unrighteousness, evil, covetousness, malice. They are full of envy, murder, strife, deceit, maliciousness. They are gossips, slanderers, haters of God, insolent, haughty, boastful, inventors of evil, disobedient to parents, foolish, faithless, heartless, ruthless . . . those who practice such things deserve to die.*
>
> —Romans 1:29–32 ESV

Before God healed my depression, I had suffered severe diabolic onslaughts for many years. I frequently felt someone constantly stabbing my heart. The stab came to me in intervals. When they came, it would trigger the urge to kill myself because the pain was *intolerable*. It was usually accompanied by a voice that said, "Look how pathetic you are! You used to come to this store with your husband. Now, where is he? He does not want you anymore and is married to another woman. No one wants you! *How pathetic!* Everybody is looking at you and mocking you. You are filthy and dirty. Even Jesus loathes you. Why don't you just *kill yourself now!*"

When the stabbing and the voice came, I would be out of breath and literally felt severe pain in my heart area. Then I would be paralyzed for a while. Imagine this, my beloved readers: I went through such whipping and stabbing since I was six years old until the day Jesus took over the ownership of my life in 2014. The pinnacle of this experience would be after my divorce—sheer torment, anguish, and desperation!

I cry out to you, my beloved readers, please listen to me! If you are suffering the same kind of torments, *run to Jesus now!*

I now know that those torments were from the demons. *I hate, hate, and hate the demons and the devil!* They are my Father's enemies, and they are my enemies too. Now, it is my turn to torment them. I frequently remind Satan, "Have you forgotten your address? I know that you have dementia. So, let me remind you. Your address is: *Number One, Lake of fire street, Hell.*"

Beloved brothers and sisters in Christ, do not be deceived by the saying, "Once saved, forever saved." There is no such thing! Often, out of our foolishness, we become *"Salad-Bar Christians."* We only want to know God's kindness but ignore His severity. Many churches and ministers do not preach the whole truth—only *"some truth."* They do not teach their congregations about hellfire and demonic torments because they fear losing income (tithes). They merchandise the body of Christ (church) for their selfish ambitions and love of mammon (money).

Deliverance—Casting out Demons from My Body

Beloved readers, you may wonder why I have spent all these times talking about demons. It is because I was under demonic bondage for many years and understand how real they are. All my symptoms of sexual immorality, bitterness, pride, and jealousy were the manifestations of demons inside of me. These characteristics are never from God.

When demons dwell in one's body, they control that body. When I shared with Melisa (the Indonesian girl) all the things I had done, she told me, "You need deliverance, have demons cast out of your body, and my pastor can do that for you."

A few weeks later, Pastor Rudi of the Indonesian church (JKI Hosana Miracle Center) scheduled my deliverance. Yet, right before the scheduled day, he canceled the appointment. The pastor said that his whole family was sick—his four sons, daughter, wife, and himself. Therefore, he could not perform the deliverance. Soon, he rescheduled another one, yet again, he had to cancel it because his whole family was sick once more.

The third time Pastor Rudi scheduled the deliverance, he asked Melisa to help me fill out the six-page questionnaire (all in Indonesian).

The pages were ledger size (11 x 17 inches), which is even bigger than legal size (8½ x 14 inches). At which time, the pastor went to another room to pray. When he came back into the sanctuary, where we were waiting, my countenance changed. I became fearful of him. I kept backing off to the corner, but it was not me who was frightened; it was the demons inside of me—they were *terrified!*

Pastor Rudi looked at the questionnaire and glanced over all the sinful things I had done. He was shocked and said, "Ying, is this you? I can't believe it! You look so innocent. Wow, you have done all these? No wonder my whole family was sick every time I planned to do the deliverance for you. Satan attempted to hinder me from setting you free of demonic bondage."

The pastor then poured some anointing oil on my head and laid his hands on me. Immediately, I felt God's power on me, and I fell to the floor. The deliverance had started. Since he spoke in Indonesian, I could not understand anything he said. The only thing I understood was "Fire... Fire... Fire!" As I lay on the floor, my hands began punching in the air, and my legs began kicking. I kept saying, "No, no, no, no more, no more!" It was not me speaking, but the demons inside of me.

The deliverance took about two hours. Through Pastor Rudi, the Holy Spirit cast out eleven demons out of me. I felt these evil spirits coming out of my right foot one by one. In the end, I could not even move, as if I had just had a major surgery. I could not even sit up. Pastor Rudi and Melisa held my back and pulled me up to a sitting position. I suddenly burst out with a loud cry. The cry filled the entire sanctuary—it was a cry of gratitude and freedom!

Thanks to God's mercy and grace. He set me free from years of demonic bondage. As a matter of fact, while Jesus was on the earth, one-third of His ministry was spent casting out demons. He commanded His disciples to cast out demons wherever they preached. He also gave power and authority to His believers to cast out demons in His name.

[Jesus said,] Go into all the world and preach the gospel to every creature. He who believes and is baptized will be saved; but he who does not believe will be condemned. And these signs will follow those who believe: In My name they will cast out demons; they will speak with new tongues; they will take up serpents; and if they drink anything deadly, it will by no means hurt them; they will lay hands on the sick, and they will recover.

—Mark 16:15–18

After Jesus rose from the dead early on Sunday morning, the first person who saw him was Mary Magdalene, the woman from whom he had cast out seven demons.

—Mark 16:9 NLT

When the seventy-two disciples returned, they joyfully reported to him, "Lord, even the demons obey us when we use your name!"

—Luke 10:17 NLT

Encountering a Real Demon

After Pastor Rudi delivered the eleven demons out of me, these foul spirits lost control over me, and *they were infuriated!* They kept trying to win me back through every chance they might get. They were eager to ensnare me into their possession again. A few months later, I was in my prayer room praying. God spoke to me and said, "Call Pastor Rudi. He needs help." I then called him right away.

"Pastor Rudi, God told me to call you. Is there anything I can do for you?"

"Ying, the church air conditioning is broken. Someone fixed it a few days ago, but now it is broken again. We need money to fix it. The church is very hot. We have to stop the Sunday school because of this."

I asked, "How much do you need, Pastor Rudi?" He told me the amount.

"Where shall I give you the money, pastor? I can drop the money at your workplace if you prefer."

We then arranged to see each other (along with his son) at a restaurant inside Pastor Rudi's teaching facility—he used to be an Olympic champion of badminton for Indonesia. As we were eating dinner, something happened unexpectedly. A woman sat down next to me, and she did not even ask for permission. She just forced herself at our table. It was late at night. Many empty tables and chairs were available, but this woman was determined to sit next to me.

She was about forty-five years old and had tattoos on her arms and neck. The strange thing about her was her eyebrows—they were golden color. I had never seen such a person like that. As soon as she sat down, she started to talk:

"Who is this guy?" She said to me and pointed at Pastor Rudi.

"He is my pastor," I said.

Then she said, "Look at him. He does not look like a pastor. He does not know what he is talking about. Why do you even listen to him? You, on the other hand, are so beautiful, young and smart. Look, your face is glowing. You are more knowledgeable than he is. You do not need him. Do not even listen to him. You are so much better."

At that moment, I immediately knew that she was not from God. I thought she could be a witch, but her face was not human-like. I said to Pastor Rudi, "I have to go. I am not hungry." She quickly held my arm and insisted on me staying. "Do not go. Let him go. You stay with me and let me chat with you."

As we walked out of that place, I said to Paster Rudi, "That woman is a demon." The pastor said, "Yes." Pastor Rudi made sure that I got into my car and drove away before he took off.

Beloved readers, from the time I called Pastor Rudi, the demons were already in motion to stop me from giving the money to fix the church air conditioning. They were determined to hinder me from helping the church as well as winning me back. Demons are everywhere, and so are God's angels. We live in the natural realm, but they operate in the supernatural realms. Even though we cannot see them, it does not mean they do not exist.

My real-life encounters with these evil spirits have mostly been through people in my life. I have experienced demonic attacks through my bosses, employees, coworkers, and friends. Sometimes through Christians. But I had never seen a real demon in human form as I saw in the restaurant that night. The demons lost their battle over me. They kept trying to entice me back under their control. But that is not possible because *I love Jesus*. My life belongs to *Jesus now and forever!*

Understand Spirit, Soul, Body, and Flesh

How to describe a human identity accurately? Some Christian ministers often teach us to say, "I am a spirit, I have a soul, and I live in a body." What is the difference between spirit, soul, body, and flesh? In this chapter, I will do my best to explain this knowledge. Nevertheless, I am only a baby Christian; my understanding is limited and far from mature. Hence, I implore you, beloved readers, to do your own research.

Spirit

Our spirits came from the heart of the Father God. He has been carrying us for eons like a pregnant Mother. Inside the Father, there are no organs, but an eternal world—mountains, rivers, rainbows, gemstones, trees, flowers, etc.—far more brilliant than the beauty of Planet Earth and the entire universe. God is a Spirit. Therefore, please do not identify Him with our human intellect.

Our spirits are mini stature of us. They are translucent and tiny. Many people, such as Jesse Duplantis and Kat Kerr, have seen millions of little spirits flowing in and out of the Father's heart and nostrils during their heavenly visits.

At a person's conception, the Holy Spirit takes a spirit from Father God and puts it inside the mothers' womb. Unfortunately, our spirits are spiritually dead at birth because we are born into this fallen world—defiled by Adam and Eve's sin against God. In order to be accepted by heaven at a person's passing, that person's spirit must be "born again," which means accepting Jesus Christ as Lord and Savior. What does it mean by "born again" or "rebirth"? Jesus explained well in the following scripture.

> *Jesus answered, "Nicodemus, listen to this eternal truth: Before a person can even perceive God's kingdom, they must first experience a rebirth."*
>
> *Nicodemus said, "Rebirth? How can a gray-headed man be reborn? It's impossible for anyone to go back into the womb a second time and be reborn!"*
>
> *Jesus answered, "I speak an eternal truth: Unless you are born of water and the Spirit, you will never enter God's kingdom. For the natural realm only gives birth to things*

that are natural, but the spiritual realm gives birth to supernatural life!"

—John 3:3–6 TPT

One may ask, "Knowing that our spirits will be born dead, why does God even bother to let us be born into this corrupted world?" The answer is that God already had a solution before sending us to the earth. Before God ever created the universe, He already planned to send His Son, Jesus, to redeem humanity—this is His gift to mankind. It is up to us to decide whether we want everlasting life in heaven or hell. God never forces us to choose His Son, Jesus.

Beloved readers, whether you believe it or not, you are a dead spirit unless you are "born again" into Christ. All who refuse to accept Jesus Christ as Lord and Savior will go to hell. You are not allowed to enter God's Kingdom of heaven! Any false religion teaches you otherwise; *your blood is on their hands.*

Soul

Beloved readers, remember: you are a spirit, you have a soul, and you live in a body. Your soul is your "mind," "will," and "emotion." At the time of spiritual "rebirth," your spirit is made alive and surrenders to God, but your soul is not. It has not been "born again" to comply with God's will. Our souls must be disciplined (day by day) to obey God's commandments. How do we do that? It is done by transforming and renewing our minds through the teaching of the Holy Spirit and the Word of God—the Bible (see Romans 12:2).

Do not be conformed to this world [any longer with its superficial values and customs], but be transformed and progressively changed [as you mature spiritually] by the renewing of your mind [focusing on godly values and ethical attitudes], so that you may prove [for yourselves] what the will of God is, that which is good and acceptable and perfect [in His plan and purpose for you].

—Romans 12:2 AMP

Renewing our minds means restructuring how we think. To do this, we must forsake worldly wisdom and seek only God's wisdom. Ironically, it is very hard to renew the minds of religious fanatics or scholars because they are deeply grounded in human intelligence. On the contrary, it is fairly easy to teach an uneducated person. When Jesus was on the earth, He did not choose kings, queens, or religious leaders as His disciples, but fishermen, prostitutes, and so-called lower-class people.

The soul is our decision-maker. Daily, the soul stands at the crossroad, directing traffic of our conducts. It can lead us to satisfy our fleshly desires, such as drugs, alcohol, sexual immorality, murder, lie, pride, self-ambition, greediness, etc. Or it can lead us to righteousness, holiness, and blamelessness. Therefore, training our souls to obey God's will is vitally important.

Body

The body refers to our physical bodies. It was made of *dust* (see Genesis 3:17), and it will return to dust when we die.

To Adam the Lord God said, "Because you have listened [attentively] to the voice of your wife, and have eaten [fruit] from the tree about which I commanded you, saying, 'You shall not eat of it'; the ground is [now] under a curse because of you; in sorrow and toil you shall eat [the fruit] of it all the days of your life.

> "By the sweat of your face you will eat bread until you return to the ground, for from it you were taken; for you are dust, and to dust you shall return."
>
> —Genesis 3:17, 19 AMP

God is the *only* life-giving source to our mortal bodies. If He decides to withdraw life and breath from humans, we will all die and return to dust (see Psalm 90:1).

> Lord, you have always been our eternal home, our hiding place from generation to generation. Long before you gave birth to the earth and before the mountains were born, you have been from everlasting to everlasting, the one and only true God. When you speak the words "Life, return to me!" man turns back to dust.
>
> —Psalm 90:1–3 TPT

Beloved readers, please understand this truth: when believers of Jesus Christ die, their spirits and souls will go to heaven to be with God. Their earthly bodies will return to dust; just as the scripture says, "*The dust [out of which God made man's body] will return to the earth as it was, and the spirit will return to God who gave it*" (Ecclesiastes 12:7 AMP). In heaven, the believers will be given brand-new spiritual bodies made by light.

On the other hand, for the unbelievers (people who refuse to accept Jesus Christ as their Lord and Savior), their spirits will be taken back to heaven by God when they die. But their souls will descend to hell for eternal punishment.

Flesh

The Bible clearly tells us that people who are still under the control of their sinful nature (flesh) are hostile to God.

> *The mind governed by the flesh is death, but the mind governed by the Spirit is life and peace. The mind governed by the flesh is hostile to God; it does not submit to God's law, nor can it do so. Those who are in the realm of the flesh cannot please God.*
>
> —Romans 8:6–8 NIV

> *Walk in the Spirit, and you shall not fulfill the lust of the flesh. For the flesh lusts against the Spirit, and the Spirit against the flesh; and these are contrary to one another.*
>
> —Galatians 5:16–17

The *"Spirit"* in the above scriptures refers to the Holy Spirit. The following scripture defines *flesh*:

> *The works of the flesh are evident: sexual immorality, impurity, sensuality, idolatry, sorcery, enmity, strife, jealousy, fits of anger, rivalries, dissensions, divisions, envy, drunkenness, orgies, and things like these. I warn you, as I warned you before, that those who do such things will not inherit the kingdom of God.*
>
> —Galatians 5:19–21 ESV

The acts of the flesh are also described in Romans 1:29 and 1 Corinthians 6:9. The consequence of walking in the flesh is *death*—meaning when these people die, they cannot go to heaven, but to hell.

> *They have become filled with every kind of wickedness, evil, greed and depravity. They are full of envy, murder,*

strife, deceit and malice. They are gossips, slanderers, God-haters, insolent, arrogant and boastful; they invent ways of doing evil; they disobey their parents; they have no understanding, no fidelity, no love, no mercy.

—Romans 1:29–32 NIV

Don't you realize that those who do wrong will not inherit the Kingdom of God? Don't fool yourselves. Those who indulge in sexual sin, or who worship idols, or commit adultery, or are male prostitutes, or practice homosexuality, or are thieves, or greedy people, or drunkards, or are abusive, or cheat people—none of these will inherit the Kingdom of God.

—1 Corinthians 6:9–10 NLT

In Galatians 5:19 and 1 Corinthians 6:9, the phrase *"will not inherit the Kingdom of God"* means *cannot go to heaven*. All the scriptures listed above are the behaviors of the flesh.

But what is the *flesh* really? The flesh is our worst enemy. It is a state of mind, heart, and emotion contrary to God. It came from the consequences of Adam and Eve's sin—when they ate the fruit of the Tree of the Knowledge of Good and Evil. The defiled nature of mankind is rooted in the poison of that tree.

The Tree of Life leads us to God's grace, but the Tree of the Knowledge of Good and Evil leads us to bondage—refers to the Old Testament's Law. The law brought death to the human race. As the scripture says, *"The sting of death is sin, and the power of sin is the law"* (1 Corinthians 15:56 ESV).

The flesh draws our eyes inward to ourselves, such as self-centeredness, self-righteousness, self-consciousness, and selfishness. It draws our eyes away from Jesus Christ, who is the source of life and grace.

When we walk in the flesh, we walk in the likeness of Satan. When we walk in the Spirit (Holy Spirit), we walk in the likeness of Christ.

The flesh is like a data warehouse. It stores the bad memories we have had throughout our lives, such as pain, sorrow, rejection, abandonment, injustice, resentment, etc. These memories keep us in a sorrowful and hopeless mindset. The flesh is extremely selfish. It cannot be redeemed because it is incapable of loving and forgiving. It is hostile to God because *"God is love"* (1 John 4:8), and He is a forgiving God.

When we act in the flesh, we give demons legal rights to enter our lives and bodies to torment us. When Jesus died on the cross and redeemed our sins, the strength of our flesh lost its power. As long as we walk in the Spirit and the likeness of Christ, our flesh has no power to control us. Yet, habitually, we do not walk in the Spirit, but allow our flesh to manifest its power. This is why Jesus commanded us to crucify our flesh by saying, *"If anyone desires to come after Me, let him deny himself, and take up his cross daily, and follow Me"* (Luke 9:23). To deny ourselves means to crucify our flesh.

Noticed, the Lord commanded us to crucify our flesh *daily*. It is a slow process—*a slow death*. It can be very painful and difficult. The worst part of our flesh is *pride*. It was pride that caused Lucifer to fall. In any given situation, our souls must choose between satisfying our flesh or obeying the Holy Spirit. It is a *daily choice*, and it is *not easy!*

In the process of crucifying my flesh, I often failed because I was not depending on the Holy Spirit and drawing from His power. I learned that we could not crucify our flesh based on our own strengths. We *must* lean on the Holy Spirit.

For many years, demons used my flesh to control me, attack me, and torment me. My life was *miserable!* But after I was born again in Christ, the closer I am to God, the less power my flesh has. Before, I could not love anyone; I could not even love myself. Gradually, I started practicing love. When we act in love, we know that our flesh is dead because the *flesh cannot love*.

Rats and Garbage

Because of my painful and traumatized childhood, the manifestations of my flesh were very strong. My soul was like a computer memory storage; it remembered all the pains, sorrows, abandonments, rejections, loneliness, and abuses I had experienced. Even though the demons were cast out of my body, I was still not totally free from their bondage. The root of my problem was not removed because the wounds in my soul were still there. In other words, those wounds were not deleted from my soul's memory storage.

It is like pulling the weeds without destroying the roots. The demons are like the weeds, and the injuries in my soul are like the roots. Even though I have accepted Jesus Christ as Lord and Savior, the process of growing my trust in Him and crucifying my flesh has been a long journey. My soul was still bleeding at that time—it still attracted the sharks—demons.

Charles H. Kraft describes in his book, *Deep Wounds Deep Healing*, how a wounded soul can still attract demons after deliverance. In most cases, myself as an example, demons can come back after being cast out. Demons are like rats, and the wounded soul is like garbage. Unless the garbage is cleaned up, the rats will keep coming back. The real problems are the soul wounds, not the demons.[9]

In order to live in people, demons must be given legal rights to do so. The rights are passed on to the demons when we sin—give them footholds. When sins are repented, we take the legal rights back from them. At which point, the demons are fairly easy to be cast out from our bodies. Most deliverance ministries focus on casting out the rats rather than cleaning the garbage—the root cause.

Deep-level healing is necessary and essential before driving out demons. I have witnessed some ministries keep casting out the same demon from the same person over and over again. They fail to realize that *demons* are always *secondary*—soul healing is primary.

Demons can only attach to conditions that already exist. They are not stupid. They do intensive research on each person whom they what to attach to. They use our flesh, weakness, and vulnerability to infiltrate us. If we keep on sinning and harboring garbage in our lives, we open doors to welcome demons.

Many Christian ministers disbelieve deep-level healing. Their argument is that Jesus did not perform inner healing before casting out demons. True, I agree. The Bible did not document any deep-level healing done by Jesus. But it is also true that many Christians have gone through multiple deliverances, yet the demons still come back to their bodies. If you need an example, read the following scripture:

> [Jesus said,] "When an unclean spirit goes out of a man, he goes through dry places, seeking rest, and finds none. Then he says, 'I will return to my house from which I came.' And when he comes, he finds it empty, swept, and put in order. Then he goes and takes with him seven other spirits more wicked than himself, and they enter and dwell there; and the last state of that man is worse than the first."
>
> —Matthew 12:43–45

In this scripture, the *"unclean spirit"* refers to the demon, and the *"house"* refers to the man's body. We noticed that the same demon which was cast out from the man's body came back with seven more wicked demons. As a result, the man's condition is worse than before. Therefore, healing the wounded soul before casting out demons is *absolutely essential*.

My Second Deliverance

I am living proof of the rats and garbage theory. After my first deliverance, some demons, such as sexual immorality, anger, and outbursts of rage, were indeed cast out. But some of them came back. Pastor Rudi provided spiritual counseling; he even performed a water baptism again, but the situation did not improve. The spirits of rejection, bitterness, offensiveness, unforgiveness, and self-pity returned. Still, I heard lots of demonic voices and suffered some horrible dreams.

After pleading with God, the Holy Spirit sent me to a Christian deliverance ministry called Moriah Freedom Ministry. They specialized in inner healing and deliverance. I called the office many times, but no one called me back. Finally, a lady called me back saying, "Very strange, I called you nine times, but the call did not go through. However, the Holy Spirit kept asking me to call you." We both knew that the demons were preventing her from reaching me. Right after she scheduled me to see the owner, Mr. James Hanley, the demons threatened me with a dream. They are bullies and gangsters. *They are sheer evil!*

The Dream

I was walking into a long and deep forest trail. The trees in this forest formed a long cave. All the overhanging branches were intertwined tightly together. There were no leaves, just huge stems. They were closely knotted and blocked the sky. I was puzzled why the trees were so tightly interlocked and also moving. When I looked closely, they were millions of serpents—large ones and small ones. But from a distance, they looked like branches.

As soon as I realized they were not branches, one of the serpents descended toward me, landed on my shoulder, and bit me. It was an extremely poisonous one—about eight feet long, with red, orange, and black patterned skin.

Instantly, Mark 16:17 came into my mind. At that moment, I was not afraid of the serpent. Instead, I just wanted to kill it. For I knew it was a demonic spirit who intended to hinder me from being set free.

> *In my [Jesus'] name they will cast out demons; they will speak in new tongues; they will pick up serpents with their hands; and if they drink any deadly poison, it will not hurt them.*
>
> —Mark 16:17–18 ESV

At that moment, the serpent was still biting me, but I yanked it off of my shoulder and wrapped its head with my jacket. With all the energy I had, I smashed the serpent's head on the ground and shouted, "Die! Die! Die!" I kept pounding and stepping until it was dead. I, on the other hand, was not harmed at all—just as Jesus said in Mark 16:17.

Before our meeting, James Hanley asked me to read his book *Healing the Shattered Soul*. He also instructed me to do a week-long intensive repentance. In doing so, I could take the legal rights back from the enemies. This was the prerequisite before the healing sessions began.

James has helped more than six thousand Christians who needed inner healings and deliverances. Each session was one hour long. After my first session, I asked, "James, why didn't you cast out the demons?" He said to me, "If I cast out the demons without healing your wounded soul, the demons will come back right away. I have seen thousands of cases. It has happened to every Christian that I helped. You must go through the deep-level healing first. Then, at the last session, I will drive out the demons."

I went through more than twenty sessions of inner healing. Each time was like having a major surgery—James was digging the root problems from my childhood to adulthood. He searched for every pocket of pain, sorrow, rejection, bitterness, fear, abandonment, etc., from my soul.

Close to the end of the deep healing process, the demons became very weak because they had nothing to cling to. The garbage (soul wounds) was emptied out. Therefore, the rats (demons) lost their legal ground to possess and control me. Then at the last session, the demons were cast out. After that, I felt *light* and *free*. Pure joy filled my heart, which I had never felt before. All these works were done by the Holy Spirit through Moriah Freedom Ministry. *To God be the glory!*

All my deliverances were performed by the Holy Spirit. Without Him, there was no deliverance. God created us in His own image and rendered us in His likeness. He did not create defective children. Originally, we were perfectly made, just as He is perfect. After mankind fell from God's divine glory by Adam and Eve, God's earnest desire is to restore us to His perfection—holy and blameless. Thus, it is His greatest pleasure to heal our wounded souls and deliver us from demonic bondage. He does this out of His absolute mercy, grace, goodness, and love. Thus, *our ultimate deliverance is to rest in Him!*

Even though we are being attacked ruthlessly by our enemy in these end-time seasons and going through the most intense demonic onslaughts, God will never allow the enemies to stretch us beyond our limits. Just like the biblical character of Job. He was tested to the ultimate limit—physically, mentally, and spiritually. But God eventually restored Job with sevenfold blessings. Our God is the *Expert* in restitution, restoration, and deliverance!

Discerning the Voice of Demons

After rebirthing into Christ, I could be more productive and closer to God if I knew how to discern demonic voices. Daily, I heard many voices, but I could not distinguish them. Some of them were from God, some were from me, and others were from demons. Since I was a baby Christian, I had not learned how to differentiate these voices. I was easily manipulated and discouraged by the demonic voices.

Demons are spirits. They know my past and present. They also do intensive studies on a person whom they want to attack. From our ancestors to the current generations, they know where the entry points are to penetrate a person. They know which button to push and make a person disheartened.

I noticed a pattern of how the demons operated on me. Day and night, I was bombarded by these voices, especially after I became a Christian. Unfortunately, for a long time, I truly believed the messages I heard. I was miserable by the enemy's deceptions.

Lies

There are only two facts: *truth* or *lies*. The truth is always from God, and lies are always from the devil. Hebrews 6:18 says, *"It is impossible for God to lie"* (NLT). Satan has to lie to draw us away from the truth (Jesus). The entire human race fell and lost our divine nature because Satan (the serpent) lied to Eve. Satan, the father of lies, has never stopped lying to us (see John 8:44). I was a victim of his lies for many years.

> *[Jesus said to the religious leaders,] You are of your father the devil, and you want to do the desires of your father. He was a murderer from the beginning, and does not stand in the truth because there is no truth in him. Whenever he speaks a lie, he speaks from his own nature, because he is a liar and the father of lies.*
>
> —John 8:44 NASB

Many times, I would hear voices and get so discouraged because I believed them wholeheartedly. I would stay away from my prayer room for weeks because I thought God was mad at me. The voices caused me to believe that God had an angry face and a stick in His hand, that He was always ready to punish me whenever I came to Him. Every time, as I was about to go to my prayer room, I would hear the following voice:

"Jesus thinks you are filthy, dirty, and disgusting. You are a sexually immoral woman. Jesus is pure. He cannot stand a filthy woman like you. Do not even go to the prayer room. He absolutely loathes you!

"God is so disappointed with you. You did not pray and study the Bible for two days. He does not want to see your face. You are an unfaithful child. Do not bother to go to your prayer room. He will turn His face away from you. He is ready to whip you!"

After my second divorce, my biggest fear was stepping out of my front door. Every time I opened my house door, a voice would tell me:

"Do not go out! Your neighbors are watching you. They are gossiping about you. Saying, 'look at that pathetic woman, abandoned by her husband, still single, and no one wants her.'"

When I heard such a voice, I felt a sharp knife stabbing in my heart, and I had to shut the door quickly. I would be literally out of breath, and my body would shake violently. I would wait until night, when no one was on the street, to pick up my mails or take a walk. To avoid shame, I pushed away all my friends. Sometimes, they came to visit me and knocked on the door; I would duck and crawl on the floor so that they would not see me through the windows. I shut out all my contacts, avoided phone calls, and built a huge wall between myself and society. The spirit of shame and guilt completely crippled me. They were like heavy chains wrapped around my neck, making me hard to breathe.

One of my coworkers' husbands worked at the same company that my husband worked. After learning my husband had abandoned me, he told his wife about the news. Unfortunately, his wife treated this as a juicy message. She started to spread the news around my office. Some of the kind coworkers told me about what she said. It hurt me deeply.

One day, I saw this woman at a supermarket (she did not see me). Fear, shame, and self-pity suddenly gripped me. The word she spread about me turned into an *ugly giant* and terrified me. I said to myself, "Run, Ying, run from her!" I grabbed some tomatoes, ran to the cashier, paid, and dashed out of the supermarket. Then the cashier chased after me and said, "Miss, you left your purse, credit card, and tomatoes on the counter. Don't you want them? You paid for them. Why are you running?"

I now understand the *ugly giant* was the enemies' lies and trickery. They tried to isolate me from people and paralyze me. Just like wild beasts attack a herd of deer, they first separate the most vulnerable one from the herd, then attack and kill. Unfortunately, for many years, I believed the lies of the enemy. I had a tough time going outside. I literally imprisoned myself inside my own house.

Doubt

After believing so many lies, I started to doubt whether God was angry at me or pleased with me, whether He loved me or hated me. I used to say, "Lord, yesterday You told me You love me, but today You told me I am disgusting. I am so confused!"

During the preparation for my missionary training and service in Brazil, I decided to take nine months off from work, dive deeply into God's Word, and spend time with Him. Every day, I spent eight to ten hours praying and studying the Bible. During that time, I asked God to give me an evaluation. I wrote many categories about my walk with God and genuinely sought His opinions about my performance. I had ratings of one through five, with five being the highest. Out of twelve categories, I rated myself mostly ones, twos, hardly ever threes—not to mention fours or fives.

Then I asked, "Father, I have done my self-rating. Now, would you please rate me? What do you think about my performance?" To my astonishment, He gave me a few threes and many fours. I said, "How can this be? I constantly hear that I am lazy, not good, and You are disappointed with me. How can you give me threes and fours? Are You doing this just to encourage me, while in reality, I don't deserve it?" Then the Father spoke:

> "You listened to the lies of the enemies. You were constantly beating yourself. I don't see you as you see yourself. You always look down on yourself. You have the spirit of self-pity, self-criticism, and self-condemnation."

He then continued . . .

> "My beloved child, this is how I see you . . . You are very precious to Me! Your love for My Son always touches My heart. Not many of My children on the earth love My Son the way you do. This is very important to Me. Your worship and prayers always melt My heart. I am deeply touched by Your love for Me. You are a child who is after My own heart. I have chosen you to do mighty works for My Kingdom."

I was *stunned* by the Father's message! The demons were tenacious. Their only goal was to destroy me. Regularly, my ears were filled with their lies which made me doubt. They would say:

> "Are you really sure Jesus likes the flowers, poems, and gifts that you gave Him? Are you really sure He is pleased with you? What makes you think that Jesus loves you? You are neither a superstar nor a church leader. How can He pay attention to you? *You are so ugly!* How can God even stand your *ugly face*?

> "Are you really sure that God will allow you to go to heaven? What makes you think that your name is on The Book of Life? You have not done anything for His Kingdom. You often disobey His commandments. You sin all the time. Many Christians are in hell now. What makes you think that He will allow you to go to heaven?"

Confusion

Doubt is a deadly weapon of Satan. It often paralyzed me and led me to question God's love and salvation. Eventually, it led me into deep confusion and uncertainty. I would say to God:

> "My Lord, yesterday You said You are pleased with me. Today You are disappointed with me and even think that I am filthy, dirty, and ugly. I am so confused."

Deception

Reading the Bible or receiving prophecies without the Holy Spirit can be devastating. I had been pondering over Bob Jones's prophecy. He had a near-death experience in 1975; that was when he witnessed something astounding. He saw people in two lines: one was to hell, and the other was to heaven. The sad news was that 98 percent of the people were in the line to hell. In other words, only 2 percent of the people were in the line to heaven (he was in this line). He literally saw the gods of 98 percent of people—the gods of money, fame, idol, drug, and sexual immorality. These gods were like patches on their bodies.[10] These people did not accept the true God—Jesus Christ. Therefore, they were on the way to hell.

Bob Jones was an anointed seer and well-known prophet. I trusted his prophecy wholeheartedly. But what bothered me was whether or not I would be in the line of 2 percent. Out of fear, I started making assumptions: as of June 2020, the world population was 7.8 billion, and 2 percent of 7.8 billion is 156 million. I was terrified about this number. As soon as the demons sensed I was confused, they started deceiving me:

> "It is extremely difficult to go to heaven. Only those who are true ministers of God can go. Look at you. What are you? You have not done anything for God's Kingdom yet. What

makes you think that Jesus will allow you to go to heaven? Don't believe what He said. In the end, He will surely send you to hell!"

I was very much troubled by this voice. I cried out to God and asked Him the truth. Then the Father said to me:

"My beloved child, you *break My heart* by asking such a question! Why should I send you to hell? What makes you think that I will abandon you? Why do you put yourself among those who reject My Son and deserve eternal punishment? For what reason should I punish you? You are a precious darling to Me, and I love you so dearly. It is time for you to have faith in Me, trust Me, and stop listening to the lies!"

Beloved readers, from Genesis to the present time, Satan has never stopped deceiving God's children. The entire human race was separated from God because Satan deceived Adam and Eve. As for me, day and night, the demons tried all kinds of tricks. They caused me to doubt my salvation and believe that I would go to hell no matter what I did.

> *The great dragon was cast out, that serpent of old, called the Devil and Satan, who deceives the whole world.*
>
> —Revelation 12:9

Condemnation

After the demons bombarded me with lies, doubts, confusions, and deceptions, they would use another deadly weapon: condemnation.

Satan often quotes scriptures to condemn God's children. His primary scheme is to turn the Bible into law (legalism) and draw us away from God's grace (Jesus). The old serpent (Satan) has never stopped enticing us to eat the fruit from the Tree of the Knowledge of

Good and Evil, which is legalism and law. The scripture says, *"The sting of death is sin, and the power of sin is the law"* (1 Corinthians 15:56 ESV), and *"The wages of sin is death"* (Romans 6:23). Satan uses law (letter) to condemn God's children. For *"The letter kills, but the Spirit gives life"* (2 Corinthians 3:6). Below is how the enemy used to condemn me:

> "You should have studied the Bible for three hours, but you only did one hour. You were supposed to worship God for five hours, but you only did thirty minutes. By now, you are supposed to be a mature Christian, but you are still a baby! God has moved on and chosen someone else to do His biddings because He thinks you are useless!"

Beloved readers, God never condemns His children (see John 3:17). Anything that makes us feel confused, doubtful, and condemned is not from God. Unfortunately, I did not have the discernment until later years. I suffered terribly because of the enemies' condemnations.

> *God did not send His Son [Jesus] into the world to condemn the world, but that the world through Him might be saved.*
>
> —John 3:17

Shame and Guilt

After being condemned, I felt guilty and ashamed. I would stay away from my prayer room for weeks. I was afraid the Lord might say, "You are an unfaithful and a lazy servant." At this point, the evil voice still would not give up:

> "Shame on you! God loved you so much, but you took His kindness and love in vain. He is so disappointed in you. What a Shame!"

The enemy even used Christians to condemn me. After being born again, my life was in a warzone. I experienced countless failures, trials, and tribulations. I was in constant persecution and attacks from all directions. As Apostle Paul said in 2 Timothy 3:12, *"All who desire to live godly in Christ Jesus will suffer persecution."*

One day, I shared my failures with a Christian friend. To my astonishment, he said, "You must have offended God, and He is punishing you." I then remembered the book of Job in the Bible. While Job underwent the most brutal assaults from Satan, his best friends mocked him and imposed shame on him. That day, I felt my body was covered with wounds; instead of comforting me, this friend poured vinegar on my wounds—just as the Proverbs says,

> *Singing cheerful songs to a person with a heavy heart is like taking someone's coat in cold weather or pouring vinegar in a wound.*
>
> —Proverbs 25:20 NLT

Kill

Satan's only goal is to kill, steal, and destroy. By the time I was very much manipulated, intimidated, and weakened, the demons finally pulled the trigger like this:

> "Why don't you just kill yourself. What is there to live for? God has rejected you. Don't even bother to study the Bible and pray. He has removed your name from The Book of Life. You will go to hell anyway."

Demons are pure evil! Satan knows that he cannot hurt God, so he hurts us instead. Humans are the only species that were made in God's image. Satan is deadly jealous of humankind. He is responsible for all destructions to the human race, such as depression, suicide, wars, etc.

Use suicide as an example. According to CDC and the World Health Organization, suicide is the tenth leading cause of death in the United

States of America—about 1.4 million people attempted suicide in 2019. Globally, more than eight hundred thousand people commit suicide each year—approximately one death every forty seconds.[11] The truth is that God never lies, deceives, devastates, and condemns His children. When so many senseless deaths occur, they are definitely from the devil.

Beloved readers, it took me years to learn how to discern demonic voices. The key is that the more time we spend with God, the less demonic attacks we encounter. When we are engulfed by God's glory and light, the enemies are blinded by His blazing radiance. When we stay close to God, we even smell good—carry His fragrance. As soon as the demons smell the fragrance of holiness, they do not come close.

Understand the Power of Humans over Demons

To my understanding, there are four types of enemies that are under Satan's command:

- Demonic principalities
- Diabolic Powers
- Rulers of darkness
- Spiritual hosts (armies) of wickedness

These enemies are not made of flesh and blood; they are spiritual beings—invisible to human eyes. Therefore, we cannot use our earthly weapons to battle against them. The scriptures say:

> [Apostle Paul said,] *We do not wrestle against flesh and blood, but against principalities, against powers, against the rulers of the darkness of this age, against spiritual hosts of wickedness in the heavenly places.*
>
> —Ephesians 6:12

> *[Jesus said,] I have imparted to you my authority to trample over his [Satan's] kingdom. You will trample upon every demon before you and overcome every power Satan possesses. Absolutely nothing will harm you as you walk in this authority.*
>
> —Luke 10:19 TPT

According to Luke 10:19, God has given us *total authority* over *all the power* of the enemies. There are maybe trillions upon trillions of satanic armies. Even though they are powerful, God's children can trample them all. The principalities of darkness are actually afraid of humans if we use the authority that God gives us. Unfortunately, most humans do not know this truth.

Humans Were Created Higher Than Angels

Who are we really? The Bible clearly tells us that we are made in God's image and according to His likeness. *In His image* means we look like Him. *In His likeness* means we have His attribute, character, and intelligence. Among all the creatures God created in the cosmos, only the human species was made in His image. Although the angelic kingdom, animal kingdom, and plant kingdom are all God's artworks, humans are special to God.

God created angels out of His holiness; hence, they are called "holy angels." But God created humans out of His love. Angels are intended to be God's servants, but humans are intended to be His family. We humans are not beggars, cowards, or weaklings; we are the sons and daughters of Almighty God. We are the princes and princesses of His Kingdom.

Beloved readers, I want you to know this *absolute truth*: human beings were created higher ranking than angels. We were made just a little lower than God Himself—*Elohim* (God in Hebrew). When Elohim gave Adam the total authority and dominion to govern the earth (see Genesis 1:26), Satan was furious and utterly jealous. He then approached the Court of Heaven to question God (see Psalm 8:4) regarding the authorities God granted to humans. Satan hated the fact that human beings were made higher than the angelic beings—himself included.

> *God said, "Let Us make man in Our image, according to Our likeness; let them have dominion over the fish of the sea, over the birds of the air, and over the cattle, over all the earth and over every creeping thing that creeps on the earth."*
>
> —Genesis 1:26

> *[Satan questioned God,] Why would you bother with puny, mortal man or care about human beings? Yet what honor you have given to men, created only a little lower than Elohim, crowned with glory and magnificence. You have delegated to them rulership over all you have made, with everything under their authority, placing earth itself under the feet of your image-bearers. All the created order and every living thing of the earth, sky, and sea—the wildest beasts and all that move in the paths of the sea— everything is in submission to Adam's sons [the human race].*
>
> —Psalm 8:4–8 TPT

Out of Satan's sheer rage, he boldly challenged God for creating humans. His *pride* and *jealousy* destined his eternal downfall. In other words, the existence of the human race triggered Satan and his fallen angels to rebel against God. We, Adam's descendants, do not realize how valuable we are. We idolize angels, worship demons, and make statues of animals as gods—not knowing that we are created higher than them all. We often devalue ourselves for lack of understanding of our true identities.

Therefore, we need to declare who we are in Christ. Not only to remind ourselves, but also to remind the enemies. We must let them know that *they cannot mess with us!* I wrote the following declaration and read it out loud from time to time.

Declaration of Who I Am

I am a daughter of the Most High God.
Jesus Christ is my Lord and Savior.
Holy Spirit is my Helper and Comforter.
I am wonderfully and remarkably made in God's image.

I have been redeemed by Jesus Christ.
I have been washed by the blood of the Lamb.
I am the righteousness of God through Jesus Christ.
All my sins are forgiven at the cross.

I am a Heavenian!
The earth is my temporary residence.
I am seated with Jesus Christ in the heavenly place.
My name is written in The Book of Life.

I am the apple of God's eyes.
He hides me under His wings.
I am highly favored, greatly blessed, and deeply loved,
by the Father, the Son, and the Holy Spirit.

I am a soldier of the Lord's end-time army.
The hosts of heaven are on my team.

JESUS, MY FOREVER LOVE

The Lord goes before me, and guards behind me.
He will never leave me nor forsake me.

I am a child of light.
I am the salt of the world.
I am the display of God's glory.
He shines through me everywhere I go.

As Jesus is, so am I in this world.
I choose to be holy, for He is holy.
I choose to be perfect, for my Father is perfect.
I choose to be joyful, for joy is a weapon.

I am a bondservant of Jesus Christ.
I serve my Master with fear and trembling.
I obey His commandments and walk in His ways.
I lay down my life at His feet!

I belong to Christ, and He is my Maker.
I am His sheep, and He is my Shepherd.
If I live, I live for Him. If I die, I die for Him,
Whether I live or die, I belong to Him.

The Spirit of God lives in me.
I am the temple of the Holy Spirit.
He sealed me for the day of redemption.
He anointed me with the oil of gladness.

I take authorities to trample demons under my feet.
I have power over all satanic armies.
No evil shall befall me, for the Lord is my shield.
No plague shall come to me, for the Lord is my safeguard.

I am exceedingly joyful when facing trials of many kinds.
I am not afraid of tribulations or persecutions,
Because God's grace is perfect for my weakness.

I shout *grace, grace, grace* to all my troubles.

The Lord is the Vine, and I am the branch.
Without Him, I can do nothing.
The Lord is the reason for my existence.
He is the source of my breath!

I choose life, not death.
I choose light, not darkness.
I choose God, not Satan.
I choose to lay down my life for Jesus Christ.

I hold the sword of the Spirit in my hand.
I have the burning coal of heaven in my mouth.
I have the eagle's wings on my back.
I am filled with the Holy Ghost!

I am baptized by Holy Fire.
My heart flows with the rivers of life.
I am no longer a slave of bondage.
I am a child of the Almighty God!

The Lord gives me beauty for ashes.
He anoints me with oil of joy.
He plants me as a tree of righteousness,
That I may yield fruits of holiness.

I am a warrior of the Lord's army.
I report duty at His command.
I pledge allegiance to His Kingdom,
And take up the cross to follow Him daily.

I am commissioned to do Father's business—
Preach the gospel, heal the sick, and cast out demons.
For His Kingdom's sake,
I live and exist every single day!

Very often, we are easily deceived by our enemies because we do not know our true identities. Thus, knowing our identities is Satan's number one nightmare. If idolaters, false religious believers, murderers, homosexuals, corrupted politicians, and satanic followers understand who they are in God, and how valuable they are in their Creator's eyes, they will not sell their souls to the devil.

Daily, many people end up in hell because they refuse to accept Jesus Christ as Lord. God said, *"My people are destroyed for lack of knowledge. Because you have rejected knowledge"* (Hosea 4:6). The *"knowledge"* God refers to is knowing who Jesus is, and what He had offered to humanity. If people accept Jesus Christ as Lord and renounce Satan, they will go to heaven. *It is that simple!* But many are stubborn to accept this fundamental truth and end up in hell!

Our Commander

The Lord of hosts (Jesus Christ) is the Supreme Commander of heavenly armies. But the Holy Spirit is the One who executes God's battle plans on the earth. Without the Holy Spirit, we cannot win wars over Satan. It is the Holy Spirit who carries the "Dunamis Power" and *"The powers of the age to come"* (Hebrews 6:5). The Holy Spirit is Jesus unlimited.

Without the Holy Spirit:

- We cannot fully understand God.
- We cannot truly comprehend the Bible.
- We have no wisdom and discernment.
- We have no spiritual gifts and power.
- We do not know the deep secrets of God.
- The churches are no better than some social clubs.

What Weapons Do We Use?

We should never go to battles without putting on the armors of God.

> *Take up the whole armor of God, that you may be able to withstand in the evil day. . . . Having girded your waist with truth, having put on the breastplate of righteousness, and having shod your feet with the preparation of the gospel of peace; above all, taking the shield of faith with which you will be able to quench all the fiery darts of the wicked one. And take the helmet of salvation, and the sword of the Spirit, which is the word of God.*
>
> —Ephesians 6:13–17

Helmet of Salvation

To protect our heads, we must put on the helmet of salvation—this is fundamental. To receive this helmet, one must be "born again" by accepting Jesus Christ as Lord and Savior. *Unbelievers* cannot have this helmet. Hence, they are the easy targets for demonic arrows.

The word "salvation" refers to "deliverance" or "redemption" of a person's soul from sin and its consequences. What Jesus did on the cross was the redemption of our sins from past, present, and future—He paid them all. Nonetheless, this does not give us the green light to sin freely.

Through the blood of Jesus Christ and His salvation, Christians have become righteous and blameless before God. However, Satan constantly reminds our past sins to condemn us, making us feel guilty for the sins that Jesus has already redeemed. Therefore, putting on the helmet of salvation will protect our minds from believing the lies of the devil.

Breastplate of Righteousness

Without righteousness, no one shall see God. As Apostle Paul said in 1 Corinthians 6:9, the unrighteous people could not inherit the Kingdom of God, but go to hell.

> *Don't you realize that those who do wrong will not inherit the Kingdom of God? Don't fool yourselves. Those who indulge in sexual sin, or who worship idols, or commit adultery, or are male prostitutes, or practice homosexuality, or are thieves, or greedy people, or drunkards, or are abusive, or cheat people—none of these will inherit the Kingdom of God.*
>
> —1 Corinthians 6:9–10 NLT

Righteousness is one of the principles that God operates in His Kingdom. It is the moral quality or state of being upright. *"Righteousness and justice are the foundation of God's throne"* (Psalm 89:14, author's paraphrase).

Gird Your Waist with Truth

"Jesus" is His earthly name; His heavenly name is "Word." He is the "Word of Truth." Truth comes from Jesus Christ. As the scripture says, *"The law was given through Moses, but grace and truth came through Jesus Christ"* (John 1:17).

The unbelievers consider Jesus as one of the prophets, such as Muhammad, Buddha, or Hindu deities. This belief is *a lie from hell!* Whoever believes this saying *cannot go to heaven, but to hell!*

The truth is:
- Jesus is God—He is part of the Godhead.
- He is the King of kings and Lord of lords.

- He is the only Gateway to heaven.

In the beginning [before all time] was the Word (Christ), and the Word was with God, and the Word was God Himself.

—John 1:1 AMP

Jesus said to him, "I am the [only] Way [to God] and the [real] Truth and the [real] Life; no one comes to the Father but through Me.

—John 14:6 AMP

Beloved readers, why does God repeatedly tell us to know the truth, only because He does not want people to go to hell. So, wake up, *all unbelievers (sleepers)!*

[God says,] Arise, you sleeper! Rise up from your coffin and the Anointed One [Christ] will shine his light into you!

—Ephesians 5:14 TPT

Shield of Faith

Faith is the assurance of things we hope for and the certainty of things we cannot see. In order for us to win combat in the spirit realm, we must have faith in God. For the battle is not ours, but God's. Throughout Bible history, many triumphant battles were the result of people putting their faith in God. For example:

- Walls of Jericho fell because Joshua put his faith in God.
- Gideon defeated Midianites because he had faith in God.
- David killed Goliath because he put his faith in God.
- One angel killed 185,000 Assyrian armies because King Hezekiah put his faith in God.

- God destroyed the mighty armies of Moabites, Ammonites, and Edomites because King Jehoshaphat put his faith in God.

A true believer of Christ does not put faith in signs, wonders, or miracles, but in the One (Jesus) who does the miracles. Truth faith is acknowledging who Jesus is—nothing more and nothing less.

Feet Shod with Preparation of Gospel of Peace

In any warfare setting, soldiers must have well-designed shoes or boots in order to engage in the rough battlefield. Christ believers: evangelists, prophets, and missionaries must rely on the anointing of the Holy Spirit for solid and firm footings to withstand bumpy roads and harsh battlegrounds when preaching the gospel of peace to the whole world.

> *How beautiful are the feet of those who preach the gospel of peace, who bring glad tidings of good things!*
>
> —Romans 10:15

Sword of the Spirit

When Jesus was being tested in the wilderness for forty days and forty nights, He defeated Satan by using the Word of God. He quoted scriptures three times: "It is written . . . It is written . . . It is written . . ." (see Matthew 4) in responding to Satan's temptation. Those scriptures were like sharp two-edged swords pierced into Satan's evil schemes (see Hebrews 4:12).

"It is written, 'Man shall not live by bread alone, but by every word that proceeds from the mouth of God.'"

"It is written again, 'You shall not tempt the Lord your God.'"

"It is written, 'You shall worship the Lord your God, and Him only you shall serve.'"

—Matthew 4:4, 7, 10

The word of God is living and powerful, and sharper than any two-edged sword, piercing even to the division of soul and spirit, and of joints and marrow.

—Hebrews 4:12

File Lawsuits Against Satan

We know that heaven is in the spiritual realm, and the earth is in the natural realm. Planet Earth is just a shadow of heaven. Whatever we have here, heaven has much more. Many prophets, who have visited heaven, revealed information about heaven's Highest Courts of Justice. We, the children of God, have access to these Courts.

Unfortunately, Satan also has access to the Courts of Heaven. When Adam and Eve sinned and disobeyed God, they deserted God and switched allegiance to Satan. Ever since, Satan has been legally entitled to file claims against mankind in heaven's Highest Courts of Justice.

We cannot sue Satan and his demons in our human courts, but we can sue them in the Supreme Courts of Heaven. We can ask the Father to be our Judge and Jesus to be our lawyer. Actually, the court proceedings in the Courts of Heaven were already documented in the book of Daniel, which was written in 536 BC.

> *I [Daniel] watched till thrones were put in place, and the Ancient of Days [God] was seated; His garment was white as snow, and the hair of His head was like pure wool. His throne was a fiery flame, its wheels a burning fire; a fiery stream issued and came forth from before Him. A thousand, thousands ministered to Him; ten thousand times ten thousand stood before Him. The court was seated, and the books were opened.*
>
> —Daniel 7:9–10

In Daniel 7, the *"Ancient of Days"* refers to God the Father. He is the supreme Judge of all ages. For thousands of years, Satan—the accuser of God's children—has never stopped accusing us (see Revelation 12:10). Day and night, he sues many Christians who are called to fight in the end-time battle. Millions of Christians and their books were brought to the Highest Courts of Justice by Satan. He abused the Courts of Heaven by bombarding the Chief Justice of Councils with false accusations about God's generals, warriors, and intercessors on the earth.

> *Then I heard a loud voice saying in heaven, "Now salvation, and strength, and the kingdom of our God, and the power of His Christ have come, for the accuser of our brethren, who accused them before our God day and night, has been cast down.*
>
> —Revelation 12:10

Satan is terrified about the upcoming movement of the Holy Spirit. He knows that heaven is about to invade the earth. Trillions of hosts of heaven have already been deployed by Jesus to assist His sons and daughters on the earth.

Beloved children of God, if Satan can sue God's servants using the Highest Courts of Justice, why can't we also sue him by utilizing the same legal tool?

Many humans, such as members of the secret societies—the Illuminati, the Skull and Bones, the Khazarian Mafia, the elites, the cabals, and the God-haters—have sold their souls to Satan for self-ambition, money, power, and fame. They have committed many unspeakable and heinous crimes against humanity. I consider them as satanic agents in our government and society. We can sue them using the Courts of Heaven because many *judges* on the earth are *totally corrupted.*

Upon understanding the Courts of Heaven and my legal rights to utilize these courtrooms, I have been suing Satan and his earthly agents ever since. In the last eight years, I have filed many lawsuits against Satan and his earthly followers. The list below is some of the recent cases that I submitted to the Highest Courts of Justice:

- Government officials (worldwide), CDC, and pharmaceutical companies lie and manipulate the citizen of the earth regarding the Covid-19 vaccine. They violate God-given liberty and human rights by mandating vaccination. Their evil crimes have caused many people to lose jobs, be hospitalized, and die.

- Secret societies, cabals, Hollywood stars, and satanic networks have sexually abused and killed millions of children through sex trafficking, pedophilia, spirit cooking, organ harvesting, and satanic rituals.

- Organizations, such as Planned Parenthood and government officials, enforce abortion or late-term abortion, which is actually sacrificing God's children to Molech and Baal (demons).

- Satan and his earthly agents (the U.S. and foreign countries) stole the 2020 election from the duly elected President Donald J. Trump.

- Individuals who sponsored street riots through Antifa and Black Lives Matter.

- Mainstream media groups spread fake news and false accusations toward President Donald J. Trump.

- A country that has manipulated many nations and committed countless inexcusable crimes, such as infiltrating other nations' presidential elections, stealing intellectual properties, bribing government officials, conducting sexual enticement, espionage, and spreading man-made pandemic.

As Satan is suing us day and night, I will also sue him day and night. I sue him based on facts, but he sues us based on lies. Between truth and lies, *truth always prevails!* Furthermore, Satan is a defeated foe. He will always lose in the end! The best resource to understand the Courts of Heaven is Robert Henderson's book *Operating in The Courts of Heaven*.

An Example of How the Heavenly Court Operates

One of the best examples of how the heavenly courtroom operates is Dr. Maurice Sklar's vision. Dr. Sklar carries divine anointing from the Holy Spirit for healing and prophetic ministry. God is frequently releasing prophecies through him.

On December 27, 2018, Dr. Sklar was taken to heaven by an angel to attend a courtroom session at the Highest Court of Justice. He was one of the five prophets called to heaven as witnesses for a court proceeding. His job was to document what he saw. Then the documentation would be added to "The Eternal Ledger of Legal Proceedings" in heaven.

The courtroom was conducted by a very tall angel—called Lady Justice. Judges seated on the left were Enoch, Abraham, Moses, David, Elijah, and Daniel. Judges seated on the right were John the Baptist, Peter, James, John, Andrew, and Paul. All of them were either prophets or apostles in the Bible, and now they are in heaven. God the Father was seated in the center. Jesus, the defense lawyer, was seated at the defense table. Satan and his diabolical lawyers were seated at the prosecution table.

Lady Justice announced the case. It was about the timing of the end-time tribulation. Satan declared that the six-thousand-year lease to Adam and his descendants (us) was coming to an end. He demanded the ownership of Planet Earth be handed over to the Antichrist for seven years. The whole case was about Satan pushing the starting date of the last seven years of tribulation (a period before the second coming of Jesus Christ to judge the earth).

Jesus, the lawyer of the human race, defended God's children on the earth. He emphasized that He had paid the death penalty for mankind. On the cross, He overtook Satan's authority over the church. Therefore, the gates of hell would not prevail against the body of Christ (the church).

On behalf of the Christian intercessors and His bride (church) on the earth, Jesus asked the Highest Court of Justice to allow the *fullness of the harvest*—meaning the gospel of the Kingdom to be preached to the whole world—then the end will come. He petitioned the Court to extend another period of time until every citizen of the earth has the chance to receive the gospel of Christ. He desired none shall perish but to be with Him in heaven eternally.

All thirteen judges read the scroll that Jesus provided, which was the supporting evidence of His petition. The letters on the scroll were *red*—they were written in His *blood*. Based on the defense lawyer's evidence, Satan and his prosecutors failed to provide legitimate reasons to support their demand. The Court session ended with the Father (the Supreme Judge) slamming His gavel. Instantly, thunders, lightning, and rainbows flashed the whole courtroom. The Father declared that the time of grace should be extended—as the defense lawyer (Jesus) had requested—to complete the *full harvest*.[12]

A Sample Lawsuit I Submitted to Heaven

Heavenly Father:

I come before Your Highest Court of Justice today on behalf of the righteous citizens of Planet Earth, in Jesus' name.

First, I invite the Councils of Justice in heaven, holy angels, and saints to witness this legal proceeding. According to Psalm 89:14, *"Righteousness and justice are the foundation of Your throne"* (NLT). I, therefore, come before You, seeking Your righteous judgment over crimes committed against the children of the earth by Satan, demons, and the wicked people.

Father, I acknowledge You as the Judge of All Creation, the King of All Ages, and the Most High God Almighty. I ask You to be the judge for this case. I ask Jesus Christ (our Eternal High Priest and Advocate) to be my lawyer. I believe that You have the dominion and authority over the heavens, the earth, and under the earth (hell). Therefore, all satanic principalities, powers, rulers of darkness, hosts of wickedness, and Satan's earthly followers must respond to Your Court orders.

The Complaint:

More than forty million people are suffering from sex slavery worldwide today. A substantial number of them are child sex slavery. Child trafficking has become the fastest-growing epidemic in the world.

In recent years, there has been a 5,000 percent increase in child sex videos on the internet. Many of these children are not minors, rather, as young as five years old. They are being sold over and over again (online) from pedophile to pedophile. According to Tim Ballard, the founder of Operation Underground Railroad (an organization that rescues trafficked children), a child can be raped more than sixty thousand times before being rescued. Yet, in most cases, they may never be rescued.[13]

Annually, human trafficking generates about 150 billion dollars.[14] In recent years, tens of millions of children have been kidnapped, sold, and forced into sex slavery and organ harvesting (body parts being sold for money). Many of their blood is used for producing Adrenochrome (extracted from brutally abused children) to get high or stay young by Hollywood celebrities, corrupted politicians, billionaires, etc.

Hence, I now ask the Highest Court of Justice to stop this horrendous crime and heinous violation of innocent children. I hold the devil, the demons, and all satanic followers who have committed this crime accountable.

Repent, Decree, and Declare:

On behalf of the righteous citizens on Planet Earth, we repent for not doing our diligence to fight against child trafficking. We repent for not defending these vulnerable children, but allowing demons and wicked people to violate these children's God-given rights. We repent for the sins of those who committed this crime, who foolishly fall into Satan's entrapment.

We decree and declare that Satan and his earthly agents (those child rapists) have no right to ravish and kill the defenseless children. We have zero tolerance for any satanic assault on these precious youngsters. We condemn the spirit of sexual perversion and human trafficking. We reprimand the demons behind these spirits. We now put Satan, his demonic force, and all who have participated in child-raping under notice.

We ask the Highest Court of Justice to convict these criminals and make them pay for their due penalties—even death penalties. We command the hosts of heaven to enforce this court proceeding and summon Satan, demons, child rapists, and child traffickers to this Courtroom.

In the meantime, we ask the hosts of heaven to tear down human trafficking networks, rescue children from sex slavery, and abolish all demonic weapons used to promote child trafficking and organ harvesting. We declare any-and-all forms of satanic plans related to child trafficking to be terminated.

Thank You, Father.

In Jesus' name, Amen!

Divine Restraining Orders

In conjunction with filing lawsuits against Satan and his principality of darkness, the Lord instructed Dr. Francis Myles to use Divine Restraining Orders as another weapon to combat the enemy.

What is a restraining order? When should we use it? And how do we file a restraining order in the Courts of Heaven?

A restraining order is a command used by the court system which prohibits a person from performing threats or harm to another person until the courtroom hearing is held. This legal procedure is utilized to protect an individual or a business in situations of sexual harassment, intimidation, domestic violence, stalking, and the like. If the defendant fails to comply with the court mandate, he or she will be charged, arrested, and penalized.

As I said before, to stop demons from harassing humans, we cannot sue or restrain them in our human courts. But we can certainly restrain them by using heavenly Courts. When we request the Courts of Heaven to issue a restraining order, we are not only asking the Highest Court of Justices to stop demonic crimes, but also to stop their human agents on the earth from helping Satan to destroy the earth.

Filing lawsuits or requesting Divine Restraining Orders from the Highest Courts of Heaven is our privilege given by God. We use these legal procedures to stop the devil from attacking us. This is one of the useful weapons to combat against the enemy, *so use it!*

Team Up with the Hosts of Heaven

Beloved readers, we are not fighting the end-time battles on our own. God has dispatched the hosts of heaven to help us. The Bible mentions "Hosts of Heaven" 20 times, "Lord of Hosts" 235 times, and "God of Hosts" 35 times. "Lord" and "God" refer to Jesus Christ. He is the Supreme Commander of the armies in heaven. The word "Hosts" refers to the heavenly armies. Sometimes the Christians call them the "Warrior Angels."

> *If you make the Lord your refuge, if you make the Most High your shelter, no evil will conquer you; no plague will come near your home. For he will order his angels [hosts] to protect you wherever you go. They will hold you up with their hands so you won't even hurt your foot on a stone.*
>
> —Psalm 91:9–12 NLT

The commander of the heavenly hosts is the archangel Michael (see Revelation 12:7). He is directly under Jesus' command. Michael is an extremely powerful commander. His showcase moment will be when he and the armies of heaven kick Satan and the demonic hosts (armies) out of the second heaven—mentioned in Revelation 12:7.

> *There was war in heaven. Michael and his angels [hosts] fought against the dragon and his angels. And the dragon lost the battle, and he and his angels were forced out of heaven. This great dragon—the ancient serpent called the devil, or Satan, the one deceiving the whole world—was thrown down to the earth with all his angels.*
>
> —Revelation 12:7–9

The hosts of heaven are not the regular angels, who are under other archangels' supervision, such as archangel Gabriel. But the hosts of heaven are combat warriors. They are enormous, some bigger than Planet Earth. As Revelation 10:5 says, an angel stands one foot on the sea and the other foot on the land. They literally can transform their bodies into objects or disguise themselves in the cloud. They are mighty, powerful, and fearsome. They are not made of flesh and blood; they are made with metal. The Bible mentions the power and magnitude of these heavenly hosts in the following scripture:

> *Then the angel [host] I saw standing on the sea and on the land raised his right hand toward heaven.*
>
> —Revelation 10:5 NLT

> *God sent an angel [host] to Jerusalem to destroy it . . . Then David lifted his eyes and saw the angel of the Lord standing between earth and heaven, having in his hand a drawn sword stretched out over Jerusalem. So David and the elders, clothed in sackcloth, fell on their faces.*
>
> —1 Chronicles 21:15–16

> *That night the angel [host] of the Lord went out and struck down 185,000 in the camp of the Assyrians. And when people arose early in the morning, behold, these were all dead bodies.*
>
> —2 Kings 19:35 ESV

From the above scripture, we can see that one host killed 185,000 Assyrian soldiers. The duty of these hosts is to do God's biddings, protect good and eliminate evil, battle against Satan, and defend God's children on the earth.

These hosts are spiritual beings and were created magnificently by God Himself. They often change themselves into various physical forms as they carry out their missions. They are intelligent, obedient, and well-trained. They are the fellow servants and co-worshipers of God with human beings (see Luke 2:12). They do have feelings, opinions, and emotions. They love to worship God.

> *You will find a baby [Jesus] wrapped in cloths and lying in a manger. Suddenly a great company of the heavenly host appeared with the angel, praising God and saying, "Glory to God in the highest heaven, and on earth peace to those on whom his favor rests."*
>
> —Luke 2:12–14 NIV

God has deployed trillions of angelic hosts onto Planet Earth to assist mankind during the end-time battle. The hosts were positioned primarily in two countries: Israel and America. During November 2020 U.S. presidential election, a few seer-prophets saw trillions of hosts of heaven in Washington, D.C. Their job is to expose voter fraud, remove the illegitimate Biden administration, and restore President Donald J. Trump (the actual winner). At the right time, when Jesus gives the command, these hosts will speedily cease the illegitimate Biden administration—God calls them "villains." Thanks to God and the hosts of heaven for helping us to get the *swamp drained!*

God has also assigned these hosts to Christians. We are God's ambassadors, commanders, and generals on the earth. The angelic hosts are ready to take our commands and fight on our behalf. They are highly effective for pulling down strongholds and tearing down satanic altars. Initially, God assigns a few hundred hosts to each believer. This is not automatic; we have to ask for it. As we team up with these hosts frequently, the Lord will assign more to us.

I initially had a few hundred angelic hosts assigned to me. Now, I may have thousands or millions. I have been deploying them frequently. I release them to China, Iran, Germany, Israel, Ukraine, North Korea, and many nations to pull down demonic strongholds. I also deploy them to different U.S. states, companies, government officials, organizations, such as the deep state, satanic societies, mainstream media, Hollywood, satanic churches, and witchcraft meeting places.

I command them to locate underground bunkers or secret gathering places used for sex trafficking and spirit cooking. I ask the hosts to rescue children who are caged, tortured, and raped by pedophiles and sex traffickers. I regularly deploy them to certain individuals, such as nations' presidents, prime ministers, high-level government officials, terrorist leaders, or leaders in the secret society. These individuals have been fulfilling Satan's assignments on the earth. They are helping him to fight against God.

Since 2016, I have been commanding these angelic hosts to stop the wicked people in U.S. Congress and foreign nations from doing harm to God's anointed, hand-picked President Donald J. Trump. I order the hosts to destroy satanic weapons, block communications between Satan's headquarters and his earthly agents, and shut the mouth of the witches who have been harming President Trump.

These angelic hosts travel at the speed of light. They are extremely organized by their ranking orders. Sometimes, I command them to destroy nuclear facilities in China, North Korea, and Irian; other times, I deploy them to stop satanic mobs, such as Khazarian Mafia, Antifa, and Black Lives Matter. I dispatch them to guard our borders against illegal immigrants. I often release them to individuals who are homosexual and unbelievers. I ask the hosts to arrest the demonic spirits from tormenting them.

Prophet Sadhu Sundar Selvaraj also witnessed how angelic hosts operate. He shared the following event in multiple church sermons:

One day, while Sadhu was waiting on God, Jesus told him to worship God at midnight because something would happen in the spirit realm during that time. The Lord warned him that a Hindu priest was plotting to kill him that night. At exactly midnight, Sadhu started to worship God. Immediately, a commander of the hosts of heaven came to Sadhu's room and said, "The battle is ready, Sir." Sadhu did not know how to respond. He then asked the Holy Spirit, "What should I say, Holy Spirit?" The Holy Spirit told him, "Just say proceed!" Then Sadhu said to the commander of hosts, "Proceed!" Immediately the commander disappeared from Sadhu's room.

At that moment, Sadhu saw a vision. An intense battle went on between God's army and the demonic army. The battle lasted about an hour. Finally, the commander of the hosts cut off the head of the satanic commander. The war ended.

Sadhu relaxed and was about to go to bed, but the commander of the Lord's army came back to Sadhu's room. He said, "The battle is over, Sir!" Sadhu asked the Holy Spirit, "What should I say to him. If the battle is over, why does he come back again?" The Holy Spirit said to Sadhu, "Just say proceed!" As soon as Sadhu gave the command, the commander disappeared from his room. Information about prophet Sadhu's teaching can be found on Angel TV.

This incident teaches us that the hosts of heaven treat us as their commanding officers. They see us as part of their team. What an awesome privilege for us! Let us thank God who gives us these magnificent angelic hosts to fight wars on our behalf. We should be grateful for their help and honor them after each battle.

One thing I have been pondering about is how the hosts are organized when Christians give commands. To my understanding, millions of Christians have been working with the hosts of heaven and giving them commands to pull down demonic strongholds. Very possible that we may send the same command at the same time. This may confuse the hosts and cause them to bump into one another.

For example, in May 2021, I ordered the hosts of heaven to block thousands of rockets from Gaza Strip to Israel—launched by Hamas and Palestinian militants. If millions of other Christians give the same order simultaneously, what will the hosts do? They may collide within themselves.

I thus asked Jesus, "Lord, even earthly battles are strategically organized by central command; how can heavenly armies be dispatched randomly? Isn't that the armies in heaven are far better organized than the earthly armies?" Jesus said, "Do not worry about how I manage My army. You just give your command, and let Me worry about how the hosts are deployed." I guess the central command in the Lord's army is at the speed of light. The hosts will never collide with one another or be confused because Jesus is the Lord of order.

What Makes Satan Fear the Most?

Have we ever thought about what makes Satan fear the most? Unlike God, who always operates in love, Satan operates in fear. He is the most fearful, paranoid, and miserable person in the universe. In order to defeat the devil, finding his weakness is essential.

Is It Worship?

We know that worship is a powerful weapon to fight against our enemy. When we worship God, Satan gets exceedingly jealous because he wants us to worship him. During worship, we literally send millions of missiles and atomic bombs to Satan's second heaven. Worship causes devastating damage to satanic armies. When we dance and sing to God, the demons are chained with iron shackles. When we worship God during hardship, distress, prosecution, and tribulation, it pleases Him the most and makes Satan *absolutely crazy*. When we clap hands during worship, we send tornados and tsunamis to Satan's headquarters—making demons *scream in terror!*

Our worship also enables God to fight on our behalf, just as God did for King Jehoshaphat. At that time, Judah was facing attacks from three mighty armies—the Moabites, Ammonites, and Edomites. Judah was significantly outnumbered. By the time King Jehoshaphat found out about the invasion, the enemy's troops had already crossed the Dead Sea and left him with very little time to prepare. King Jehoshaphat then proclaimed a fast throughout all Judah and Jerusalem. He pleaded with God for help.

> *Jehoshaphat stood and said, "Hear me, O Judah and you inhabitants of Jerusalem: Believe in the Lord your God, and you shall be established; . . ." He appointed those who should sing to the Lord, and who should praise the beauty of holiness, as they went out before the army and were saying: "Praise the Lord, for His mercy endures forever."*
>
> *Now when they began to sing and to praise, the Lord set ambushes against the people of Ammon, Moab, and Mount Seir, who had come against Judah; and they were defeated.*
>
> —2 Chronicles 20:20–22

This story confirms the power of worship. That day, on the way to the battlefield, the only thing that the army of Judah did was worship and praise the Lord. They did not fight at all. It was after the Lord received the worship; He caused the enemies to fight among themselves—they were all killed by their *own swords!* By the time King Jehoshaphat's army arrived at the battleground, all they saw were dead bodies. It took them three days to gather the spoils. To this day, that place is called the *Valley of Blessing*.

Even though worship is important, it is not the number one thing that Satan fears the most.

Is It Faith?

In the book of Matthew and Luke, Jesus taught us that if we have faith as small as a mustard seed, we can command mountains to move, and they will move. We can order trees to be uprooted, and they will obey.

> *[Jesus said,] "If you had faith even as small as a mustard seed, you could say to this mulberry tree, 'May you be uprooted and be planted in the sea,' and it would obey you!"*
>
> —Luke 17:6 NLT

> *Jesus told them. "I tell you the truth, if you had faith even as small as a mustard seed, you could say to this mountain, 'Move from here to there,' and it would move. Nothing would be impossible."*
>
> —Matthew 17:20 NLT

Indeed, faith is important because *"Without faith it is impossible to please God"* (Hebrews 11:6 NIV). The Bible tells us that we can do even greater miracles than what Jesus did if we have faith in God. Although faith is important, it is not the number one thing that Satan fears the most.

Is It Love?

The greatest commandment that God has given to mankind is love. Jesus said, *"'You shall love the Lord your God with all your heart, with all your soul, and with all your mind.' This is the first and the great commandment. And the second is like it: 'You shall love your neighbor as yourself'"* (Matthew 22:37–39).

> *[Apostle John said,] Dear friends, let us continue to love one another, for love comes from God. Anyone who loves is a*

child of God and knows God. But anyone who does not love does not know God, for God is love.

—1 John 4:7–8 NLT

Love is God's number one nature. "*Three things will last forever—faith, hope, and love—and the greatest of these is love*" (1 Corinthians 13:13 NLT).

[Apostle Paul said,] If I speak in the tongues of men and of angels, but have not love, I am a noisy gong or a clanging cymbal. And if I have prophetic powers, and understand all mysteries and all knowledge, and if I have all faith, so as to remove mountains, but have not love, I am nothing. If I give away all I have, and if I deliver up my body to be burned, but have not love, I gain nothing.

—1 Corinthians 13:1–3 ESV

Obviously, love is essential. It is the greatest weapon to destroy Satan's work. However, love is still not the number one thing that Satan fears the most.

Then What Is It?

Is it humility? Is it wisdom? Is it joy? Is it peace? Is it patience or endurance? Is it courage? All these are important, and they do cause the enemy to fear. But still, these are not what Satan fears the most.

It is Obedience!

- We can passionately worship God.
- We can have faith in God and move mountains.
- We can have sound wisdom and understanding.
- We can have love and compassion.
- We can humble ourselves before God Almighty.
- We can seek the peace of God.
- We can have patience and endurance.
- We can be bold and courageous.

But, if we do not obey God and heed His commandments, the enemy is not threatened by us. As soon as we obey the Holy Spirit, Satan knows that he is powerless over us! *Obedience* is the number one mandate for a soldier in the military. We are at war; we are God's end-time army. Therefore, it is vitally critical to obey the Lord and pay attention to the commands of the Holy Spirit. Jesus said, *"If you love Me, obey My commandments"* (John 14:15 NLT).

God rejected King Saul because of his disobedience (see 1 Samuel 15:22). He removed Saul's kingship and gave it to David—a man who obeyed God at every turn. Throughout the history of the Old and New Testaments, we see that God delights in those who obey Him and fear Him. The Israelites disobeyed God. As a consequence, an eleven-day journey to the promised land turned into forty years—what a painful lesson for them and us to learn! Our God can be extremely kind, but He can also be extremely strict and severe. Thus, let us not test God's temper, only *obey* Him and *fear* Him!

> *Samuel replied [to King Saul], "What is more pleasing to the Lord: your burnt offerings and sacrifices or your obedience to His voice? Listen! Obedience is better than sacrifice, and submission is better than offering the fat of rams. Rebellion is as sinful as witchcraft, and stubbornness as*

> *bad as worshiping idols. So because you have rejected the command of the Lord, he has rejected you as king."*
>
> —1 Samuel 15:22–23 NLT

When we obey God, we send a sweet aroma to the heart of the Father. When we obey God, we release the fragrance of Jesus Christ because He is the ultimate example of total obedience. *"Jesus humbled Himself and became obedient to the point of death, even the death of the cross"* (Philippians 2:8, author's paraphrase).

God did not create us for us; He created us for *Himself*. Obedience is not a choice, but a command. We must train ourselves to be in total obedience to all God's commandments, even unto death. We must love our God enough to choose obedience rather than self-indulgences. We humans are often careless about God's severity and treat Him with little fear and respect. In contrast to angels in heaven, they prostrate before His throne in reverent fear.

Jesus promised that He is coming soon to take His children home. However, most of us are not ready for His return. He has been warning us for thousands of years. He will not wait for us forever. Those who are ready to go to His Kingdom must be obedient, pure-hearted, and eagerly waiting on Him. He desires none to perish, but all to be with Him in heaven. However, He cannot take those who do not obey Him.

Whoever is ready for Jesus will hear the trumpet sound on the *"rapture"* day (see 1 Thessalonians 4:16). But those who disobey Him and continue entangling themselves in sin will have to go through the great tribulation—this is when Satan is cast down to the earth in his great wrath. Billions of people will either be killed or surrender to him. Many will take the mark of the beast, which will guarantee them to hell.

> *The Lord Himself will come down from heaven with a shout of command, with the voice of the archangel and with the [blast of the] trumpet of God, and the dead in Christ will rise first. Then we who are alive and remain [on the earth] will*

simultaneously be caught up (raptured) together with them [the resurrected ones] in the clouds to meet the Lord in the air, and so we will always be with the Lord!

—1 Thessalonians 4:16–17 AMP

Beloved readers, this is a *serious matter!* Are you ready for Jesus' second coming? If you are not ready now, what makes you think you will be ready on the *"rapture"* day? Are you prepared to see the King of kings and Lord of lords? Are you prepared to face the judgment seat of Christ? Are you waiting on Him daily? Are you abiding in His love and obeying His commandments? I am saying these to the Christians.

To the non-Christians: why are you risking your eternal life? Do you not know that you will be judged by Jesus on the *day of judgment?* Do you not know that you will be condemned (see John 3:18)? Heaven and hell are right at your door. *Make your choice today!* Repent your sins, and accept Jesus Christ as your Lord and Savior!

Whoever believes in him [Jesus] is not condemned, but whoever does not believe is condemned already, because he has not believed in the name of the only Son of God.

—John 3:18 ESV

James Bond

Espionage is an important tool for winning wars. In WWII, there were tens of thousands of spies from the allied countries, as well as Nazi Germany. Some of the most effective spies were women.

In fact, WWII's most effective spy was a woman—with a wooden leg—named Virginia Hall. Her code names were Marie and Diane. She was also called "The Limping Lady." The Gestapo gave her the nickname

"Artemis" and considered her to be the most dangerous spy. However, they never caught her.

Virginia was an American who worked with England's Special Operations Executive (SOE) against Nazi Germany. She organized sabotage and rescue operations across France. She became an expert in supporting the resistance and supplying agents with weapons and medical supplies. Her heroic work paved the way for the allied invasion. Yet, the Nazis only knew her as "The Limping Lady." [15]

Believe it or not, God put many of His secret agents (angels from heaven) on the earth. Some prophets revealed that God put these spy-angels inside the U.S. Pentagon. The spy-angels are not the hosts of heaven (warrior angels); rather, they look like human beings. Most likely, they are under the archangel Gabriel.

In 2017, I resigned from my job and planned to join Heidi Baker's missionary base in Brazil. Months before my trip, I hid myself in the prayer room to spend time with God. One afternoon, the Holy Spirit said to me, "You will be My James Bond. I need you to go to Berlin and do warfare intercessions there." I was puzzled and said, "Holy Spirit, did I just hear You right? Did You say James Bond?" I thought God was joking with me, because the Holy Spirit jokes with me sometimes. He is a very humorous Person. Then He mentioned the name James Bond a few more times later that week. I really thought He was being funny, so I did not pay much attention.

A few months later, God mentioned to me again: "You will be My James Bond and go to Berlin to pray." By then, I knew the message was from God, and He was not joking. I said to the Holy Spirit, "James Bond is a man. I am a woman," but He did not respond. History tells us that some of the best spies were women. Therefore, out of my obedience, I quickly booked the airline ticket to Berlin, Germany.

Antichrist and the Spirit of Hitler

I couldn't help but wonder—*why pray in Berlin?* Later I learned: prophet Sadhu Sundar Selvaraj prophesied that the spirit of Hitler would once again come out of Germany in the last days. Only this time, there will be much greater slaughters to the Jews and the Christians. It will make the Holocaust look like child's play. Other prophets also prophesied the same—the Antichrist will come out of Berlin, Germany.[16]

The Throne of Satan—Pergamon Altar

In the book of Revelation, Jesus revealed that the throne of Satan was in Pergamon—near modern-day Izmir, Turkey.

> [Jesus said to Pergamon church,] I know your works, and where you dwell, where Satan's throne is. And you hold fast to My name, and did not deny My faith even in the days in which Antipas was My faithful martyr, who was killed among you, where Satan dwells.
>
> —Revelation 2:13

One of the most famous architectures in Pergamon is the Altar of Zeus, which was built around 166–156 BC. It was situated on a terrace of the acropolis, overlooking the ancient Greek city. This enormous altar—a Hellenistic Greek sculpture—was built during the reign of King Eumenes II. This beautiful structure was not a temple but merely an altar.

Eventually, the Pergamon Altar was moved to the Pergamon Museum in Berlin by the German archaeologist Carl Humann in 1886. The reassembling was finished in 1889, which was the same year Hitler was born. Later, Hitler had his architect Albert Speer build an altar called Zeppelinfeld by copying the Altar of Zeus from Pergamon. Prophetically speaking, Hitler's altar was really the altar of Satan. Most of his speeches were given at Zeppelinfeld. This altar was the Nazi party's rally ground, located southeast of Nuremberg, Germany.

Many believe that Hitler and the nation of Germany were orchestrated by Satan. WWI and WWII were both started by Germany, where the altar of Satan was. In WWII, the Nazis killed six million Jews to fulfill Satan's plan. "Holocaust" means "religious sacrifice" or "burnt offering." Hitler used six million Jews as burnt offerings to Satan. The devil's purpose was to wipe out the Jewish people from Planet Earth in order to counter God's plan for the Jewish nation, Israel.

Originally, the Altar of Zeus in Pergamon was built as the altar of burnt offerings, where many Christians were killed. One of the courageous martyrs was Saint Antipas. He was a bishop of the church of Pergamon during the reign of the Roman Emperor Nero. Antipas was martyred around AD 92. He was slowly roasted to death inside a brazen bull-shaped oven—the most brutal and violent killing device.

Ishtar Gate

In addition to the Pergamon Altar (throne of Satan), the Ishtar Gate is also displayed in the Pergamon Museum in Berlin.

Ishtar (also known as Astaroth, Ashtaroth, Astarte, Inanna, Esther, Aster, Easter, Isis, and Irnini) was worshiped as a goddess by the Assyrians, Babylonians, Phoenicians, Greeks, and other pagan religions. Astaroth (Ishtar) is a powerful demon in the ranking of Lucifer (Satan).

In Jeremiah 7:18, the *"queen of heaven"* refers to Ishtar. She was portrayed as the wife of the false god Baal, also known as Molech. In Babylonian culture, she was called Semiramis—the wife of Nimrod. Worshiping the *"queen of heaven"* was widespread throughout the pagan cultures, which provoked God to anger.

> *[God said,] The children gather wood, the fathers kindle the fire, and the women knead dough, to make cakes for the queen of heaven; and they pour out drink offerings to other gods, that they may provoke Me to anger.*
>
> —Jeremiah 7:18

Ishtar in English is called Easter. Long before the Roman Catholic Church mixed the celebration of the resurrection of Jesus Christ with pagan spring fertility rituals, Ishtar (Easter) was already celebrated as the goddess of fertility and sex. She was the woman with many breasts in ancient sculptures. During the festival, people baked cakes for Ishtar, got intoxicated with wine, and engaged in orgies in the temple of Ishtar.

The truth is that the celebration of Ishtar (Easter)—fertility and sex—have nothing to do with Christianity or Jesus. Biblically speaking, there is definitely no connection between the resurrection of Jesus Christ and the so-called Easter Sunday—eggs and bunnies' tradition.

In 575 BC, during the reign of King Nebuchadnezzar II, the Ishtar Gate was built in Babylon (present-day Iraq). It was excavated in the early twentieth century, and it is now displayed in Berlin's Pergamon Museum.

The picture is very clear—both the throne of Satan (Altar of Zeus) and the Ishtar Gate (monument of demonic deity) are in the Pergamon Museum. Obviously, Germany is ready to welcome the Antichrist—the Bible calls him *"the man of lawlessness"* (see 2 Thessalonians 2:7). In fact, the spirit of the Antichrist is already working in secret. The only Person who restrains him from surfacing is the Holy Spirit.

> *This lawlessness [Antichrist] is already at work secretly, and it will remain secret until the one who is holding it back steps out of the way. Then the man of lawlessness will be*

revealed, but the Lord Jesus will slay him with the breath of his mouth and destroy him by the splendor of his coming.

—2 Thessalonians 2:7–8 NLT

To this day, I still cannot believe that the Holy Spirit selected me (an inconspicuous Chinese woman) to pray in Berlin. I am honored by God's calling. I am a soldier of the Lord's army. I am His James Bond— *the female 007!*

Part Four

Unique Journey with Jesus Christ

Encountering Jesus and Falling in Love

As I mentioned before, I became a Christian in February 2014. Two months into my spiritual journey, I encountered something unexpected. These divine meetings have fundamentally changed my life ever since.

I made one of the rooms in my house an *"Encounter Room"* to be with God. I set up a chair for Jesus to sit on. Most of the time, I was on my knees. I would usually sing and worship God for about two hours before praying. One day, in April 2014, I saw a vision during my worship time (not with my eyes opened, but closed). I saw it with the eyes of my heart. The vision was very clear, as though seeing it with my natural eyes.

I saw myself as a three-year-old girl playing in a beautiful garden. From a distance, I saw Jesus walking toward me with a big smile on His face and open arms. He wore a white robe and had long curly hair down to His shoulders. His beard was neatly trimmed. He seemed very tall—about six feet or taller.

I ran toward Him. He bent down and scooped me up with such a delighted smile on His face. I giggled with excitement and kissed His face all over. I played with His beard and hair, but He did not mind, rather allowing me with amusement. I wrapped my little arms around His neck, kissed His cheeks, and squeezed Him with hugs (see Figure 5). He appeared to enjoy it very much!

Figure 5: Meeting Jesus in my three-year-old spiritual body.

Night after night, I saw myself as this three-year-old girl with Jesus—loving Him, kissing Him, hugging Him, and playing with Him in that garden. He laughed a lot but said very few words.

Sometimes, on the way back home from work, I had not even parked my car yet, but this three-year-old girl would urge me to run to my prayer room and kiss Jesus. She would say, "I want to see Him. I miss Him. *Hurry up!*" Most of the time, I was too tired to go upstairs. I just wanted to lie down on the sofa for a while. But this little girl would not wait or let me rest; she wanted to see Jesus *so badly.*

When this happened, I would say to her, "You have to wait. I need to eat dinner and rest a little bit before going to the prayer room." But I could sense that she was not happy with me. Beloved readers, I think this little girl is my spirit. The Bible says:

> *He [God] chose us in Him before the foundation of the world.*
>
> —Ephesians 1:4

> *[God said,] I knew you before I formed you in your mother's womb.*
>
> —Jeremiah 1:5 NLT

Our spirits existed inside the Father long before He created the heavens and the earth. He created our souls before the foundation of the world. If God knew who I was before I was born, I would assume I also knew who He was before becoming a human. Otherwise, how could this three-year-old girl run to Jesus without any introduction, as though she knew Him all along? Usually, little girls run away from strangers, but not in my case. She loved Jesus at first glance, as though she saw her own father. It was amazing to see myself so thrilled to be with Jesus. My spirit knew then and knows now who He is!

> *In him [God] we live and move and exist. As some of your own poets have said, "We are his offspring."*
>
> —Acts 17:28 NLT

As I stated in the previous chapter: many prophets, who have visited heaven, witnessed something phenomenal. They saw millions of spirits flowing in and out of the Father's nostrils and heart area. These spirits were translucent—like the size of gingerbread. This tells us that our spirits come from inside the Father. No wonder the scripture (Acts 17:28) says that *we live, move, and exist* in God before the foundation of the world.

God the Father carried our spirits with Him for eons (see Isaiah 46:3). Inside the Father, there are no organs but another world. The Father is usually portrayed as "El Olam" (Eternal God) because inside the Father is an eternal world. God is a Spirit. We, as His offspring, lived with Him, breathed with Him, moved with Him. With childlike voices, we asked Him to send us to Planet Earth to glorify Him. No doubt, I was one of those spirits. That was why I knew Jesus at my first encounter.

> *I have cared for you since you were born. Yes, I carried you before you were born. I will be your God throughout your lifetime—until your hair is white with age. I made you, and I will care for you. I will carry you along and save you.*
>
> —Isaiah 46:3–4 NLT

Believe it or not, I somehow (vaguely) remember the touching moment of saying farewell to the Father before coming to the earth. The Father held me (a little spirit) in His palms and looked at me tenderly. With tears running from His face, He uttered His good-bye words. He told me that I would have a very tough childhood. I would suffer things beyond a normal child could bear. I would take care of my own parents at a very young age. He told me not to be afraid because He would be with me through troubles and dangerous times. I told Him I was ready to fulfill His will and glorify Him on the earth. We both cried—sorrowful tears—not wanting to be apart from each other.

Beloved readers, whether you believe it or not, we were inside the Father God for ages. He carried us for eons. *He is our real Father!* Sometimes, during my worship, when my spirit is in total *oneness* with God, I can see myself dancing with Jesus inside the Father. I have also seen the Holy Spirit there. Inside the Father is exceptionally bright—it makes my colored dress and hair turn into white light. This usually happens when my worship reaches its *crescendo* and touches the heart of the Father.

Back to the garden—I, as a little girl, ran to Jesus daily for about a month. Then one day, I said to Him, "Jesus, I love you so much, I want to marry you." I was just too innocent to say such a thing at that age, but my spirit knew my desire for Him—just as Isaiah 54:4 says, the Lord (Jesus), our Creator, will be our Husband:

> *[God said,] Fear not; you will no longer live in shame. Don't be afraid; there is no more disgrace for you. You will no longer remember the shame of your youth and the sorrows of widowhood. For your Creator will be your husband; the Lord of Heaven's Armies is his name! He is your Redeemer, the Holy One of Israel, the God of all the earth.*
>
> —Isaiah 54:4–5 NLT

Fourteen Years Old

Soon, during my time with Jesus, the three-year-old girl turned into a ten-year-old, then to a twelve-year-old. After that, she turned into a fourteen-year-old teenager. The jumping, kissing, and hugging with Jesus disappeared. She became a quiet and docile young woman.

Every night, I (the young woman) would come to the garden and wait for Jesus. When He came, I would hug Him. He also changed His way of greeting me. He became very gentle and tender—a different manner from holding the three-year-old child. He would gently kiss my forehead and hands. It was extremely heartwarming. I had never had such an experience before—*a divine kiss from God!*

Every time I went to see Him, I could see myself with long silky hair. I looked a little taller than I am now and always wore very colorful dresses—like Cinderella dresses. Most of the time, they were baby blue; sometimes, they were pink, red, yellow, lavender, or white. Each visit was in a different dress. The fabric was not earthly. It was super lightweight, and the textures were shimmering and dazzling.

Jesus usually wore a white robe with gold trim on it. Sometimes, He wore a dark red sash or a gold sash. Other times, He wore a blue robe. No matter which robes He wore, He always looked *exceptionally handsome!* There was not much talking, but lots of dancing, hugging, and holding hands. Beloved readers, our Lord loves to dance because He created dance!

Sometimes, Jesus took me to a field with the most fragrant and exquisite flowers. We danced in this beautiful flower bed. When He got excited, He would pick me up and swing me in the air to express His joy. This kind of encounter went on for about a month.

Meanwhile, the Holy Spirit directed me to read the Bible and Christian books. The reading started changing my life and brought me into a deeper dimension of knowing God. From the day I became a Christ believer until now, the Holy Spirit has led me to read more than fifty Christian books. Out of which, the following three books taught me how to pursue an intimate relationship with Jesus:

- *Heaven Awaits the Bride* by Anna Rountree.
- *Visions from Heaven* by Wendy Alec.
- *Heaven Is So Real* by Choo Thomas.

These books had significant impacts on my life because my experiences were similar to these women's encounters with Jesus. They had been taken to heaven by the Holy Spirit many times, and all had very personal, loving relationships with Jesus. In fact, Anna Rountree had a wedding ceremony with Him in heaven.

I do not believe it was a coincidence that the Holy Spirit introduced these books to me. He wanted me to fall in love with Jesus. Many people have received different callings from God, such as the missionary, pastor, prophet, seer, etc. But for me, my *primary calling* from God is to be *Jesus' lover*. Jesus created me for Himself. Only He can truly satisfy my desire, and *my desire is Him* and *Him only!*

Believe it or not, I somehow remember my life in heaven before coming to the earth. During many of my worship times, I often see myself (in a fourteen-year-old spiritual body) kissing, hugging, and dancing with Jesus inside the Father. I was not merely a spirit that existed inside the Father—*I was Jesus' lover.* In other words, we were in love long before I came to Planet Earth as a human.

Seventeen Years Old

After being fed ample spiritual food by the Holy Spirit, in June of 2014 (four months after becoming a believer), I began to see myself turning into a seventeen-year-old young woman. Beloved readers, I cannot tell you why the Holy Spirit revealed Jesus to me in such a gradual way.

By then, when I saw the Lord, my manners had changed. I was very submissive and shy—almost as if He became my Lover and I was dating Him. The relationship turned into fairly romantic. I was constantly yearning for Him. The desire and hunger to be with Him were so painful and unbearable because the longing was too intense. I literally felt heartaches all the time. By then, I realized that *I had fallen in love with Him!*

Every night, after worshiping God, I would say, "I want to see You, my Lord. I have missed You so much!" When I closed my eyes, there I was, in my spiritual body, with a beautiful Cinderella dress. As I looked to the distance, there He was, walking toward me. I would run toward

Him, throw myself into His arms, and give Him a squeezing bear hug. I could not control my feelings, for *I was crazy about Him!*

Jesus always had a big smile on his face and usually opened His arms while walking toward me. When He reached me, He would lift me up and swing me in the air to express His happiness. Then, He would hold me close to His chest for *a long time* with His eyes closed. I could literally hear His heart saying, "How I have missed you, My darling, My precious lover. Oh, you are Mine!" After that, He would kiss my forehead and hands.

Beloved readers, Lord Jesus is an *extremely emotional* Person. He never hides His feelings. He is real and honest. His passion and love are genuine. He is pure and authentic with child-like innocence. Even though He is exceedingly tough, He is also the gentlest Person I have ever known. He is the best *Lover* one can ever dream of, and *He is my Lover!*

Every time Jesus held me, even though I saw myself in the spirit, my earthly body would shake and cry; because hugging Jesus was an exceptionally emotional experience. I could feel my blood boiling and my heart pounding.

Routinely, after hugging, He would sit on a big rock in our garden—He created this garden just for us. I would sit on the ground and lift my face to Him with sheer adoration. Sometimes, I would lay my head on His lap and enjoy the romantic moment (see Figure 6).

"I have missed you so much, my Lord!" I would say.

"I have missed you too, my beloved!" He would reply.

Figure 6: Jesus and I in the garden.

Most of the time, Jesus would kiss my hands and forehead. We would look into each other's eyes without saying a word because our eyes and hearts could communicate much deeper than words.

Beloved readers, I would assume each of you had your first love—the first butterflies-in-the-stomach feeling, the first spark with your lover, and the first romantic moment one can never forget. Well, the romance between Jesus and me is ten times more intense than any human's first love.

I usually asked Him about His well-being, news from heaven, or events happening on the earth. He would talk about my life, nations, world leaders, and His plans. During my time of despair, failure, and trials, He would comfort me in this garden. We usually talked for thirty minutes or so; then we would go to other places.

Our Meeting Places

These are the few unique places that Jesus has taken me, and He still does to this day. None of these places are earthly, but celestial. These sceneries' inexpressible beauty and marvelous colors cannot be found on Planet Earth. I did not pick these meeting locations, but Jesus did.

The Beach

Sometimes, Jesus takes me to a beach where the seashore seems endless. I have never seen anyone else on this beach, only He and I. The sky has the most brilliant colors. The hues are orange, lilac, blue, lavender, and silver. The ocean is also amazingly colorful because it reflects the sky. This is the most gorgeous beach I have ever seen. I don't think it is earthly.

Often, I will lean on Jesus' chest while sitting on the sand and watching the ocean waves (see Figure 7). He dances with me a lot on this beach. At sunset, the yellow, orange, and red colors will cover our faces and clothes—stunningly beautiful and romantic—as though we are dancing with ribbons of fire and bands of love that tie us together. Just as God said in Hosea 11:4 about how He drew His beloved children of Israel to Himself: *"I drew them with gentle cords, with bands of love."*

Figure 7: With Jesus at the beach.

Other times, we ride horses on this beach. These white horses are the most regal and splendid (they are not earthly). We often ride at a fairly fast speed. My long dress will flow with the wind, and so will His hair and robe (see Figure 8). This is the most romantic moment.

There are times we ride together on one horse. I will sit behind Jesus and hold His waist.

Figure 8: Horseback riding with Jesus at the beach.

Jesus and I also walk a lot on this beach. We stroll barefoot and always hold hands. There are lots of laughing and hugging. Our Lord loves to laugh. He has the *most beautiful smile!* Whenever we come to this beach, whether walking, dancing, or horseback riding, I always feel the profound romance between us. I can hear the Song of Solomon—like sweet melodies in our hearts—*the psalms of love.*

The biblical characters of *"The Bridegroom King," "The Beloved,"* or *"The Shepherd King"* in Song of Solomon are the personification of Jesus Christ. *"The Shulamite"* is the personification of His bride on the earth. These songs reveal the love stories between God and mankind. They are the melodies that God sings to His lovers on the earth. The lyrics are incredibly romantic, intimate, and personal. They are the innermost heart yearning of God Almighty to His beloved children on Planet Earth. Our God does not hide His feelings from His brides. The Song of Solomon is the *masterpiece* of the Holy Spirit.

The Shulamite:

The voice of my Beloved! Behold, He comes leaping upon the mountains, skipping upon the hills. My Beloved is like a gazelle or a young stag. Behold, he stands behind our wall; He is looking through the windows, gazing through the lattice.

—Song of Solomon 2:8–9

Now he comes closer, even to the places where I hide. He gazes into my soul, peering through the portal as he blossoms within my heart.

—Song of Songs 2:9 TPT

The Bridegroom-King:

Aris, my dearest. Hurry, my darling. Come away with me! I have come as you have asked to draw you to my heart and lead you out. For now is the time, my beautiful one. The season has changed, the bondage of your barren winter has ended, and the season of hiding is over and gone . . . Arise, my love, my beautiful companion, and run with me to the higher place. For now is the time to arise and come away with me.

—Song of Songs 2:10, 11, 13 TPT

O my dove, in the clefts of the rock, in the secret places of the cliff, let me see your face, let me hear your voice; for your voice is sweet, and your face is lovely.

—Song of Solomon 2:14

Just as the intense romantic fires flare up between *"The Shulamite"* and *"The Bridegroom King,"* so do the romantic flames burn between Jesus and me.

I rarely see Jesus' face is troubled. But one day, while we were walking on the beach, He was very quiet. He seemed somewhat upset. He did not say a word but just held my hand and walked. I did not say anything either, knowing that something might have been troubling Him. For a while, He was still quiet. In order to cheer Him up, I scooped some ocean water in my hand and splashed it on Him. He laughed and pulled me into His arms, and hugged me. He knew I was not being disrespectful, but rather to cheer Him up. Even though He did not tell me why He was troubled, deep inside, I could sense His aching heart for mankind.

Beloved readers, there is a burden in Jesus' heart regarding the salvation of the human race. He will always bear this burden until all the scriptures are fulfilled. His deepest longing is to bring mankind back to His Father. This is His gift to His Father, and the very reason He died for. He wants to please and glorify the Father. He knows the Father's heart will not be complete until all His sons and daughters on the earth reconcile to Him.

In addition, the governments of the heavens and the earth are all on Jesus' shoulders. *"All things were created through Him and for Him"* (Colossians 1:16), *"and the government will be upon His shoulder"* (Isaiah 9:6). Ever since He departed from the earth, He has never stopped interceding for His earthly children. He feels the pains and sorrows from each and every one of us. His heart is often grieved when the devil deceives His children. Jesus' burden is the temporal and the eternal well-being of all the offspring of the Father.

> *Unto us a Child [Jesus] is born, unto us a Son is given; and the government will be upon His shoulder. And His*

name will be called Wonderful, Counselor, Mighty God, Everlasting Father, Prince of Peace.

—Isaiah 9:6

On the cross, Jesus did all He could to redeem us—nothing more or nothing less. All we have to do is accept Him as our Lord and Savior, yet many of His children still go to hell because of their unbelief—this is why the heart of Jesus is often grieved.

Our God cries for us. Every drop of His tears is gathered in bottles, so as our tears. People, who have been to heaven, witnessed something astounding—all our tears, along with God's own tears, are collected by angels and put into glass bottles. They are stored in the *Rooms of Tears* in heaven and documented in *The Book of Remembrance.*

> *[King David said to the Lord,] You've kept track of all my wandering and my weeping. You've stored my many tears in your bottle—not one will be lost. For they are all recorded in your book of remembrance.*
>
> —Psalm 56:8 TPT

Jesus frequently cries for us. He will continue crying and carrying the burden for the lost souls until His gift to His Father is fulfilled. In the meantime, Jesus has been preparing homes for us and *eagerly* anticipating our arrival in heaven (see John 14:2).

> *[Jesus said,] In My Father's house are many mansions; if it were not so, I would have told you. I go to prepare a place for you. And if I go and prepare a place for you, I will come again and receive you to Myself; that where I am, there you may be also.*
>
> —John 14:2–3

My relationship with Lord Jesus is like dating between two lovers. This divine love burns in our hearts. I have shared my love story with some Christians. Yet, most of them do not believe in the romance between Jesus and me. For those people who tend to put God in a box and use human minds to restrain God's ways, I have this message for you. If you do not believe Jesus can fall in love with a human—such as me—and be my Lover, you'd better remove the Song of Solomon out of the Bible, because those Songs describe the most intense love between *"The Bridegroom King—Jesus"* and His lovers on the earth.

Dancing on the Ocean Surface

One day during my prayer time, I said, "Lord, I want to see You. I miss You!" Immediately, I saw myself in my spiritual body, with long silky hair, wearing a beautiful peach-colored dress. There was Jesus, walking toward me, smiling. I ran to Him, and He picked me up in the air with excitement. Then He held me tightly in His arms for a long time. I heard His heart saying, "Oh, how I have missed you, my lover, my beautiful bride!" Then He gently held my face with both of His hands and *kissed my lips*. Instantly, fire ran through my whole body. This was the first time that He ever kissed me on my lips.

Beloved readers, speaking about "kiss," you must remove your earthly thought and replace it with *pure divine* thought. Human beings did not create "kiss," but God did. Kissing by God is the most *sacred* and *holy* thing! The true lovers of Jesus Christ long for His kisses, just as the Shulamite woman said to her Bridegroom-King, *"Let him kiss me with the kisses of his mouth—for his love is better than wine"* (Song of Solomon 1:2, author's paraphrase).

Then Jesus took me to our beach. Only this time, He took me down to the ocean surface and danced on it. As I described previously, this beach was not earthly. It was too beautiful and colorful to describe. The ocean reflected the sky in orange, purple, lilac, silver, and blue—almost like we were dancing on a color palette. However, water is water; it moves. I started panicking. Jesus was holding me in a ballroom dance position and said, "Look at Me, darling, just look at Me. Do not look at the water!" At that moment, I instantly remembered Peter, who walked on water and sank because of his doubt.

> [Jesus said,] "Come!" And Peter got out of the boat and walked on the water, and came toward Jesus. But seeing the wind, he became frightened, and when he began to sink, he cried out, "Lord, save me!" Immediately Jesus reached out with His hand and took hold of him, and said to him, "You of little faith, why did you doubt?"
>
> —Matthew 14:29–31 NASB

Not making the same mistake as Peter did, I trusted the Lord completely. I kept my eyes on Jesus at all times. We danced gracefully. The choreographies of the dance were like a combination of Foxtrot and Quickstep. We moved with elegant dance rhythms on this beautiful ocean dance floor (see Figure 9). With our feet, we painted the perfect artwork of *romance of love*. I enjoyed it very much, and He was very pleased because I trusted Him.

Figure 9: Dancing with Jesus on the ocean surface.

I knew He was testing my faith. He was teaching me never to doubt or fear whenever I am in His presence. He was training me never to remove my eyes away from Him, even in the raging ocean (see Hebrews 12:2). All living beings, whether in heaven or on earth, were created by Jesus Christ. He is greater than all. *"He is before all things, and in him all things hold together"* (Colossians 1:17 NIV). If we behold Him, fear has no power over us. But if we feel fearful, it is because we are not beholding Him.

> *Let us fix our eyes on Jesus, the author and perfecter of our faith, who for the joy set before Him endured the cross, scorning its shame, and sat down at the right hand of the throne of God.*
>
> —Hebrews 12:2 BSB

The Garden

Jesus and I have a secret garden where only He and I have access. There are many kinds of flowers, fruit trees, and fountains in this garden. The fragrance is unbelievably aromatic—one can get drunk from it.

I often sing the song "I Come to the Garden Alone" while waiting for Him. As soon as I hear the key opening the garden gate, my heart begins to race. Then, there He is, my Beloved, *dazzling* and *handsome*. I will run to Him, hug Him, kiss Him, and cling to Him, as though I can possibly lose Him. He is always excited to see me. The very first thing He always does is hug and kiss me passionately. I can tell that He enjoys every moment of embracing me.

Beloved readers, our Lord Jesus is incredibly romantic—He created romance. Being in love with Him is a *full-time job* because I feel lovesick all the time. My heart aches frequently because of my yearning and longing for Him. I am *helplessly in love* with Jesus. He is the true love of my soul—*my forever love!* I truly understand the Shulamite's longing for her Beloved.

The Shulamite:

Night after night I'm tossing and turning on my bed of travail. Why did I let him go from me? How my heart now aches for him, but he is nowhere to be found! So I must rise in search of him, looking throughout the city, seeking until I find him. Even if I have to roam through every street, nothing will keep me from my search. Where is He—my soul's true love? He is nowhere to be found. Then I encountered the overseers as they encircled the city. So I asked them, "Have you found him—my heart's true love?" Just as I moved past them, I encountered him. I found the one I adore! I caught him and fastened myself to him, refusing

> *to be feeble in my heart again. Now I'll bring him back to the temple within, where I was given new birth—into my innermost parts, the place of my conceiving.*
>
> —Song of Songs 3:1–4 TPT

Our dances in this garden are mostly close and intimate. Under the silvery moonlight, there are lots of hugging and kissing. Sometimes, Jesus places my head on His arm and gently runs His fingers through my hair. He treasures our time together so dearly, and I adore Him beyond my heart can bear.

I usually say to Him, "My dearest Darling, my Sweetheart, I love You with all my heart. I want to kiss all the scars that You took for me. I want You to feel loved. I want to romance You and make You feel wanted. I want to give You everything that I have."

His eyes will get sparkly, and He just quietly takes my love into His heart without a word. There are times, He says, "My beloved, your love for Me melts My heart." I did not know that I could melt the Lord's heart. I take delight in melting His heart because I want Him to feel adored and loved!

I love to worship God. Whenever I am with Him, I will spend at least two to three hours in worship alone. I usually close my eyes, mostly on my knees, and sing my heart songs to the Trinity (Father, Son, Holy Spirit).

Ninety-five percent of the time, during my worship, Jesus has physically come to my prayer room. He usually sits on the chair, looks at me, and enjoys my worship. Even though my eyes are closed, I can see Him with my spiritual eyes.

I am not shy to sing intimately to my Yeshua Hamashiach (Jesus the Messiah). He usually sits there for hours and lets my voice warm His heart. I often say, "Lord, let my voice kiss your heart and let the music hug you. Would You open Your heart and let me walk in, and be with

You in *oneness*? Please take me away, my Lover; take me to the end of the universe. Let us fly to our secret chamber of love."

Many times, Jesus will stand right in front of me while I worship Him. When that happens, I will gently kiss His hair, His forehead, His eyes, His nose, His beard, His shoulders, His arms, His hands, His feet, and His heart. Lastly, I will kiss His lips. He just stands there and receives my kisses. Then, He will kiss me back passionately. These are the most intimate moments—*the pin-drop moment!*

The Shulamite:

Let him smother me with kisses—his Spirit-kiss divine. So kind are your caresses, I drink them in like the sweetest wine! Your presence releases a fragrance so pleasing— over and over poured out. For your lovely name is "Flowing Oil." No wonder the brides-to-be adore you. Draw me into your heart. We will run away together into the king's cloud-filled chamber.

—Song of Songs 1:2–4 TPT

I believe this is a spiritual garden that Jesus planted in me. I am the garden, and He is the Gardener. He is the only One who can unlock the gate of this garden. He planted the seeds for flowers, fruit trees, and vineyards. He created fountains and streams. He has nourished the garden with His love and watered it with His patience, gentleness, grace, and faithfulness. I was just a baby Christian when He created this garden. Ever since, He has patiently waited for my garden to flourish.

He has waited for my flowers to bloom, so that He can enjoy the fragrance of love and grace. He has waited for my trees to bear fruits, so that He can taste the holiness, righteousness, and faithfulness. He has waited for my fountains to bubble, so that He can enjoy the springs of joy, peace, and purity. He has waited for my vineyards to produce lush grapes, so that He can taste the wine of gentleness, meekness, and obedience. He has waited for me to smell like Him, look like Him, taste like Him, think like Him, and act like Him. Upon His nurture and caring, this garden has been flourishing. One day, He will come to drink the finest wine—the wine of my innermost love for Him.

What Jesus has been doing is to create a secret paradise within me. The paradise of our dating place, the paradise of our private chamber, the paradise of our wedding bed, and the paradise of *oneness* with Him! He and I are one—*inseparable*! The following scriptures describe perfectly how Jesus (The Bridegroom King) desires me (His bride) to be.

The Bridegroom-King:

How satisfying to me, my equal, my bride. Your love is my finest wine—intoxicating and thrilling. And your sweet, perfumed praises—so exotic, so pleasing. Your loving words are like the honeycomb to me; your tongue releases milk and honey, for I find the promised land flowing within you. The fragrance of your worshiping love surrounds you with scented robes of white.

My darling bride, my private paradise, fastened to my heart. A secret spring that no one else can have are you— my bubbling fountain hidden from public view. What a perfect partner to me now that I have you. Your inward life is now sprouting, bringing forth fruit. What a beautiful paradise unfolds within you. When I'm near you, I smell aromas of the finest spice, for many clusters of my exquisite fruit now grow within your inner garden.

Here are nine: pomegranates of passion, henna from heaven, spikenard so sweet, saffron shining, fragrant calamus from the cross, sacred cinnamon, branches of scented

> *woods, myrrh, like tears from a tree, and aloe as eagles ascending. You are a fountain of gardens. A well of living water springs up from within you, like a mountain brook flowing into my heart!*
>
> —Song of Songs 4:10–15 TPT

Jesus is my Gardener, Maker, King, and God. He will prune the dead branches within me—the branches of pride, bitterness, and unforgiveness; the branches of self-righteousness and self-pity; the branches of my flesh—the fallen nature of mankind.

In the spiritual realm, sin has a horrible smell. It has a rotten and filthy odor because it resembles Satan's character. Sin also has color— it is ugly and dreadful. When we walk in transgression, sin, and iniquity, such as pride, bitterness, jealousy, sexual lust, and rebellion, we look like Satan and smell like Satan. When we walk in the fruits of the Holy Spirit, such as *"love, joy, peace, longsuffering, kindness, goodness, faithfulness, gentleness, self-control"* (Galatians 5:22–23), we look like Jesus and smell like Him.

The aroma of love, obedience, and humility surpasses the finest perfume. The color of righteousness and holiness exceed the most beautiful paintings. The taste of gentleness, patience, and kindness is better than the most delicious delicacy. Our Lord has the most beautiful fragrance. Many Christians have experienced His fragrance—it literally smells like the sweetest roses, because He carries the *aroma of holiness!*

> *Thanks be to God who always leads us in triumph in Christ, and through us diffuses the fragrance of His knowledge in every place. For we are to God the fragrance of Christ.*
>
> —2 Corinthians 2:14–15

My greatest desire is to please Jesus, understand His heart, romance Him, and let Him feel loved. He deserves our love. He gave everything for us, died on the cross, redeemed our sins, and paid our death penalty, so that we can have everlasting life. If I can lay down my life, pour it out as a drink offering, and please Him in any shape or form, even unto death, I will do so because *He is worthy!*

Everywhere I go, I want to look like Jesus, smell like Jesus, and act like Jesus. I want to diffuse His fragrance and shine as light in this fallen world.

Jesus is the Lover of my soul. I am lovesick all the time, for He is so beautiful and irresistible. He has told me many times, "You are so precious to Me. Your worship and your voice touch My heart. They also touch My Father's heart. As you are in love with me, I am also in love with you—more than you can imagine. I have put you in *a very special place* in My heart!"

Jesus's love has made my lips the lyric writer—full of the sweetest words. I often say, "Jesus, my Love, I am Your crimson rose and elegant lily. I am Your Shulamite—Your crazy lover!"

The Shulamite:

I am truly his rose, the very theme of his song. I'm overshadowed by his love, like a lily growing in the valley!

The Shepherd-King:

Yes, you are my darling companion. You stand out from all the rest. For though the thorns surround you, you remain as pure as a lily, more than all others.

—Song of Solomon 2:1–2 TPT

The Shulamite:

Suddenly, he transported me into his house of wine—he looked upon me with his unrelenting love divine. Revive me with your raisin cakes. Refresh me again with your apples. Help me and hold me, for I am lovesick! I am longing for more—yet how could I take more? His left hand cradles my head while his right hand holds me close. I am at rest in this love.

—Song of Songs 2:4–6 TPT

Beloved readers, my heart *melts* whenever I think about Jesus!

The Green Meadow

Sometimes, Jesus takes me to a very beautiful and paradise-like meadow. It is surrounded by gorgeous trees. The grass is pure green, well-manicured, and extremely pleasing. In the background, there are snow-capped mountains, which give a perfect contrast to the blue sky and lush greenery. There is a large pond with clear blue water, reflecting the snow-capped mountains and surrounding scenery. This place is too perfect, exceptionally breathtaking. It is not from the earth.

He usually takes me there to rest. We will lie down on the grass, breathe in the fresh air, and enjoy the charming scenery. I always wear colorful, gossamer-like dresses. Sometimes, I wear a purple princess dress. Other times, I wear a white or yellow dress. The fabrics of the dresses are not earthly. They are exceptionally light, sheer, feathery, and glimmering. When Jesus holds me and kisses me, I always feel like a princess in Prince charming's arms.

Jesus usually wears a white robe with different colored sashes, such as red, blue, or gold. Sometimes, He wears a blue robe that complements

His piercing-blue eyes—they can penetrate my heart and cause me to be speechless. He is about thirty years old.

Jesus is *incredibly handsome*. His build is masculine with broad shoulders. Yet, He is also exceptionally soft, gentle, and romantic. He is a person of very few words. Most of the time, He communicates through His eyes and heart. When His eyes talk, *one cannot resist!*

Whenever we come to this green meadow, I always have a flower garland on my head. These garlands are made from fragrant flowers. We will dance barefoot on this green carpet-like pasture. As I said before, we speak very few words. Instead, we mostly look into each other's eyes and let the eyes talk. It is an exceptionally peaceful and pleasant place—too perfect to be adequately described. Most of the time, I am like wax melting in my Lover's arms. It is the *best feeling ever*!

Jesus is holy and profound, yet very approachable. His voice is incredibly calm, yet resolute and confident. One can fall in love with Him just for His demeanor. His face is more like Akiane Kramarik's painting—*Prince of Peace*. He has olive skin, a neatly trimmed beard, and brown curly hair. He is very attractive—inside and outside. Just like the Song of Solomon says, *"He is altogether lovely"* (5:16).

I describe Jesus from a human point of view, but He is so much more! He is greater than all—He holds the universe in His hands. *"For by Him all things were created that are in heaven and that are on earth, visible and invisible, whether thrones or dominions or principalities or powers. All things were created through Him and for Him"* (Colossians 1:16). Also, Job 26:7 describes Jesus: *"He spreads out the northern skies over empty space; he suspends the earth over nothing"* (NIV). This means when Jesus created the earth, He stretched the sky like a curtain with His hands and hung Planet Earth on it like a Christmas ornament.

Jesus is a Spirit wearing a human body. He is the image of the invisible Father. In the Song of Solomon, the Shulamite woman described Jesus (the Beloved) much better than I am able.

The Shulamite:

My beloved is white and ruddy, chief among ten thousand. His head is like the finest gold; His locks are wavy, and black as a raven. His eyes are like doves by the rivers of waters, washed with milk, and fitly set. His cheeks are like a bed of spices, banks of scented herbs. His lips are lilies, dripping liquid myrrh. His hands are rods of gold set with beryl. His body is carved ivory inlaid with sapphires. His legs are pillars of marble set on bases of fine gold. His countenance is like Lebanon, excellent as the cedars. His mouth is most sweet, yes, he is altogether lovely. This is my beloved, and this is my friend.

—Song of Solomon 5:10–16

The way Jesus loves me makes me feel like I am the only woman in the universe. Beloved readers, our Lord is *very personal*. He will make you feel that you are the only one in His heart. He loves all His children. He is our Husband and Lover! Each child is important to Him. He has perfect plans for each of us. If you seek Him, He will make Himself available to you. If you search for Him with all your heart, He will be found by you (see Jeremiah 29:13). He desires to be found more than we desire of Him. He is waiting for each of us to seek Him and have an intimate relationship with Him.

You will seek Me and find Me, when you search for Me with all your heart. I will be found by you, says the Lord.

Jeremiah 29:13–14

Our Lord Jesus wants us to know His very Person, not just know Him through His Word—the Bible. He is a personal God! He once told me, "Do not compare yourself with other children of Mine or be jealous of them. You are unique to Me personally. I made each of my children with a distinct fingerprint because each of them is special to Me."

Once you find Him, He is all yours! You will be drenched in His ocean of love, covered by His hugs and kisses, and enclosed by His glory. Then you will be utterly and helplessly falling in love with Him. You will be His prisoner of love. *Forever undone!*

Jesus once said to me, "My heart is for you to access. It is open for you anytime you seek Me. I am open to anyone who is willing to seek My heart. I have been waiting for My children for ages. I have longed for them. My heart can be very lonely because of the longing for My children. You have found My heart; keep seeking deeper—it is yours!"

Dancing inside the Sun

There have been multiple times that Jesus has taken me to a celestial galaxy where I can see the sun just about fifty feet away. He usually leads me to dance inside the sun. Brilliant light and intense glimmer radiate inside this massive fireball. Our faces and clothes turn to orange color. Amazingly, I am neither hot nor burned. I can actually touch the sun—it feels like silk. We have danced in this gigantic burning sphere many times.

It is common knowledge that the temperature of the sun (inner core) is about 27,000,000°F (15,000,000°C). Usually, a human being can suffer third-degree burns by exposure to 150°F for two seconds. But how come Jesus and I are not scorched by the unbelievable amount of heat in the sun?

A possible explanation relating to this experience can be found in the book of Daniel. When King of Babylon, Nebuchadnezzar, commanded his mighty army men to cast Shadrach, Meshach, and Abed-Nego into a burning fiery furnace, he discovered something phenomenal. Even though he commanded the furnace to be heated seven times more than usual (could be 3,000°F), the three young

Hebrew men were not burned. Instead, the flames killed those army men who threw them in the fire.

Subsequently, something even more astonishing happened. Nebuchadnezzar saw a fourth man standing with the three Hebrews inside the scorching furnace. He said, *"I see four men loose, walking in the midst of the fire; and they are not hurt, and the form of the fourth is like the Son of God"* (Daniel 3:25). He then commanded Shadrach, Meshach, and Abed-Nego to come out of the furnace. People were amazed. They noticed that the blazing fire had no power over the three young men. Their bodies were not burned, *"the hair of their head was not singed nor were their garments affected, and the smell of fire was not on them"* (Daniel 3:27).

Just like those Hebrews, I was not burned in the sun when I was with Jesus. Beloved readers, the *"Son of God"* in Daniel 3:25 refers to Jesus Christ in His pre-incarnate body. God is not bound by time. He can be at any time and place as He wishes, because He created time.

Autumn Poem for Jesus

On November 22, 2018, Thanksgiving Day, I wrote the following poem for Jesus:

Thinking of You!

Autumn is here,
Brown, yellow and red.
Walking in this colorful forest,
Thinking of You.

Season is changing,
Foggy, rainy, and gray.
Walking on this chilly road,

Thinking of You.

Looking at my neighbor's house,
Kids are running around the fireplace.
Families are greeting with hugs and kisses,
Yet, I am alone, thinking of You!

I lift up my soul,
Calling Your name.
My Beloved, would You take me away?
And let us find our own fireplace.

Looking at the stars,
They are singing and dancing.
I ask, "Have you seen my Beloved?
If you see Him, tell Him, I am looking for Him!"

Candlelight,
Pumpkin pie,
Tears are running, heart is yearning.
Where are You, my Beloved?

You have stolen my heart.
You have grieved my soul.
For You are far away,
And I cannot hold You and kiss You!

How I long for You, my Beloved.
I am in love with You, my Darling.
How desperate and feeble I am,
Because I am lovesick for You.

My heart is burning with flames,
The flames of love for You.
My soul is singing beautiful songs,
The songs of adoration for You!

JESUS, MY FOREVER LOVE

I am mad,
I am crazy,
I am helpless,
And I am hopeless!

Oh, my Beloved,
"Set me as a seal upon your heart,
As a seal upon your arm;
For love is as strong as death." *

You are like the wind,
Coming and going.
I run to catch You,
But I cannot find You!

Do not torture me, my Beloved,
Have mercy on me, my Darling.
Come and let us run away,
To our secret dating place.

"Make haste, my Beloved,
And be like a gazelle
Or a young stag
On the mountains of spices." *

Come quickly, my Darling,
Like the eagle in the sky.
Take me upon Your wings,
And fly to the end of the heavens!

Let our hearts sing in the sky.
Let our love release fragrance to the cloud.
Let our hands compose
A symphony of divine romance!

I am Your rose of Sharon.
I am Your lily of the valley.
I am Your Shulamite—
Your passionate lover.

I am a gorgeous garden,
Filled with vibrant flowers.
Come, my Sweetheart,
Pick any as You please.

I am a lush vineyard,
Produce the finest wine.
Come, my handsome Lover,
Drink until your heart is satisfied.

Rise up, my Beloved,
My beautiful One,
Come away with me—
Away from this cold and rainy world.

There You come,
Descending from the cloud.
Your face is as radiant as the sun,
Walking toward me with Your open arms.

I run to Your embrace,
Resting on Your heart.
Do not let me go, my dearest Lover,
For I cannot live without You!

I am no longer myself,
I am no longer of this world.
I am Yours, forever Yours.
For I am deeply and utterly in love with You!

Your lover,

Ying

* Song of Solomon 8:6; 8:14.

No Woman Can Get Pregnant by Reading a Book

Beloved readers, knowing Jesus from reading the Bible is one thing, but knowing Him in person is another. Indeed, He was written in the Bible from the Old Testament to the New Testament, but He is also a *living Person*.

No woman can get pregnant by reading her husband's book. There must be intimacy involved, such as kissing, hugging, and lovemaking. In the same manner, if we want to know the Lord, we must spend time with *His Person*. Our Lord would like us all to know Him intimately and personally. Without *spiritual lovemaking* with God, we cannot get pregnant and bear fruit for the Kingdom.

> [Jesus said,] You must remain in life-union with me, for I remain in life-union with you. For as a branch severed from the vine will not bear fruit, so your life will be fruitless unless you live your life intimately joined to mine. "I am the sprouting vine and you're my branches. As you live in union with me as your source, fruitfulness will stream from within you—but when you live separated from me you are powerless.
>
> —John 15:4–5 TPT

The fruits that Jesus wants us to bear are: "*love, joy, peace, longsuffering, kindness, goodness, faithfulness, gentleness, self-control*" (Galatians 5:22–23). Many Christians spend more time reading the Bible than with the Lord Himself. We fail to realize that the Lord is very much alive.

Jesus' heart can be grieved because we neglect His Person. So many believers embrace His book (the Bible) more than embracing the Lord of the book. We often place the Bible above the Lord and proclaim that we know Him. We study the Bible for hours, yet we hardly spend ten minutes with the Lord Himself.

In other words, if I have a husband and someone wrote a book about him. Daily, I spend more time reading the book than kissing him, hugging him, and making love to him. I am sure this marriage will not last long. Therefore, when we seek the Lord, we must seek *His Person*. We must desire to see Him *face to face*. He is not an idea, nor an imagination; He is a real Person. Only if we fellowship with Him intimately and communion with His Person daily, will we give birth to spiritual fruits for the Kingdom of God.

Twenty-One Years Old

Guiding by the Holy Spirit, I had been feasting on spiritual food—the Bible, sermons, and Christian books. It was truly a life-changing experience. God's Words, combined with many Christian authors' testimonies, enriched my spiritual life to a different dimension. The Holy Spirit caused me to hunger for divine wisdom, knowledge, and understanding. I was like a sponge absorbing as much spiritual food as I could.

On June 28, 2014, during my time with God, I found myself becoming a twenty-one-year-old woman (in my spiritual body). At this point, Jesus and I had already been very close. We were lovers. As the relationship matured, my intimacy with Him intensified.

Routinely, in my spiritual body, I would kneel and wait quietly in the garden for the Lord to come. When I saw Him coming, I would run to Him and hug Him passionately. During these emotional moments, there were not many words, just intimate love between us. Jesus is an extremely *passionate Person*. Every time we hugged, I could feel His immense inner Joy.

White Eagle, Birthday Cake, and Flowers

Many times, the Lord has taken me to different places on His Eagle's wings. Every so often, Jesus turns Himself into a White Eagle and carries me to our usual meeting places—the beach, the garden, the meadow, the sun, the flower field, or the winter flower forest. I usually hold the Eagle's neck as He flies. I can see the earth from a bird's-eye view. Sometimes, it looks like places in Europe; other times, the scenery is celestial.

On the Eagle's back was the most intimate time. I would murmur in my heart, "I love You so much, Yeshua, my Love. Take me away, far, far away, to the end of the heavens." And the Eagle would say, "I love you, my precious lover! Where would you like Me to take you?" We could hear each other's voices by heart.

It is not a strange thing that God carries His children on His Eagle's wings. In fact, the following scripture confirms that God had indeed taken the children of Israel on His wings:

> *The Lord called to him [Moses] from the mountain and said, "Give these instructions to the family of Jacob; announce it to the descendants of Israel: 'You have seen what I did to the Egyptians. You know how I carried you on eagles' wings and brought you to myself. Now if you will obey me and keep my covenant, you will be my own special treasure from among all the peoples on earth.'"*
>
> —Exodus 19:3–5 NLT

> *"When I passed by you [Jerusalem] again and looked upon you, indeed your time was the time of love; so I spread My wing over you and covered your nakedness. Yes, I swore*

an oath to you and entered into a covenant with you, and you became Mine," says the Lord God.

—Ezekiel 16:8

He [God] will cover you with his feathers. He will shelter you with his wings. His faithful promises are your armor and protection.

—Psalm 91:4 NLT

March 2016, on my birthday, the Lord put me on His Eagle's wings and flew to a place where was like a big cave—it could be His Eagle's nest. Inside this place was filled with flowers, dazzling lights, and colors of all kinds. I would describe this place as a cartoon-like wonderland. Flowers were singing, butterflies were dancing, and glittering lights were encircling us.

Jesus was in a pure white garment, and I was in a baby blue Cinderella dress. There was enchanting music in the background. He held me close and danced with me. Our eyes locked on each other. His eyes were *piercing* and *irresistible!* This place picturized the royal Prince and His lover's secret meeting place. Jesus is an exceptionally romantic Lover. He always expresses His emotions genuinely. And my heart was melted like wax. I was *madly in love* with Him!

Then the Lord held my hand and walked further into this cave-like place. He put a big bouquet of red roses in my hand. His eyes were filled with affection, and He said to me, "Happy Birthday, My darling!" I was speechless by His fiery passion.

On a nearby table, there was a huge birthday cake. The size of the cake was the same size as the round table. It was decorated with pastel baby-green icing and garlanded with white flowers—gorgeous.

My jaw dropped and said, "For me? Oh, my Lord, You did all these for me?" I jumped with joy and hugged His neck with a squeezing kiss on His cheek. I kept saying, "Thank You, my Love! I am so overwhelmed. The flowers are beautiful. And the cake is so lovely; I have never seen a cake that big. Thank You, my Darling!"

Jesus is the desire of my soul. His affection *enraptures* my heart. I am frequently drunk in His flaming passion. Being romanced by Him is beyond description. Everything He does for me is to purify me, cleanse me, and beautify me. He is preparing me for my eternal life with Him. While the King is in love with me, all I need to do is obey Him, lay down my life for Him, be submissive to Him, surrender to Him, be His bondservant, and let Him *unlock* my heart! The following scriptures describe our love better than I do.

The Bridegroom-King:

Arise, my love. Open your heart, my darling, deeper still to me. Will you receive me this dark night? There is no one else but you, my friend, my equal. I need you this night to arise and come be with me. You are my pure, loyal dove, a perfect partner for me. My flawless one, will you arise? For My heaviness and tears are more than I can bear. I have spent myself for you throughout the dark night.

—Song of Songs 5:2 TPT

The Sleeping Bride:

My Beloved reached into me to unlock my heart. The core of my very being trembled at his touch. How my soul melted when He spoke to me!

Most sweet are his kisses, even his whispers of love. He is delightful in every way and perfect from every viewpoint. If you ask me why I love him so, O brides-to-be, it's because there is none like him to me. Everything about him fills me with holy desire! And now he is my beloved—my friend forever.

—Song of Songs 5:4; 5:16 TPT

My holy desire for Jesus burns in my heart. I sincerely hope all God's children on Planet Earth have the same desire toward our King. From the Song of Songs, we know that The Bridegroom King (Jesus) takes delight in romancing His earthly lovers. He treats each of His children—who longs to have an intimate relationship with Him—special. Each has a unique place in His heart. His Eagle's wings are for all who desire to fly with Him.

Two White Eagles

On January 31, 2020, as I was soaking in Christian music, I saw Jesus as a big White Eagle and myself as a small white eagle flying in the sky. We were cruising here and there—over mountains, rivers, oceans, green pastures, flower beds, etc.

We first landed on the beach—the one with orange, silver, lilac, and purple colored sky and ocean floor. At the time of landing, we changed back to human forms and began to dance barefoot on the sand. He looked at me intently. Our eyes remained locked, refusing to look away. The romance between us was intensified to a deeper dimension.

When it comes to romance, Jesus is surpassing all human romance imaginable. He seldom uses words but His body language. Most of the time, Jesus speaks to me with His eyes. Please do not ask me why; I somehow understand His eye expression.

We danced from the sand to the surface of the ocean. Our clothes reflected the color of orange, purple, lilac, silver, and blue in the sea. Jesus pushed me for some distance, and then He gestured for me to come to Him. I ran to Him, and He lifted me up in the air with my arms stretched out like an airplane. We both laughed and laughed . . .

We then took off and landed on the sun. Each time we took off, our bodies turned into the white eagles again, and when we landed, we would turn back into human forms. We danced a little while in the sun. As we were twisting and turning, the fire of our love resembled the temperature of the sun. My dress reflected the colors of the sun, but it was not burned—*Amazingly beautiful!* Then we turned into the white eagles again, cruised inside the sun for a while, and flew away.

We landed on a beautiful flower field. It was filled with light pink and orange flowers. As we danced, the flowers encircled us like many colored ribbons. They began to dance with us. The hues of the flowers formed swirling celestial aurora. At that moment, I saw my dress turning light pink and orange. It resembled the color of the flowers. Everything around the presence of Jesus was alive—even my dress was alive (see Figure 10).

Jesus was excited and lifted me up in the air. Once in a while, He would make a big dance move; other times, He would do a close dance. As for me, I just enjoyed being His lover, resting in His arms, and letting Him lead. It was truly *a dance of romance* and *a dance of love!*

Figure 10: Dancing with the flowers.

After that, we took off and landed on an ocean of dazzling stars. They made a welcoming and glittering dance floor for us. I saw myself in ballet clothes and pointed shoes. Although I had never learned ballet, I was doing *en pointe, fouetté, arabesque, and pirouette*. Jesus was in a male ballet position and supported my moves. We were like the ballet stars in *Swan Lake*. Our clothes were sparkling among the alluring stars. Heavens were hushed! The only sound that could be heard was the two lovers' heartbeats—Jesus and Ying—*a ballet of love!*

Jesus Gave Me a New Name

Once, as we were walking in the garden, Jesus called me by the name "Mei Lin." I was surprised and wondered why the Lord called me by this name. He always calls me "darling," "sweetheart," or "beloved," but this time was different.

"Mei Lin" in Chinese means "Forest of Winter Flowers." The Chinses people call it "Plum Blossom in Snow." The shape of the flower looks like a cherry blossom, but the color is red. They only bloom in the winter during snowtime, and symbolize beauty and strength. Actually, giving a new name by God is not a strange thing. This is documented in both the Old and New Testaments of the Bible:

> *[Jesus said,] To everyone who is victorious I will give some of the manna that has been hidden away in heaven. And I will give to each one a white stone, and on the stone will be engraved a new name that no one understands except the one who receives it.*
>
> —Revelation 2:17 NLT

> *[The Lord said,] I am changing your name. It will no longer be Abram. Instead, you will be called Abraham, for you will be the father of many nations.*
>
> —Genesis 17:5 NLT

After Jesus gave me the new name, He frequently took me to a forest of winter flowers. I would wear a white dress with red plum blossoms imprints on it. He would wear a white robe with a red sash. We danced in this snow-white forest, decorated with gorgeous red winter flowers—incredibly charming.

Other times, He just held me in His arms under the snow-frost branches. Although it was cold, He kept me close to His chest to keep me warm. Talk about romance, more than romance! *I am His winter flower—His precious Mei Lin.*

On July 29, 2021, during my devotion time, I saw the following vision:

Jesus was walking toward me in the garden. I ran to Him (in my spiritual body), and He picked me up with intense joy. When He put me down, He placed a winter flower on my hair (see Figure 11). I was wearing the same white dress with red plum blossoms on it. Only this time, I noticed these flowers were alive.

Figure 11: Jesus holding me in the forest of winter flowers.

"My Mei Lin," He whispered and gently hugged me with His eyes closed. Then He kissed me intimately. With both of His forearms, He picked me up (like a groom carries the bride on the wedding day) and ascended into the sky. We landed in the forest of snowy winter flowers. Millions of plum blossom trees were in full blooms. There He kissed me again. This kiss was different from any other kiss before—currents of love poured into my heart like warm oil, causing my earthly body to breathe heavily.

Then we got into a snowball fight. We were running and throwing snowballs at each other. Our hair and clothes were muddled with snow. We laughed so hard and couldn't stop the excitement. Beloved readers, Jesus is an amusing and innocent Person—*pure like a child.*

He then put me on His Eagle's back and took off with His large wings, soaring high into the sky and cruising among the thick cloud. He said to me, "I want you to believe that I love you beyond you can comprehend. I also receive your love and take it deep in my heart. You were not mistaken; we were indeed lovers before you came to the earth as a human. We were very close and deeply in love!" I was silent and in tears—profound tears dropping on the Eagle's feather.

We then landed on our beach. Jesus held my hand and led me to the ocean. There, we swam with all kinds of fish and flipped with dolphins. We also danced in the water like those synchronized swimmers in Olympics. Jesus is an adventurous and exuberant Person to be with.

I then saw millions of multi-colored waters erupting into the sky and forming a beautiful water pillar. Suddenly, out of this pillar, a white dove and a pink butterfly came out and flew into space. The white dove was the Holy Spirit, and the butterfly was me. I will explain more about me being a pink butterfly in a later chapter.

Make Love to Me!

October 8, 2019, on the day of Yom Kippur, I took three days off just to be with God. Each of them (Father, Son, Holy Spirit) spoke to me. I know their voices. Even though they are One, they have their distinct characters and voices. The following message was from Jesus:

> "I know you are in love with Me. You have desired to carry My fragrance of humbleness and gentleness. You have asked me to teach you holiness. I will teach you and will not let you walk by yourself. I am your Husband, and you are My responsibility.
>
> "Love Me means to give everything to Me, obey my commandments, and pick up the cross and follow me! You are My lover. I have always enjoyed being with you. I really do! Carry My fragrance, for I desire to give you all My fragrances and make you beautiful. *Make love to Me* and *Me only*, not to this world or idols.
>
> "Pursue Me into a deeper dimension. Pursue me with all your heart. I desire to be intimate with you more than you can understand. I created you to love Me and be My lover. You are Mine! I am your Beloved, your Husband, your King, and your God. Honor Me with your love and devotion, for I am waiting for you and welcoming you deeper into My heart!"

Beloved readers, I have received many messages like this since the day I became a Christian. They filled many of my notebooks, but I had never heard the word *"Make love to Me!"* In my human mind, it sounded very strange. How could an Almighty God say such a thing? But as I thought it deeper—beyond human comprehension—I understood.

Love-making is the ultimate union between a husband and wife. It is the climax of worshiping God. God created man and woman to make love, multiply, and populate the earth. When Jesus said, *"Make love to Me,"* it meant *"Union with Me"* and not to the world. He wanted me to bear spiritual fruit. Just as He said in John 15:

> *You must remain in life-union with me, for I remain in life-union with you. For as a branch severed from the vine will not bear fruit, so your life will be fruitless unless you live your life intimately joined to mine.*
>
> *I am the sprouting vine and you're my branches. As you live in union with me as your source, fruitfulness will stream from within you—but when you live separated from me you are powerless.*
>
> —John 15:4–5 TPT

The Lord desires to have my whole life. He is a jealous God; He does not share. He doesn't want me to give part of my life to Him and part to the world, because the god of this world is still Satan. The following scripture describes the *climax* of *union with God*:

> *My old identity has been co-crucified with Christ and no longer lives. And now the essence of this new life is no longer mine, for the Anointed One [Jesus Christ] lives his life through me—we live in union as one! My new life is empowered by the faith of the Son of God who loves me so much that he gave himself for me, dispensing his life into mine!*
>
> —Galatians 2:20 TPT

Jesus in My Dining Room

*E*ver since the day I was born again in Christ, each holiday, such as Christmas, Thanksgiving, Valentine's Day, and Father's Day, I have purchased cards and gifts, and have written poems to God the Father, the Son, and the Holy Spirit. Even though they might not use the gifts that I bought for Them, it was my way of showing love.

In December 2015, during preparation for Jesus' birthday, I ordered a birthday cake with *"Happy Birthday Jesus"* on it. I also wrote a love letter and bought Him the following gifts:

- A man's winter scarf
- A set of wood carving tools (Jesus did carpentry when He was on the earth)
- A box of Lindt Lindor Chocolate Truffles
- A beautiful birthday card

On Christmas Eve, 2015, I attended the church service at JKI Hosana Miracle Center (the Indonesian church). Right after, I invited Melisa (the Indonesian girl) to come to my house and celebrate Jesus' birthday with me. Melisa is a "seer." The Lord has opened her eyes to see the spirit realm with her natural eyes. During the church service, she told me that Jesus was standing behind pastor Rudi and wearing a red robe with gold embroideries all over the robe. He also had a beautiful crown on His head.

After the church service, I put all the gifts on my dining room table, decorated with festive colors. I arranged a chair for Jesus on my right and Melisa on my left. Then I presented the gifts, opened the card, and read my love letter to Him. The birthday cake was placed in front of His chair with lighted candles. We started singing happy birthday. I did all these out of my faith, yet in reality, I was not sure Jesus would come to receive His birthday gifts because I could not see Him with my natural eyes.

While I was singing happy birthday, Melisa said to me, "Ying, the Lord is pleased with you. He likes the gifts, the card, and the cake." A few minutes later, she said again, "Ying, the Lord is very pleased with you."

About an hour later, I asked Melisa, "Do you really think the Lord sees what I bought for Him? Do you think He paid attention to my gifts? He has so many other children who celebrate His birthday this night." Melisa said, "Ying, remember I kept telling you that the Lord is pleased with you? When you sang happy birthday, He was sitting on the chair you arranged and looking at the cake with a big smile. He sat there for a while to receive your gifts and listened when you read the love letter. After that, He left."

I was stunned and cried out, "Oh, Jesus, I did not know You really came to see me and receive my gifts in person." My body was shaking with joy. Melisa then said, "Jesus wore the same red robe and the crown, just as I saw Him in the church." I was overwhelmed with joy.

All my encounters with Jesus have been with my eyes closed—seeing Him with the eyes of my heart, but Melisa can see Him with her natural eyes. Beloved readers, our Lord takes delight in receiving His children's gifts. He longs for our attention and puts Him first above all else. From the day I bought His birthday gifts, He could not wait to receive them. Jesus is so real, sweet, and innocent with a *childlike* heart.

Conversely, the devil was deadly jealous of my love for Jesus and created a drama right after the birthday celebration. A voice spoke to me, "You are such a naïve fool! Jesus did not come to see you. He came to see that girl. It is Melisa whom He loves, not you! You prepared the celebration for nothing because He delights in Melisa."

Beloved readers, in 2015, I was a one-year-old baby Christian. I had not learned how to distinguish God's voice from the devil's voice. At that moment, I was so confused. I thought Jesus came to see me. It was I who bought the gifts, the card, and the cake. Why would Jesus come to see Melisa in my house and not me? I ran upstairs, hid in the closet, and cried bitterly. I said to Jesus with tears:

"Lord, why are You hurting me like this? Have I not shown You that I love You by giving You the birthday gifts? If You love Melisa, why didn't You meet her at her house? Why did you humiliate me in my house? I planned the celebration to please You, but You ended up hurting me. *Why Lord? Why?*"

While I was crying, I could sense Jesus was standing next to me. He was silent, without a word. *He was grieved!*

I was heartbroken for about two weeks until one of the Christian sisters told me, "Ying, the Lord came to see you, not that girl. He knew that you couldn't see Him with your natural eyes, so He used Melisa to tell you that He came to receive your gifts." It took me a long time to get over the hurt. That was my initial spiritual journey when the devil took advantage of my naïveness.

Beloved readers, the devil and demons will use all kinds of tricks to confuse believers, especially the baby Christians. They are jealous of every child who has intimate fellowship with God. Their goal is to deceive us in any way possible. They are *sheer evil*. The voice I heard that night was from the enemy.

Since the day Jesus came to my house and sat in the dining room, I always put flowers on the spot He sat. I will not allow anyone to sit on that chair—it is reserved for my Husband, Jesus!

Satan Often Uses Christians to Do His Biddings

Sadly speaking, Satan will use Christians to confuse other Christians every so often. In the beginning (as a baby Christian), I was overly naïve and blindly trusted other fellow believers. I innocently believed that mature Christians were trustworthy and had much closer relationships with God than I did. I was wrong!

Once, a Christian sister called me and said, "The Lord just talked to me and asked me to tell you something." I then quickly invited her to my house. She said, "The Lord doesn't prefer the way you love Him. The intimacy you showed to God was not His wish, such as giving Him flowers and gifts. The Lord wants you to show Him agape love."

I asked her, "What is agape love?" She told me the definition. I assumed her message was from the Holy Spirit. Later, when I googled agape love, I realized that she quoted exactly from Google. Perhaps she indeed got the definition online to support her point. Regardless of where the description came from, I considered her intention was good and genuine. However, her message deeply penetrated my heart and impacted my trust in God.

I was confused and angry with God. I forgot all the scriptures that I had studied. I was so hurt and discouraged by her message. I murmured in my heart, "The Lord is not pleased with me. He doesn't want me to love Him in such a way. He takes no pleasure in my flowers, cards, poems, love letters, and gifts." I could hear a voice laughing, "Ha, Ha, Ha! I told you. All that you did for Him was stupid. *So stupid. Jesus hates you!*"

Instead of confirming with the Holy Spirit about this sister's message, out of my anger, I ran to my prayer room and put away all the cards, love letters, and gifts I had bought for God. Up to that point, I had more than fifty love letters, poems, and cards, along with gifts to the Father, the Son, and the Holy Spirit. There were three-tier shelves in my prayer room. All filled with my cards and gifts. That night, my heart was *so broken*; I threw them all into a box. I was upset and miserable. My body and hands were shaking while putting things away. I felt rejected and misled by Jesus. I cried out to Him with a sobbing voice:

"Lord, if you did not like my love letters, poems, cards, and gifts, why didn't You say so? Instead, every time I presented my letters, poems, and gifts to You, You always told me that You loved them, and they were very precious to You. But now, Your message has changed. If that was the case, why didn't You just tell me from the beginning? *Why did you trick me?* Why did you torture me this long, knowing that I was helplessly in love with You? All I did was to express my intimacy with You in my own unique ways."

That night, I could not hold my peace anymore. I ran to the local store and bought a bottle of wine. I drank it until I got drunk. I felt as if my Lover had broken up with me, and I was rejected.

Beloved readers, the enemy of God has become our enemy—they hate us. They will do whatever they can to break our relationship with God. In my case, Jesus and I were extremely close and intimate; this drove the enemy *absolutely crazy*. Yet, they used my naïve nature and lack of knowledge to infiltrate my mind and deceive my heart. Let alone, he used a Christian to do his bidding, which totally took me off guard.

This taught me an important lesson: we must test *all* things according to God's Word, we must hold sound discernment, and trust in the Lord wholeheartedly. Under *all* circumstances, we must lean only on the Holy Spirit—not on what others tell us or on any unfamiliar voices, which mostly come from demons. Just as the scriptures instruct us:

> *Trust in the Lord with all your heart, and lean not on your own understanding.*
>
> —Proverbs 3:5

> *Test all things; hold fast what is good. Abstain from every form of evil.*
>
> —1 Thessalonians 5:21–22

Later, during my devotion time with God, Jesus said to me:

> "Why did you doubt about Me? Why did you listen to another person's voice? When I said I love your letters, poems, cards, and gifts, *I really meant it!* You are one of the few who know how to touch My heart and My Father's

heart. I love the flowers you bought for Me. I treasure all your gifts and poems. *Do not stop! I want more!* I desire your love and romance. They are so dear to Me. I have put you in a very special place in My heart. I am in love with you. *You must trust Me* and not doubt Me!"

Upon receiving Jesus' message, I realized that I was fooled by the enemy. As for that sister, I don't think she knew the message was not from God. Therefore, I don't blame her and have forgiven her.

Beloved readers, I longed for the Lord's love, but at the same time, I was also afraid of His love. I had been divorced twice. If Jesus ever divorced me, that would be the end of my life (not thinking rationally). Jesus knew my thoughts and fear, so He purposely kept His actions consistent. Every time I saw Him, He was always gentle and loving, as though I was the only person in His heart and the only lover in His life.

The more I wanted to trust Him fully, the harder the enemy attacked me. The voice of the enemy bombarded me day and night, causing me to doubt Jesus' love. I constantly heard voices like this:

> "He is disappointed with you. You missed the morning devotion. He is angry with you. Don't even go to the prayer room. You are an unfaithful bride. He has moved on to other faithful brides and will not see you anymore. He loathes you because you are filthy! He despises you and thinks you are disgusting. You are covered with sins, but He is pure. Therefore, He can't stand you!"

When these voices came, I was afraid of Jesus. I was terrified that He would abandon me. I could not afford to have another brokenheart divorce. I thus left some room in my heart and did not trust His love completely.

One day, when I requested to see Him, I saw Him sitting on the big rock in our garden, and I sat on the ground (in my spiritual body) and looked up to Him. His face was solemn. He kept silent for a while and said, "Have I not shown you long enough that I love you? Your doubt saddens Me. I do not love you one day and change My heart another day. I am God; I do not change. I have been faithful to you. Never doubt My faithfulness to you!"

Both of His hands held my hands firmly while speaking. I could feel He was very sad. I looked down with embarrassment and shame. At this moment, His voice was getting more solemn and resolute. I could feel that He was shaking.

"Ying, I want you to look at Me!" He insisted. By the way, He always called me darling, sweetheart, or beloved, but this time, He called me Ying. I was so ashamed and afraid; I could not look at Him. He then gently lifted my chin with both of His hands and said, "Look at Me, Ying. What do you see? Look at My eyes! What do you see?"

I timidly lifted up my head and looked at His eyes. Wow, they were sapphire blue, as deep as the bottomless ocean, piercing through my heart with intense passion. They were fearsome, divine, and tender-loving. At that moment, I wanted to run away from Him because He was too good for me, and I was not worthy of Him. I was an unfaithful lover and a doubting bride. He deserved someone much better.

He was quiet and understood my thoughts. He kept holding my chin and looking at me intently with His penetrating eyes. I could not even move or escape because He wouldn't allow me. He was determined to get His answer. "You must tell Me! What do you see?" He insisted. *"Tell Me!"*

At that moment, I began to tremble and cry. With my feeble voice, I said, "I see love, total love, nothing but love." I knew I was wrong, but I was too *chicken* to love Him.

He said, "Then why did you doubt My love? You must never doubt My love! You have no idea how much I love you! When I say I have fallen in love with you, I am telling you the truth. I am the Lord. *I do not lie!*" His voice became more and more intense. I then fell on His feet and wept uncontrollably.

I cried out, "I want to trust You, but I can't. It is too painful to fall in love. I am afraid of falling in love with You. Why do you love me, Jesus? What is it about me that makes you stay with me? Two husbands divorced me. Why are you still staying with me? Just like them, You are supposed to be gone by now. Why have you not done so yet? No one has stayed with me for long. I was supposed to be deserted because I am an unfaithful and ugly wife. Why have you not left me yet?"

Beloved readers, I wanted to trust Him *so badly*, but I was afraid to be abandoned by Him. I was not rational even though the Bible says God will never leave me nor forsake me. In reality, having been divorced twice, fear crippled me and caused me not to trust Him fully. In those days, love to me meant *pain!*

Jesus did not say anything at that moment. His hands were still holding me and would not let go. I could feel His heart was very heavy and grieved. *He was crying* and held me tightly still. With heartfelt tears, He said, "I am not a man. I am God! I will never leave you nor forsake you! You just have to trust Me!"

I had meditated on the following scriptures many times, but only until that moment, I truly understood their meaning.

> *[The Lord said,] I will make you my wife forever, showing you righteousness and justice, unfailing love and compassion. I will be faithful to you and make you mine, and you will finally know me as the Lord.*
>
> —Hosea 2:19–20 NLT

> *Be strong and courageous. Do not be afraid or terrified, . . . for the Lord your God goes with you; he will never leave you nor forsake you.*
>
> —Deuteronomy 31:6 NIV

"Hold My Back!"

One night, the Holy Spirit gave me this dream: I was on vacation, somewhere in Switzerland. After my family and I checked into the hotel, I said, "Let me buy some food from the local store." As I walked around the street, suddenly, I fell off a cliff. My hands were gripping the edge of the cliff. When I looked down, there was an exceedingly deep and endless abyss. I am notoriously afraid of heights; they can paralyze me easily. I started to shout, "Help! Help!" Somehow, I was holding a three-ring folder with one hand while the other hand continued clinging on the edge of the cliff. I realized this could be the end of my life.

Suddenly, a man showed up next to me. He was tall and robust. He said, "I want you to let go of your hands and hold my back instead; let me pull you up."

I screamed, "No, no, no, I can't. I am afraid. I can't let my hands go!" He said, almost like a command, "Let go of your folder first, be calm, close your eyes, and hold onto my waist. *Do it now!* If you do not, you will die!"

At that life-or-death moment, I had no choice; I did what he told me. I released the folder, and it fell quickly into the deep abyss. I then held his waist with both of my hands and closed my eyes. My body was literally hanging on his back. At that moment, my life was totally in this man's hands. He slowly pulled me up from the cliff and then vanished.

This dream was obvious. The Man was Lord Jesus. The cliff was the edge to hell. He came to rescue me from falling into the pit of hell. He wanted me to trust Him blindly. He wanted me to hold onto Him in the most dangerous situation. He wanted me to let go of my fear and trust Him completely. He showed me that He would hasten to rescue me under any perilous circumstances. Just as King David said, *"O Lord,*

You pulled me up from Sheol; You spared me from descending into the Pit" (Psalm 30:3 BSB).

"*Sheol*" is another word for "hell," "hades," "abyss," or "perdition." "*Pit*" refers to the prison cell in hell—there are many pits in hades for holding the lost souls. People are burning in these deep pits and unable to come out—sheer suffering! Every day, the Lord is rescuing His children from falling into the pits of hell. He is our Rescuer, Savior, and Redeemer.

The dream also implies that we live in a fallen world, where Satan still rules. If we do not obey God's commandments and walk in His ways, we will surely fall—as I did in the dream.

The endless deep is the way to perdition. Daily, we are walking around the edge of hell. If we are not clinging to Jesus, we will descend into the underworld. The enemies will keep tricking us into the abyss, just as Jesus said the following to author Rick Joyner in his book *The Call*:

> "The whole world still lies in the power of the evil one, and you walk on the edge of hell every day. Through the midst of it there is a path of life. There are deep ditches on either side of the path of life, so you must not deviate from the narrow way.
>
> "No one can find his own way out of those ditches. Following your own way is how you fall into them, and your own way will never lead you out. I am the only way out. When you fall, do not waste your time trying to figure everything out, for you will only sink deeper into the mire. Just ask for help. I am your Shepherd, and I will always help you when you call on Me." [1]

Beloved readers, heaven and hell are our daily choice, and God gives us free will to choose. He does not demand us to heaven or hell—*it is our choice*. If you end up in hell, do not blame on God, but blame only on yourself. The edge of hell is right at your door. If you keep on sinning, you will eventually end there. *"For the wages of sin is death, but the gift of God is eternal life in Christ Jesus our Lord"* (Romans 6:23). "Death" here refers to "hell."

Uncovering His Feet

At midnight, while Boaz was sleeping under the silvery moonlight, Ruth uncovered his feet at the threshing floor. She quietly lay down at his feet, hoping he would take her under his wings.

The biblical character of Boaz was the personification of Jesus, and Ruth was the epitome of a perfect bride for Jesus Christ. She was loyal, sacrificial, faithful, obedient, and humble. The Lord delights in the inner beauty of His brides—meek, pure, and submissive.

Naomi, Ruth's mother-in-law, is the personification of the Holy Spirit. It is the Holy Spirit who directs us, prepares us, beautifies us, and anoints us to be ready for King Jesus. Likewise, what happened between Jesus and me was arranged by the Holy Spirit. The following scripture describes how Naomi prepared Ruth for Boaz.

> *Wash yourself and anoint yourself, put on your best garment and go down to the threshing floor; but do not make yourself known to the man until he has finished eating and drinking. Then it shall be, when he lies down, that you shall notice the place where he lies; and you shall go in, uncover his feet, and lie down; and he will tell you what you should do.*
>
> —Ruth 3:3–4

The Bible tells us that no one can come to Jesus unless the Holy Spirit draws us near to Him. Just as Jesus said in John 6:44, *"No one can* come to me unless the Father who sent me draws them to me." The Holy Spirit prepares us for our Bridegroom King by:

- Cleansing us and making us pure for Jesus.
- Beautifying us and making us presentable to Jesus.
- Anointing us with meekness before approaching Jesus.
- Guiding us to stay low in humility before Jesus.
- Instructing us to lie down at Jesus' feet in reverent fear.

Just as Naomi arranged for Ruth to meet Boaz at midnight, so as the Holy Spirit arranged for me to fall in love with Jesus. Without the Holy Spirit, my loving relationship with Jesus is impossible. I have fallen in love with a few men in my life, but the euphoric-fresh love will not last long. It usually becomes the norm when the relationship goes into a routine, but not in my case with Jesus. Our fresh-first love and all-consuming romance intensify every day, only because our intimate relationship is not fleshly but divine.

The story continues between Boaz and Ruth:

> *After Boaz had finished eating and drinking and was in good spirits, he lay down at the far end of the pile of grain and went to sleep. Then Ruth came quietly, uncovered his feet, and lay down. Around midnight Boaz suddenly woke up and turned over. He was surprised to find a woman lying at his feet! "Who are you?" he asked. "I am your servant Ruth," she replied. "Spread the corner of your covering over me, for you are my family redeemer." "The Lord bless you, my daughter!" Boaz exclaimed. "You are showing even more family loyalty now than you did before, for you have not gone after a younger man."*
>
> —Ruth 3:7–10 NLT

Ruth is my role model for pleasing Jesus. In order to be close to Him, I desire to be like Ruth with sheer obedience and total meekness. I often say to Jesus, "Lord, I am your Ruth. Would You be my Boaz? I come to lie down at Your feet. Would You take Your maidservant under Your wings and let me please You?"

I usually spend three to five hours in my prayer room with the Lord. Seventy percent of the time, I kneel or prostrate on the floor. I must stay low when approaching God. Bowing down in humility is the place where I encounter Him. It is the place where the enemy cannot detect me.

To me, humility is beauty; lowliness is power; forgiveness is joy; obedience is gold; meekness is ruby; and pure-heart delights God. A woman with a gentle and quiet spirit is extremely precious to our Lord God. I have been asking the Holy Spirit to train me in these qualities. All I want is to please Jesus. I have no other desires—*I desire Him and Him only!*

My Dating Song with Jesus— "Draw from My Well"

Every time I wait on God, I always put Terry MacAlmon's music "Draw from My Well" in the background. I usually picture myself as the Samaritan woman at Jacob's well. It was there she encountered Jesus (see John 4:7). I love this story only because I had a similar lifestyle as this woman had. We both did sexually immoral things in our lives, and we both received the great mercy of God. Jesus did not look down on this Samaritan woman. Instead, He valued her and revealed that He was the Messiah before disclosing this amazing truth to His disciples. *"For the Son of Man [Jesus Christ] came to seek and save those who are lost"* (Luke 19:10 NLT).

> *A Samaritan woman came to draw water, and Jesus said to her, "Please give me a drink." . . . She said to Jesus, "You are a Jew, and I am a Samaritan woman. Why are you asking*

me for a drink?" Jesus replied, "If you only knew the gift God has for you and who you are speaking to, you would ask me, and I would give you living water."

The woman said, "I know the Messiah is coming—the one who is called Christ. When he comes, he will explain everything to us." Then Jesus told her, "I am the Messiah!"

—John 4:7, 9–10, 25–26 NLT

The *living water* that Jesus offered to the Samaritan woman was the spring of His everlasting love and eternal life, for the Lord Himself is *"The Lord of the fountain of life"* (see Psalm 68:26). This living water has been flowing from God's heart into my heart. Everything that Jesus has been doing in my life, He is doing in my heart—that is where His living water flows (see John 7:37).

Let all the congregations bring their blessing to God, saying, 'The Lord of the fountain! The Lord of the fountain of life!'

—Psalm 68:26 TPT

[Jesus said,] If anyone thirsts, let him come to Me and drink. He who believes in Me, . . . out of his heart will flow rivers of living water.

—John 7:37–38

While Jesus was on the earth, His heart was closer to the widows, orphans, prostitutes, and sinners than to kings, queens, and rich people. He came for those deeply entangled by the demonic bondage—the captives and the oppressed; He came to save those who were lost and brokenhearted; those who lived in delusions of self-righteousness, self-ambition, and pride; those who were despised by society; for the Lord's heart ached for the so-called *unlovely* by the worldly view.

> *[Jesus said,] The Spirit of the Lord God is upon Me, because the Lord has anointed Me to preach good tidings to the poor; He has sent Me to heal the brokenhearted, to proclaim liberty to the captives, and the opening of the prison to those who are bound; to proclaim the acceptable year of the Lord, and the day of vengeance of our God; to comfort all who mourn, . . . to give them beauty for ashes, the oil of joy for mourning, the garment of praise for the spirit of heaviness; that they may be called trees of righteousness.*
>
> —Isaiah 61:1–3

The music "Draw from My Well" has become our dating song. Many times, I have invited Jesus to dance with me with this music. It is the theme of our romance. My soul *thirsts* for Him (see Psalm 47:1). Just as the Samaritan woman drew water from Jacob's well, I too draw the living water from Jesus, so that His love can flow into my heart unceasingly.

> *I long to drink of you, O God, to drink deeply from the streams of pleasure flowing from your presence. My longings overwhelm me for more of you! My soul thirsts, pants, and longs for the living God. I want to come and see the face of God.*
>
> —Psalm 47:1–2 TPT

Once a prophetess visited a pastor's house. As soon as she entered the door, she saw a river of living water flowing in this place, and the angels were doing water sliding as if at an amusement park. Although this pastor could not see this phenomenon, the seer prophetess could see. Our God is waiting for all of us to draw from His well. As long as His fountain of love flows in our hearts, we will be engulfed by His Shekinah glory, and the enemies cannot detect us.

He Is a Jealous God

The Bible says that God is a jealous God. He does not like His children to worship idols. He is the only God in the universe—there is no other God besides Him. I have never really comprehended the nature of God's jealousy until one day...

After coming back from Brazil for a missionary school and evangelical service, I started looking for a job. However, an IT director's job was not easy to find in the city where I lived. After consulting with the Holy Spirit, He told me not to worry. He said, "Not only will you have a job, but I will give you three jobs to choose from." Indeed, in about two months, I got two job offers, and the third one was offered a week later. I was amazed and extremely grateful. I had no doubt that the job offers were the work of the Holy Spirit!

However, at the beginning of the new job, I had to learn the new business, organize my employees, and get to know business stakeholders. I was overwhelmed and started to cut back on my devotion time with God. Before the new job, I would spend three to five hours daily in my prayer room. After the new job, I only spent weekends with God. I was frustrated, but it was not done intentionally.

One day, Jesus spoke to me: "My darling, I am jealous of your new job. I am jealous of your time spent on sleeping, watching movies, and all other things. I have been waiting for you to come to see Me in the morning. What about our dates? Have you forgotten Me? Have you forgotten your own Husband?"

I could not believe my ears. Wow, God was jealous about my time spent on the new job and other things. I could sense that Jesus' voice was sad—not angry, but sad. I felt so bad. For a long time, I struggled to believe that Jesus could literally fall in love with me. I thought He was just saying it to make me feel good or encouraging me.

Later, the Holy Spirit said, "I blessed you with a new job, but you forgot about your Jesus. *You used Me!*" The tone of the Holy Spirit was very upset. I got scared of His seriousness because He had never spoken to me like that.

A few days after, the Father spoke to me, "My child, My Son really is in love with you. Do not break His heart. Be faithful to Him, for you are precious to Him. He desires your love more than you can understand. Be loyal to Him. He can be hurt, and You indeed hurt His feelings!" What the Holy Spirit and the Father intended to tell me was that Jesus must be the *first* in my life above all else. In other words, He does not like to compete with worldly things in my life. He must be the *center*—just like the following scriptures say:

> *You must not bow down to them [false gods] or worship them, for I, the Lord your God, am a jealous God who will not tolerate your affection for any other gods.*
>
> —Exodus 20:5 NLT

> *The Lord your God is a consuming fire, a jealous God.*
>
> —Deuteronomy 4:24

Our God is the Owner and Maker of the universe. He has every right to be jealous because He is jealous over His own children. We are His property. If we love earthly things, such as jobs, money, property, or material things, we are not worthy of Him. If we love our parents, children, husbands, wives, and friends more than Him, we will provoke Him to jealousy. He must be the first in our lives *at all times!* Jesus made this very clear in the following scripture:

> *Anyone who loves his father or mother more than Me is not worthy of Me; anyone who loves his son or daughter*

> *more than Me is not worthy of Me; and anyone who does not take up his cross and follow Me is not worthy of Me.*
>
> —Matthew 10:37–38 BSB

We must give God all the honor and glory by putting Him above all things. No one dares to compete with His glory. Lucifer did, and he was cast out of heaven forever. King *"Herod did not give glory to God, an angel of the Lord struck him down, and he was eaten by worms and died"* (Acts 12:23 BSB). Also, King Nebuchadnezzar did not give God glory for his accomplishments; God punished him for seven years. He lived like a beast in the field and ate grass like an ox. Similarly, the two sons of Aaron—Nadab and Abihu—did not give God the honor; they offered unauthorized fire in the censers. The Lord consumed them by fire, right in front of their Father, Aaron.

> *Moses said to Aaron, "This is what the Lord spoke, saying: 'By those who come near Me I must be regarded as holy; and before all the people I must be glorified.'"*
>
> —Leviticus 10:3

Why Can God Be Jealous, But I Am Not Allowed?

The King James Bible mentions *"jealous"* or *"jealousy"* forty-three times. Out of which, thirty-six times are related to God's divine jealousy. However, when I checked the word *"jealousy,"* I found its meaning very negative. It means *"envy," "discontent," "resentment,"* and *"bitterness."* I was perplexed and asked the Holy Spirit, "How can God be jealous, and I cannot? What is the difference between human jealousy and God's jealousy?"

Throughout my life, I have been tormented by the spirit of jealousy. On March 20, 2020, the Holy Spirit explained to me:

"Human jealousy is different from God's jealousy. Human jealousy is to crave something that they do not possess but yearn for it—to the point of violence, anger, rage, and murder. However, God's jealousy is to desire something that belongs to Him to begin with, but is robbed by His enemy, for all things are God's property. He is the Supreme Owner of all creations.

"Human jealousy came from Lucifer. It was his jealousy and pride that caused him to fall. Jealousy is a demonic spirit. It was this foul spirit that corrupted Lucifer. The same spirit will corrupt you, and I do not want you to be ruined by it.

"All creations came from God. You never created them nor own them. Therefore, you have no right to be jealous, but God does. Everything belongs to Him. He has the right to be jealous over His own creation and His offspring, but you do not!

"Jealousy is deadly—it will destroy you! Stay away from this evil spirit. It can harden your heart and block Me from helping you. Its purpose is to lead you to bitterness, anger, and unforgiveness. When you are empowered by this spirit, you will be in torment and miserable, so stay away from it!

"Open your heart and let Me in. Let Me teach you and guide you. Do not be stubborn about little things. It will hinder you from doing My will. You have limited time on the earth; each moment is precious. Do not waste on pointless things, and do not be jealous of other people.

"Look up and fix your eyes on Jesus. You have a Husband who is in love with you; you have a Father who adores you, and you have Me who watches over you. Together, We give you so much attention and love. Is that not enough? Why do you have to compete with others?"

The Father also said to me, "jealousy, envy, bitterness, and unforgiveness—these sins will lead you to hell. I love you more than My own life, but I cannot let you come to My home because there is no sin allowed in heaven." These words were strong warnings from God. *I got sacred!*

Jealousy Is as Cruel as the Grave!

The Shulamite to Her Beloved:

Set me as a seal upon your heart, as a seal upon your arm; for love is as strong as death, jealousy as cruel as the grave; its flames are flames of fire, a most vehement flame.

—Song of Solomon 8:6

Beloved readers, as I was falling deeply and utterly in love with Jesus, jealousy crept into my heart. When I watched other Christians sharing their intimate fellowship with Jesus on social media, I got very jealous. I was jealous about Jesus giving intimate attention to other believers, especially to female believers.

The very first time that jealousy triggered within me was when I saw Ana Werner on Sid Roth's show—*It's Supernatural*. She described how she danced and hugged Jesus when she visited heaven; I was extremely jealous. Thereafter, every time I saw her on YouTube, I would turn away from her. I treated her as my rival. I thought in my heart, "Jesus is my Husband. He belongs to me." I was burning with jealousy! Day and night, I was tormented by this demonic spirit. I could not be at peace for weeks. My behavior may sound silly, but that was how foolish I was when it came to jealousy.

In my mind, Jesus is *my Husband.* I promised Him that I would never get married (while I am on the earth) so that my whole heart would concentrate on Him. However, I never thought that I could be jealous of other believers who were also in love with Jesus. For a while, it got to a point where I didn't even want to see Jesus or talk to Him. I felt as though my Lover had run away with another person. I was heartbroken. I truly understood the meaning of the scripture, *"Love is as strong as death, jealousy as cruel as the grave"* (Song of Solomon 8:6).

I could not face Jesus during those days, yet, deep in my heart, I yearned for Him *terribly*. I missed Him so much. I missed kissing Him, hugging Him, and dancing with Him. After about a week, I went back to my prayer room. As soon as I got there, my tears flowed like a river. I could not refrain myself and said, *"I miss You, my Love, my darling Husband!"*

I didn't expect He would listen to my cry because my behavior was *so silly*. Yet, to my surprise, He came right away, as though He had been waiting for me. He hugged me fervently. A grief etched across His face. I felt that He was crying. Then He held my face close to His and said, "My lover, My spouse, do not *ever* leave Me like that! Do not *ever* break My heart! I missed you so much. You knew that I *yearned* for you, but you would not come to see Me." He continued. His body was shaking.

I did not know what to say. I was *speechless*. Jesus silently held me for a long time. The only thing that I could hear was His heart's cry. At that moment, my jealousy was gone. I forgot all about it. I was shocked because I made Him cry in such deep pain. Then, He said:

> "Every living soul was made through Me and for Me. There are billions of living souls on the earth. I made each of them unique, and each was made for Myself. I love each of them individually and give them My full attention equally. This does not mean that I love you less or am unfaithful to you. You must allow Me to love My other children. You must not be jealous when I do so. Have I not told you that you have a

very special place in My heart—a place no one can take or replace. *It is reserved for you!*

"Not many children of Mine want to have an intimate relationship with Me like you do. Not many children of Mine want to treat Me as their Lover or Husband like you do. They just want Me to be their Lord, and that's fine. I honor their choice. As for you, you choose to be My lover. We are indeed lovers; we are married. Our intimacy is beyond natural—it is divine. I have been faithful to you, and I want you to be faithful to Me. Under any circumstance, be loyal to Me and do not compare yourself with other children of Mine.

"My beloved, My spouse, I am your Husband, and I am always here for you whenever you need Me. When you call upon My name, I will come quickly by your side. At this time and season, be quick to repent, quick to forgive, and quick to move on. Otherwise, you will be disqualified for My end-time calling.

"Do not compare! Each child has their own calling, which was ordained before the foundation of the world. Remember what I said to James and John, *"To sit on My right or on My left, this is not Mine to give; but it is for those for whom it has been prepared"* (Mark 10:40 NASB). Your life was predestined long before the cosmos was ever created.

"It is time for you to eat solid food instead of drinking milk. It is time for you to be mature and not be a baby. It is time for you to truly understand My heart and My ways. Otherwise, you will fall behind for what I have called you to do!"

He continued:

"I desire My lovers to be pure, humble, and submissive. I desire you to fear Me with reverent fear, love Me with all your heart, and love My other children as you love Me. If you truly love Me, then be happy for whatever pleases Me. Being with My other children pleases Me. Can't you be happy for Me?"

I was ashamed and did not know what to say. Jesus understood my thoughts. He then started kissing me—a very long kiss. He hugged me passionately against His chest and held me for a long time with His eyes closed. Then He kissed me again. *My heart melted!* At that moment, my body was filled with the warm oil of the Holy Spirit. I was undone, totally undone! All I can say is that Jesus is real. He is the *best Lover— the best of the best!*

Afterward, He put me on His Eagle's wings and flew to a hill that was covered with lilac trees. The fragrance was unbelievable. He knew that my favorite flower was lilac. There, He picked me up. His right arm held my legs; His left arm held my upper body. Then He kissed me again. We danced among these gorgeous lilac trees, and our hearts merged by this precious divine love.

Then Jesus took me to our usual meeting place—the meadow. We lay down on the green grass, and He kissed me again. He is indeed in love with me, and I am indeed crazy about Him. I kissed Him back— on His hair, eyes, nose, lips, hands, and feet. Our hearts resembled the following scriptures precisely:

The Shulamite Bride:

I long to bring you to my innermost chamber—this holy sanctuary you have formed within me. O that I might carry you within me! I would give you the spiced wine of my love, this full cup of bliss that we share. We would drink our fill until . . . His left hand cradles my head while his right hand holds me close. We are at rest in this love.

—Song of Songs 8:2–3 TPT

The Bridegroom-King:

Fasten me upon your heart as a seal of fire forevermore. This living, consuming flame will seal you as my prisoner of love. My passion is stronger than the chains of death and the grave, all consuming as the very flashes of fire from the burning heart of God. Place this fierce, unrelenting fire over your entire being.

—Song of Songs 8:6 TPT

Kiss God and Let Him Kiss Me

Proskuneō —To Kiss God

According to the *King James Bible Dictionary*, the Greek word *Proskuneō* is related to worship. It expresses one's adoration to God with total surrender and profound reverence. It shows one's absolute admiration for God—like a dog licking his master's hand. It means to bow low and touch the ground with one's forehead in sheer respect and devotion. It means to kneel prostrate in worshiping God.[2]

I love to worship God. I usually sing to Him at least two to three hours before praying. During worship, I often say, "Father, would You open Your heart and receive my heart songs? Let my music notes kiss You with millions of kisses. Let my voice send flames of adoration to You. Let my songs hug You with bands of love. *Buckle Your seatbelt Daddy, and enjoy my worship!*"

Most of the time, I throw kisses to the Father, the Son, and the Holy Spirit because true worship is to kiss God—*Proskuneō*. Sometimes, I kiss each of Them in a unique way. For example, I will kiss the hair of Jesus, His forehead, nose, eyes, cheeks, shoulders, arms, hands, feet, and heart. Lastly, I will kiss His lips. I give these kinds of kisses to each of Them separately.

Almost always, when I worship God, Jesus will show up in my prayer room. I can see Him sitting on the chair that I prepared for Him. Sometimes, He will sit there for hours just to look at me and enjoy my worship. Every so often, He will stand right in front of me to receive my kisses. *Our God loves to be kissed!*

After my worship, I often remain quiet and let God speak. The Father has told me many times, "My sweetest child, I love your worship. You know how to touch My heart. You are a child who is after My own heart. Your love for My Son melts My heart. He is in love with you. Come to see Him often and be faithful to Him. Do not make Him wait, for He longs to see you!"

Jesus usually tells me, "You are so precious to Me. I love your voice. My heart is warmed and pleased by your voice. I love you very much, my precious darling. You are so special to Me. I long to see you every day." Many times, when I prostrate before His feet, I feel the Lord put both of His hands on my head.

Strangely enough, the Holy Spirit does not say much during these times, and I know why. All these genuine and profound worships are orchestrated by the Holy Spirit. He is the Conductor of my heart songs to God.

Other times, I kiss God while dancing. I lift up my hands and throw kisses to His throne. I usually dance for God in my living room. Sometimes, I invite Jesus to dance with me. My soul thirsts for God (see Psalm 42:1). When I worship Him, I try to let my spirit sing instead of flesh. Both the spirit and soul are located in the belly area.

When I sing songs to God, I can feel my spirit jumping inside of me. Usually, after three hours of non-stop singing, my voice is gone; however, my spirit is unwilling to stop, just as the following scripture says:

> *As the deer pants [longingly] for the water brooks, so my soul pants [longingly] for You, O God. My soul (my life, my inner self) thirsts for God, for the living God. When will I come and see the face of God?*
>
> —Psalm 42:1–2 AMP

God is Spirit. Our worship can only touch His heart when worshiping Him in spirit and truth. Most of the time, I do not sing in English but in tongues. I do not open my eyes but close them to concentrate on God's face. I can see Them clearly through the eyes of my heart (my spiritual eyes). Jesus, in the following scripture, teaches us how to worship.

> *[Jesus said,] The hour is coming, and now is, when the true worshipers will worship the Father in spirit and truth; for the Father is seeking such to worship Him. God is Spirit, and those who worship Him must worship in spirit and truth.*
>
> —John 4:23–24

Yishkeni—Let Him Kiss Me!

According to Rabbi Jonathan Cahn, the word for a divine kiss is *Yishkeni*, which means "Let God kiss me." [3] When our worships touch God's heart, He delights to kiss us in return.

When we worship God in spirit, we become one with God. True worship causes the Holy Spirit to release precious oil on our heads and flows onto our bodies—making us one with God. Many times, during worship, I could literally see myself inside the Father. It was there; I saw myself dancing with Jesus. I could also see the Holy Spirit there. Inside the Father is literally an eternal world—that was the place where I came from.

He Kissed the "Breath of Life" in Me

When two people are in love, the very first thing they do is kiss each other. Kissing expresses one's feelings, love, and desire. Notice that when two people kiss, they exchange breath—*the breath of life from God.*

Who created the kiss, have not by God? All things created by God are *pure* and *holy*. However, Satan often lures humans to sexualize kissing. He makes what God intended to be pure filthy.

As I mentioned in the previous chapters, the very first time Jesus kissed me, my whole being was filled with warm oil—Holy Spirit's diving anointing. Just as God exhaled the *breath of life* into Adam and made him a living being (see Genesis 2:7), so as Jesus kissed His *breath of life* into my being.

> *The Lord God formed a man from the dust of the ground and breathed into his nostrils the breath of life, and the man became a living being.*
>
> —Genesis 2:7 NIV

Dr. Brian Simmons (the lead translator for The Passion Translation of the Bible) explains the meaning of *the breath of life*. It means to breathe into someone's nostrils like two people kissing. He states that God actually kissed life into Adam. The breath from God is the *Spirit of life*. It is more than the air that we breathe. It contains God's intelligence, wisdom, knowledge, understanding, and characters.[4] God literally released His *likeness* (personality) into Adam. Just as God said in Genesis 1:26:

Let Us (Father, Son, Holy Spirit) make man in Our image, according to Our likeness [not physical, but a spiritual personality and moral likeness]."

—Genesis 1:26 AMP

The true believers of God—like the Shulamite bride—yearn for God's kiss.

The Shulamite Bride:

Let him smother me with kisses—his Spirit-kiss divine. So kind are your caresses, I drink them in like the sweetest wine!

—Song of Solomon 1:2 TPT

His lips are lilies, dripping liquid myrrh.

—Song of Solomon 5:13

"Lilies" signifies Christ's purity and innocence, and *"myrrh"* represents His suffering love on the cross.

Beloved readers, if a person stops breathing, that person expires. Nevertheless, do you know the source of our breath? Where does it come from? The truth is that we breathe only because the Holy Spirit is still breathing. He breathes *the breath of life* into all living beings unceasingly. If He stops exhaling, we will all perish, just as the scripture says, *"If God were to take back his spirit and withdraw his breath, all life would cease, and humanity would turn again to dust"* (Job 34:14–15 NLT). Hence, for every breath you inhale, thank God for it. But for those who speak lies, spread fake news, blaspheme against God, *shame on you* to defile God's breath and repay Him with evil!

He Asked Me and I Said Yes

There was a time in 2017, Jesus took me to a celestial galaxy, where I did not see any other living soul, just He and I. It was a tranquil night. Trillions of dazzling stars and nebulas were around us. He held me in His arms, and we danced intimately in the air because there was no ground to stand on.

Jesus quietly looked into my eyes. I sensed that He wanted to say something, yet He was waiting for the right moment. There was a shyness in His manner. I know I should not use the word "shyness" on Lord Jesus, but that was precisely how I felt at that moment.

The anticipation built up in my heart, knowing that whatever He wanted to say must be important to Him. Finally, He said to me softly, "Do you want to be with Me only?" I immediately understood what He meant. He was asking me not to get married again on the earth and set apart just for Him—be His lover and bride.

I could not answer Him at that moment because the question was too sudden, and I was not prepared to answer. I just kept smiling and continued our dance. He understood my thoughts and did not press my response.

I then recalled a scripture brought to me by the Holy Spirit a week before. Apostle Paul said in 1 Corinthians, *"I say to those who aren't married and to the widows—it's better to stay unmarried, just as I am"* (7:8 NLT). At that time, I was puzzled why the Holy Spirit emphasized this verse to me. I asked, "Holy Spirit, why are You showing me this scripture? Are you telling me not to get married?" He did not answer me; instead, He led me to another scripture:

> *The unmarried woman cares about the things of the Lord, that she may be holy both in body and in spirit. But she who*

is married cares about the things of the world—how she may please her husband.

—1 Corinthians 7:34

I was torn apart by Jesus' question because of my earthly desire. After my divorce, I had a strong yearning to get married again. I longed to have a companion because I was lonely. I had always been a very *needy* person. I needed a lot of attention, both mentally and physically. Even though I am a spiritual being, I am still an earthly creature. I have physical needs just as billions of other humans do.

I struggled for a week—wrestling between my flesh and spirit. I kept murmuring: "Setting apart for Jesus means I may never get married again while I am on the earth. I may never enjoy earthly pleasures, such as making love, kissing, and hugging. I will be alone for the rest of my life. What if I am old or in the hospital—who will be taking care of me? What about all the holidays and vacations—who will be spending time with me? What about every day, night, and weekend—who will be there for me? What about going out to movies, concerts, or restaurants—who will be accompanying me? It is good to be with Jesus spiritually, but I am still an earthly being."

That week, my carnal nature took over my thoughts because it desired physical pleasure, but my spirit knew that marrying Jesus would be the greatest honor and the highest calling from God.

Fear of loneliness terrified me. My mind was filled with "What about me, me, me?" When I turned my eyes away from the Lord and concentrated on myself, the Lord became very small, and I became the focal point.

A few days later, Jesus asked me again, "Do you want to be with Me only?" I smiled and still could not answer Him—pretending I did not understand His inquiry. I was not ready to answer Him. What He asked of me was a big deal. He was silent and understood my thoughts.

Beloved readers, it was very simple: Jesus wanted me for Himself. He did not want me to marry again. He was certain about what He wanted, but I was uncertain about what I wanted. We, humans, struggle every day between God and our carnal natures. We hardly ever put God first, yet He puts us first—even died for us.

I was ashamed because I could not even answer His simple question, yet He laid down His life for me. Finally, I said to myself, "Ying, are you stupid or something? What a foolish girl you are! When the King of the universe asks you to be with Him, it is an honor. What are you waiting for?"

A week later, I approached Jesus and said, "Lord, my answer to your question is yes. I will be with You, *only You,* for the rest of my life." He appeared very content with my answer.

Jesus chooses me not because of how worthy I am, but because of how worthy He is. I was created to be His bride, His lover, His worshiper, and His bondservant. My life is all about Him, not about me. Without Him, I would not even exist. He is the source of my life and my very breath. Without Him, I am nothing. My problem was that I put too much value on worldly things, such as fleshly needs, material needs, and earthly desires. But I forgot—*having Jesus means having everything!*

On March 2, 2020, Jesus said to me, "Your life is not about you. When I choose you, it is not because of how good you are; it is because of how good I am. I never created you for you. I created you for Me. Therefore, stop looking at yourself, but looking only at Me."

I have realized that I must always abide in His presence without looking at myself. Communion with Him is the very purpose of my existence every day. All creations exist through Him and for Him. Apart from Him, there is no life. I will always be weak and insufficient; however, it is not about my strength or sufficiency. It is about His strength and sufficiency. I will always be unworthy of what He calls me to do; however, it is never about my worthiness that causes Him to choose me. It is all about His worthiness.

Will You Marry Me?

*J*esus proposed to His bride (the church) on the cross. The cross was His wedding ring for His wife-to-be on the earth (see Hosea 2:19). He laid down His life to exchange for our salvation. He purchased our freedom with His own blood. Have we ever thought about how valuable we are? It cost God's own life to save mankind.

> *[The Lord said,] I will take you to be my wife forever. I will take you to be my wife in righteousness, justice, love, and compassion. I will take you to be my wife in faithfulness.*
>
> —Hosea 2:19–20 CSB

The more time I spent with Jesus, the stronger I desired to marry Him. Marriage is a union of love. It is oneness between two people. It is the declaration, dedication, and commitment of a loving relationship. Even though Jesus is my Lord, my Savior, my Redeemer, and my God, I want much more than that. I want to have the most intimate relationship with Him—like husband and wife. I want to love Him like a lover. Throughout our time together, I have learned that Jesus is very personal. He needs me to love Him personally. He needs me to be His lover.

In fact, *The Passion Translation* of the Bible mentioned countless times in the books of *Psalms* and *Song of Songs* that people who desire to know Jesus intimately are called "the lovers of God" or "the devoted lovers of Yahweh."

> *There's a private place reserved for the devoted lovers of Yahweh, where they sit near him and receive the revelation-secrets of his promises.*
>
> —Psalm 25:14 TPT

Jesus has been proposing to His brides for thousands of years. Yet, why can't we also propose to Him and make Him feel wanted? Jesus once expressed to a prophetess, "I have been pursuing and proposing to my brides on the earth relentlessly for thousands of years. Why can't my brides also purse and propose to Me?" This saying cut to my heart. It showed our Lord desired us to chase after Him intimately.

I then started forming a thought: "I will propose to Jesus and ask Him to marry me." It sounded bizarre—a woman proposing to a man. According to our earthly culture, a man always offers marriage to a woman, not the other way around, *but I did not care*. Deep inside, I somehow knew that Jesus desired His earthly children to propose to Him—making Him feel wanted and loved.

I then started looking for a wedding ring and researched the finger size of Jesus. After a while, I found a little information from Ken Peter's testimony on *Prophecy Club*. In Ken's vision, when the enemy was about to behead him, he saw a big and rugged hand holding him. That hand was the hand of Jesus. The Bible also tells that Jesus did some carpentry work while He was on the earth. Therefore, I assumed that His hands were big and strong. His finger size could be ten to eleven.

I spent a long time searching for a wedding ring for Jesus. I went to jewelry stores and searched online. Eventually, I found a perfect one. It was a gold ring with beautiful carvings in the center—simple and elegant. The size of the band was ten and a half. Inside the ring, I had it engraved *"Yeshua, My Forever Love!"* which is the title of this book. The name *Jesus* in Hebrew is *"Yeshua,"* which means *"to deliver"* or *"to rescue."*

I wrote a proposal to Jesus along with a beautiful card. I decorated my living room table with red roses, and invited the Father and the Holy Spirit to be my witnesses. On December 25, 2016 (Jesus' birthday), I knelt down in front of the chair where He sat before and asked Him to marry me.

At that moment, my heart almost jumped out of my mouth. I was *extremely nervous*. I thought in my heart, "What if Jesus says no? What am I going to do? I will run away from the room and never face Him again—too embarrassing! No human I know has ever done something like this. At least I have never heard about it. Oh, please help me, Father. Help me!" At that moment, Jesus was silent; He quietly listened to my thought.

I didn't even give Him a chance to say *yes* or *no*; instead, I kept murmuring in my heart because I was anxious. I could sense the Father and the Holy Spirit were present in the room. My hands were shaking, and my voice was trembling while reading the following proposal to Jesus.

Ying's Marriage Proposal to Jesus

I am a lilac.
Bloom in a cool-summer climate.
Beautiful in color,
Unique in fragrance,
Pleasant to behold.

I am a daisy.
Cheerful in full sun.
Wild and purple,
Pretty and lovely,
Waiting to be picked.

I am a rose.
Live in a gorgeous garden.
Crimson outside,
Flame of love inside,
Longing to be noticed.

I am a lily.
Dwell in a valley.

JESUS, MY FOREVER LOVE

Pure in white,
Distinct in splendor,
Inviting to be touched.

Oh, my Beloved, my dearest Beloved!
Come and behold Your lilac.
Come and pick Your daisy.
Come and smell Your rose.
Come and touch Your lily.

I am lovesick—
Deeply and helplessly in love.
Day and night, I am thinking of You.
You alone have occupied all my heart,
Because You are *irresistible!*

My beauty is for Your pleasure.
My exquisiteness is for You to behold.
Take me, my Beloved.
Set me as a seal upon Your heart.
And hide me under Your outstretched wings.

It has been long enough,
For me to yearn for you.
My love toward You has been intensified—
It has become *uncontainable.*
Help me, my Beloved, and tell me *what to do!*

Today, I must take the chance,
With my trembling heart,
And sheer desperation,
I extend my proposal to You, Jesus.
Will You marry me?

I want to be Your best bride—
Pure, meek, and obedient.

I want to give You joy and happiness—
The intimacy You have desired.
I want to love You forever and ever!

Whether Your answer is yes or no,
I cannot control.
But I hope it is a yes.
Do not break my heart, Jesus.
Answer me, my Love, and *say yes*!

I desire to be one with You—
For better or worse,
For richer or poorer,
For glory or suffering,
I am Yours, forever Yours!

Your lover,

With the deepest longing for an answer of yes!

Ying

Beloved readers, after reading the proposal to Jesus, I dared not to lift up my head and look at His face because I was *terrified* about what He would say. But, to my relief, His answer was *yes*. Marrying Jesus was the most honorable thing I have ever done. Since that day, He frequently tells me, "My love, I am your Husband, so let Me take care of you as a Husband should. Do not worry about anything. I will cover you under My wings."

Poem to Jesus on Valentine's Day and His Gift to Me

Ever since 2014, the year I became a Christ believer, I have been inviting Jesus to be my Valentine on every Valentine's Day. I usually dress up and put make-up on just for Him. I always buy a dozen red roses and write a romantic poem for Him. So far, I have spent eight Valentine's Days with Him. On February 14, 2020, I wrote the following poem to Jesus.

Camellia

I have a camellia tree outside my kitchen window.
It was planted in the year I got married.
When my husband and I bought it, it was just a tiny plant.
As years went by, it became a gorgeous tree.

The leaves were glossy dark green.
The flowers were bright pink.
Each year around Valentine's Day,
It would bloom with perfectly shaped petals.

They were pleasant to behold.
They smiled at me whenever I looked out the kitchen window.
I would breathe in their happiness.
Life was good.

Then a storm came.
It crushed my life into pieces.
The divorce struck me down.
I was in pitch darkness.

Strangely enough,
The camellia tree was also withered.
The leaves dried up and became yellow.
There were no flowers to behold.

The camellia was just like my life,
Dried up and ceased to flow.
Four years passed by,
The whole tree gave up its life.

Daily, my tears mingled with the camellia's tears.
We lost our wills to live.
Our happiness turned into mourning.
Our pain and sorrow seemed unceasing.

Then Jesus came into my life.
I was revived and born again!
My frozen soul started defrosting.
Pain and sorrow turned into rejoicing.

Surprisingly enough,
As my life started to recover,
The camellia tree also started reviving.
At last, our mourning turned into dancing!

Her leaves changed from yellow to green.
For the very first time,
After eight barren years,
The camellia tree started budding.

JESUS, MY FOREVER LOVE

On this Valentine's Day,
As I look out of my kitchen window,
The camellia is blooming and singing,
With thousands of gorgeous flowers.

She is singing for her Yeshua.
She is dancing for her Sweetheart.
She is smiling at her Lover.
And she is blooming for her Darling.

My Yeshua, my Sweetheart, my Lover, and my Darling,
I am Your camellia.
I was once withered.
But You brought me back to life!

I once lost my prettiness,
But You gave me "beauty for ashes." *
I once grieved with helplessness,
But you anointed me "with oil of gladness." *

Yeshua, I am Your pink camellia,
Dazzling with glossy green leaves.
I open my face with perfect petals—
They are for You, my Beloved!

On this Valentine's Day,
At this romantic night,
I put on my gorgeous pink dress,
And spread my petals all around You.

Would You come and pick Your camellia?
Would You hold her against Your heart?
Would You kiss her with Your passionate lips?
Would You hug her with Your everlasting embrace?

> Oh, my Lover, My Valentine,
> I beg You not to stay afar.
> Come closer to Your beautiful camellia—
> For she is Yours, forever Yours!

Happy Valentine's Day, Yeshua, my Husband.

Your camellia,

Ying

* Isaiah 61:3; Psalm 45:7

I bought a dozen red roses for my Valentine Jesus. He showed up in my prayer room and sat on the chair for a long time—watching me worship. Then I presented the above poem to Him. While I was reading it, He stood up and kissed me.

With my spiritual eyes, I then saw myself (in my spiritual body) dancing with Him in a field of camellia trees. All the flowers were pink, and they sang beautiful songs for us. I saw myself wearing a pink dress with camellia petals all over it. They were alive and moving. I was in His arms, dancing—*being His camellia!*

The Valentine's gifts from Jesus to me were a bouquet of red roses and a red heart-shaped box. Inside the box, there was a small square box. He opened it up; it was a ring with a big red diamond on it. I immediately understood the meaning of red—it represented His blood. He placed it on my finger, and I was speechless—it was *fabulously beautiful!*

With sheer affection, I kissed His hands, face, eyes, and lips. There were no English words that could describe my feelings toward Him adequately. It was a silent, hush moment—just hugging, kissing, and enjoying the romantic moment between the two Valentines.

My Birthday Gifts from God

March 2020, on my birthday, I had a fantastic time with God. Jesus knows my favorite flower is lilac. So on this day, He gave me a bouquet of roses, a cake with lilac flower icing, and a charming white dress with lilac flowers on it. As I said before, everything in heaven is alive—even the flowers on the dress are alive.

Later, Jesus and I went to see the Father. In Daddy's garden, my birthday gift was already displayed on a table. It was a light purple box wrapped with white ribbons. I ran to the Father and kissed Him. He was so happy to see me; He then asked me to open the gift. Inside the box was a gorgeous dress—light purple fabric with lilac flowers on it. Surely the Father knew my heart's desire. There were other things in the box: a paintbrush for me to create divine paintings and a book—that book was the book I am writing now. Evidently, it already existed in heaven.

Our God is a tenderhearted and loving Father. He knows His children's needs before we even ask Him. Just as Jesus said, *"Your Father knows exactly what you need even before you ask him!"* (Matthew 6:8 NLT). I felt so pampered that day with all the wonderful birthday gifts from the divine Trinity.

By the way, whenever I say I am with Them (Father, Jesus, Holy Spirit), I mean in my spiritual body. Sometimes as a four-year-old girl, other times as a fourteen-or-seventeen-year-old young woman. I don't know why the age switched back and force. Only the Holy Spirit knows.

"Our Wedding Bed Has Gone Cold!"

One morning, Jesus said, "My sweetheart, I love you. I am so delighted in you." He kept making sweet comments about me—like lover's talk. I said, "Lord, you just touched my heart." Being humorous, I continued, "Lord, did you eat sugar this morning? Your lips are so sweet." Jesus said amusingly, "I don't have to eat sugar to be sweet—I am naturally sweet." I laughed.

Beloved readers, do not think that Jesus is always sweet and soft-spoken; He can be intense and severe. The Bible portrays Him as the *Lamb of God*, but also describes Him as the *Lion of Judah*. He is never shy to rebuke and chasten His children if necessary. Out of His love, He disciplines us. Throughout my eight years of fellowship with Him, He has been pruning my dead branches and helping me to grow. If he chastens me, it means He loves me and treats me as His beloved.

> *Blessed is the one whom God corrects; so do not despise the discipline of the Almighty. For he wounds, but he also binds up; he injures, but his hands also heal.*
>
> —Job 5:17–18 NIV

> *"My son, do not despise the chastening of the Lord, nor be discouraged when you are rebuked by Him; for whom the Lord loves He chastens, and scourges every son whom He receives." If you endure chastening, God deals with you as with sons; for what son is there whom a father does not chasten?*
>
> *Now no chastening seems to be joyful for the present, but painful; nevertheless, afterward it yields the peaceable fruit of righteousness to those who have been trained by it.*
>
> —Hebrews 12:5–7, 11

On January 25, 2020, Jesus said to me:

"My love, you have not given Me all your heart. You have not given Me all your times, desires, wants, needs, finances, and belongings. I want them *all*—not just some of them. Your commitment to Me is *not consistent*. I need your attention just as much as you need Mine. I want to see your face; I want to kiss you and spend time with you—I need you to *come to Me daily*.

"I cannot be the second in your life; I must be the first. Either you have room for Me in your heart, or you have room for this world—you choose. If you have room for this world, you are not worthy of Me. I know you love Me; however, you do not give Me your whole life, and I want it all.

"My heart burns for you. I want more of you, do you understand? That is what a husband should be, right? But you often put Me aside and ignore My feelings. Whenever you need me, I come quickly. But whenever I need you, you are not there—this will not work in our relationship. I want a dedicated wife and a passionate lover!

"I want you to stop sinning! Remember what I told you: walk in love and humility. Treat people with kindness and respect. You are not an average person; you are My lover! You should imitate My characters wherever you go. How I desire to make you more beautiful, but you won't let me. My darling, hear Me! Obey My commandments and focus on pleasing Me.

"Do not be lazy—this is your number one problem. What did I say about the ten virgins? I will shut the door of heaven on those lazy ones; you do not want to be like those foolish virgins. Keep pressing into Me and do not stop, for the

Kingdom of heaven is at hand. I have prepared everything for you in heaven. I only want you to be diligent and finish your earthly assignments. Will you do that?

"Do not lie to Me, My child. Do not say that you will be more devoted to Me and not follow through. I have pointed this out to you *many times*, but you have not changed. Either you are with Me or this world—there is no middle ground. I have never promised that loving Me would be easy. It needs *extreme dedication*.

"You can be an average follower, or you can be *an extreme lover*. I want you to be an extreme lover. You are the darling of My heart and the darling of My Father's heart. You can change. I will help you. I am not angry with you; I just want you to know how I feel. That's all."

On March 4, 2020, Jesus said:

"My love, you started well; what has happened? You have lost your first love for Me. You have begun using Me to gain blessings instead of truly loving Me. You have started taking My kindness and love for granted. You have begun becoming lukewarm and love the world more than loving Me.

"How many mornings had I wanted to see you, but you were not there. *Our wedding bed has gone cold*, but you don't even care! Why are you calling Me your Lover, yet do not treat Me as one? Why are you calling Me your Lord, yet do not obey Me? Why do you memorize My Words, yet do not put them into action? What is your purpose on the earth? You must understand that if you genuinely want Me, you must lay down your life and follow Me.

"There are billions of children on the earth, but very few truly want Me to be their Lover. I have been searching for lovers, and I want you to be one. Spending time with Me and loving Me are not obligations or burdens; rather, it should be the desire of your heart. I do not need a duty-wife. I want a love-making wife. Come to Me with longing and yearning of My Person, not formality or checklist. I am searching for a *real lover*, not a *duty lover*.

"Do not think you are guaranteed to heaven. Many believers started well but ended in hell. Why? Because they took Me lightly. They did not walk in My ways and understand My heart. They indulged themselves in worldly things. Therefore, be careful, My sweetheart, and do not take My kindness and love in vain.

"I am not a *babysitter*; I am your Lord. I want you to pursue Me, not I consistently chasing after you. What about My desires? Do you not care? Oh, My dearest, your time on the earth is very short, so use every minute well. I have been warning you the same thing over and over again. It's time for you to be serious about My voice.

"I do not beg you to listen to Me. But when the time comes, you will regret it greatly. The sad thing is that my enemies never stop fighting. They are attacking My children aggressively. But My children are lazier than My enemies.

"I am God. I search the minds and hearts of all My children. Come back to Me, My darling. Come back to Me, My beautiful bride. I do not want to lose you. Can't you understand the deepest longing of My heart?"

When the Lord rebuked me, I felt *terrible*. My ego (pride) was hurt. Yet deep in my heart, I knew His rebukes were out of love. Beloved readers, it is easy to be with Jesus when He is happy and sweet, but it is frightening to see His serious face and be criticized by Him.

Most of my Friday evenings were spent watching movies and indulging myself with earthly desires—I love old war movies. Then, the following morning, I would sleep in and miss my devotion time with the Lord. I promised myself that I would get up at 2:40 a.m. every day to spend time with Him, but from time to time, I failed. I began making excuses and pretending God would forgive me.

I had been struggling with my flesh and desired carnal comforts. When my flesh fought with the Spirit, the flesh won. My consciousness became numb and sluggish—it led me to be complacent and lukewarm. Eventually, I will become like those five foolish virgins (see Matthew 25:1). When the bridegroom (Jesus) comes, and when heaven's door is shut, it will be too late!

> [Jesus said,] "The kingdom of heaven shall be likened to ten virgins who took their lamps and went out to meet the bridegroom. Now five of them were wise, and five were foolish. Those who were foolish took their lamps and took no oil with them, but the wise took oil in their vessels with their lamps. But while the bridegroom was delayed, they all slumbered and slept.
>
> "And at midnight a cry was heard: 'Behold, the bridegroom is coming; go out to meet him!' Then all those virgins arose and trimmed their lamps. And the foolish said to the wise, 'Give us some of your oil, for our lamps are going out.' But the wise answered, saying, 'No, lest there should not be enough for us and you; but go rather to those who sell, and buy for yourselves.' And while they went to buy, the bridegroom came, and those who were ready went in with him to the wedding; and the door was shut.

> "Afterward the other virgins came also, saying, 'Lord, Lord, open to us!' But he answered and said, 'Assuredly, I say to you, I do not know you.' Watch therefore, for you know neither the day nor the hour in which the Son of Man is coming."
>
> —Matthew 25:1–13

The Lord hates lazy and lukewarm followers. He said to the Laodicean church: *"I know your works, that you are neither cold nor hot. I could wish you were cold or hot. So then, because you are lukewarm, and neither cold nor hot, I will vomit you out of My mouth"* (Revelation 3:15–16). Beloved readers, being vomited out of God's mouth is a terrifying thing. His rebukes woke me up. I was scared!

He Is Not a Fire Hydrant

In 2014, after becoming a Christian, I used to shower God with worship, praises, and prayers for many hours daily. But one day, something unexpected happened. As usual, I said my last few prayers and walked out of the room. Then I heard a voice, "What about Me? I have not had a chance to talk yet." I was shocked and said, "Oh, I am so sorry, Lord. I did not give You a chance to talk." I went back to the room and ended up spending another two hours just letting Him talk.

It is true that we are not sensitive to His presence. We only care about what we want to say. Often, we have a list of requests or petitions, but our God has so much to speak to us too. We hardly give Him the time or chance.

Beloved readers, our God has infinite patience with us. But we often treat Him impatiently. Whenever we need something, we ask Him to fulfill our needs speedily. We treat him as a fire hydrant, a vending machine, or a drive-through restaurant—how disrespectful and insensitive we are to our God Almighty!

In my initial stage of fellowshipping with God, I ignored an important aspect: *"wait on the Lord."* The Bible says, *"Those who wait on the Lord shall renew their strength; they shall mount up with wings like eagles, they shall run and not be weary, they shall walk and not faint"* (Isaiah 40:31).

Waiting on God is to stay still and silent. It is to let Him examine, enlighten, and quicken my heart. As Psalms 37:7 says, *"Be still in the presence of the Lord, and wait patiently for him to act"* (NLT). God cannot talk to me if my mind is filled with the noises of the world. My flesh (carnal desire) cannot die unless I wait on the Lord. When I humble myself, stay quiet, empty my mind, and prostrate at God's feet, my soul will be refreshed. I will be like an eagle flying high with supernatural vision and strength.

"Wait" in Hebrew is "qavah," which means: "bind together," "entwine tightly," or "eagerly anticipating." When we wait on God, we entwine our hearts with His heart. The Passion Translation describes "wait" as "to be in labor"—giving birth to spiritual fruits.

"I Died for You Personally!"

As I was worshiping the Lord on April 12, 2020 (the Resurrection Day), a conversation took place: I said, "Jesus, I do not fully understand Your love. The level of my understanding is too shallow. I want to understand it on a deeper level. Will you please help me?" He replied, "You have been saying that you love Me, but you really don't know what love is all about." At that moment, He gave me a vision. I saw Him hanging on the cross. His face and body were covered with blood. He literally took me to the crucifixion scene. With short-and-painful gasps, He said to me while on the cross:

"Ying, I did not just die for the entire human race, but I died for you personally! Do you understand? *Personally!* If you were the only child on the earth, I would still come and die for you. That is how much I love you. That is how valuable you are to Me. My love for you is much deeper than you can ever comprehend."

I was speechless and weeping. Then, I saw Jesus sitting in my prayer room. I put my head on His feet and said, "My Lord, You are too good for me. I am not worthy of being Your lover. You are too holy, and I am too sinful. My Lord and my God, please tell me, what do you want from me?"

He paused for a moment, then said with a deep voice, "I want your love! I want to be loved. I want you to give Me everything. *I want you!*"

Beloved readers, Jesus is a Man with very few words. But when He speaks, His words mean a million—with tremendous weight. I said nothing at that moment. I just held His feet and cried like a baby. Then He continued:

> "Walk with Me, My sweet darling. Walk with Me from the wilderness to the promised land. Walk with Me from the valley of the shadow of death to the glorious heavenly places. Walk with Me in trials and tribulations. Walk with Me in mercy and love. Walk with Me in the end-time battles. During this journey, I will never leave you nor forsake you. If you move a small step, I will move a bigger step. I will lead you on this narrow road to life.
>
> "I created you to be My lover—this is *your highest calling*. So love Me and adore Me; admire Me and obey Me. Worship Me in spirit and truth. Never leave Me, and always be faithful to Me. I want you to be My best lover!"

I kept crying, feeling undone by His yearning for love from this inconspicuous Chinese woman.

Beloved readers, when Jesus was on the cross, He said to His Father, *"My God, my God, why have you forsaken me? Why are you so far from saving me?"* (Psalm 22:1 NIV). *"I am like a worm, crushed and bleeding crimson, treated as less than human. I've been despised and scorned by everyone!"* (Psalm 22:6 TPT).

The word *"worm"* in Hebrew is "tola'ath," which refers to "crimson worm," used for dyeing clothing. In the ancient Middle East, when the crimson worm is crushed, it produces a rich red dye. Garments colored with this scarlet dye can be very costly.

When Jesus called Himself a *"worm,"* He was comparing Himself to the "crimson worm," crushed for our sins. Just as He said in the book of Isaiah, *"Though your sins are like scarlet [tola'ath], they shall be as white as snow; though they are red like crimson [tola'ath], they shall be as wool"* (Isaiah 1:18). Jesus shed His blood to exchange for our pardon. The blood of Jesus has tremendous cleansing power. It can purge our sins and make us whiter than snow.

To this day, I still remember the crucifixion scene vividly—His broken body, gasping voice, and facial expression. His whole body was covered with blood—totally red—just like a *crimson worm*.

Beloved readers, my heart is *very heavy* and *sorrowful* as I am writing this chapter. Jesus shed His blood for you and me. Therefore, I ask you to please put down the book now and thank Him for His sacrifice. If you have not received Jesus Christ as your Lord and Savior yet, this is the perfect time to do so. Please find the acceptance prayer at the end of this book.

He Is a Warrior God

Most people love to know God's kindness, but very few are willing to know His severity. Jesus is the *Savior*, but He is also the *Judge*. One day, we will all stand before the judgment seat of Jesus Christ. By then, it will be too late to repent our sins. *"It is a fearful thing to fall into the hands of the living God"*

(Hebrews 10:31). If we repeatedly allow sin to rule our lives, we will face God's severe judgment.

Beloved readers, to give you a clear picture of what God's judgment will look like, read the following scriptures in Revelation 14. The bodies of those—who are against God and refuse to accept Jesus Christ as Lord and Savior—will be crushed like grapes in God's winepress (His wrath). Their blood will flow out of the winepress like a river. This blood river will be as high as a horse's bridle and stretch as far as 182 miles (293 kilometers) long.

> *I saw another angel flying through the sky, carrying the eternal Good News to proclaim to the people who belong to this world—to every nation, tribe, language, and people. "Fear God," he shouted. "Give glory to him. For the time has come when he will sit as judge. Worship him who made the heavens, the earth, the sea, and all the springs of water."*
>
> *Then a third angel followed them, shouting, "Anyone who worships the beast and his statue or who accepts his mark on the forehead or on the hand must drink the wine of God's anger. It has been poured full strength into God's cup of wrath...."*
>
> *After that, another angel came from the Temple in heaven, and he also had a sharp sickle. Then another angel, who had power to destroy with fire, came from the altar. He shouted to the angel with the sharp sickle, "Swing your sickle now to gather the clusters of grapes from the vines of the earth, for they are ripe for judgment." So the angel swung his sickle over the earth and loaded the grapes into the great winepress of God's wrath. The grapes were trampled in the winepress outside the city, and blood flowed*

from the winepress in a stream about 180 miles long and as high as a horse's bridle.

—Revelation 14:6–7; 9–10; 17–20 NLT

Righteousness and justice are the foundation of God's throne. He is a just God. He disciplines believers severely who know the truth but do not abide in it. To those He gives much, He requires much. Christians dare not test God's temper by entangling ourselves in sin continually.

For the unbelievers, the severity of His judgment is called the *"second death"*—eternal hellfire (see Revelation 21:6). *"For the wages of sin is death"* (Romans 6:23), but the wages of righteousness are joy, peace, and honor. One day, we will all face the judgment seat of Christ and receive our due reward or penalty.

[Jesus said to Apostle John,] I am the Alpha and the Omega, the Beginning and the End. I will give of the fountain of the water of life freely to him who thirsts. He who overcomes shall inherit all things, and I will be his God and he shall be My son. But the cowardly, unbelieving, abominable, murderers, sexually immoral, sorcerers, idolaters, and all liars shall have their part in the lake which burns with fire and brimstone, which is the second death.

—Revelation 21:6–8

We often portray Jesus as kind, gentle, and merciful, but He is also tough, intense, and mighty. He is called the *"Lord of hosts."* The word *"host"* refers to the heavenly army. The Bible refers to Jesus as the *"Lord of hosts"* 235 times. Moses said, *"The Lord is a man of war"* (Exodus 15:3). Jesus is the *"Lamb of God,"* but He also is the *"Lion of the tribe of Judah"* (Revelation 5:5). We often treat Jesus lightly, without reverent fear. We enlarge His kindness but minimize His severity.

Rick Joyner, the executive director of Morning Star Ministries, talks about the *martial* nature of our Lord Jesus in his book *Army of the Dawn*. He explains that Jesus Christ is a military Commander—*a Martial God*. He is the God of war (see Psalm 45:3).

> *Now strap your [Christ's] lightning-sword of judgment upon your side, O mighty warrior, so majestic! You are full of beauty and splendor as you go out to war!*
>
> —Psalm 45:3 TPT

We should never neglect the warrior aspect of Jesus' nature. All authorities have been given to Him in heaven and on the earth by the Father. On the judgment day, Jesus will judge every nation and every individual. All false prophets, sinners, and unbelievers will be cast into the lake of fire along with Satan, demons, and the fallen angels.

Let me clarify here: the *unbelievers* refer to those who refuse to accept Jesus Christ as Lord, and do not believe Jesus is part of the Godhead. Many religions believe Jesus is just one of the prophets, not God—*this is a lie from hell!* Jesus is God. The definition of the Trinity is God the Father, God the Son (Jesus Christ), and God the Holy Spirit. Although the Godhead is three distinct individuals, They are three in One.

From the book of Genesis to the book Revelation, God refers to Himself as *"Us"* or *"Our"*—the *"Triune God."* Any religion or people, who worship God but refuse to worship Jesus, are worshiping the wrong god. Consequently, they will go to hell. *It is that simple!*

Some of my Muslim friends say, "We worship the same god as you call God." Not so! If they indeed worship God, they should worship Jesus, but they don't. One thing God hates the most is idolatry. Whoever worships any other god will be executed (see Exodus 22:20). God does not tolerate His created beings to worship false gods, but Him only.

[God said,] He who sacrifices to any god, other than to the Lord alone, shall be put under a ban (designated) for destruction (execution).

—Exodus 22:20 AMP

The Scariest Scripture— "Only a Few Ever Find It"

We know that God's Words are true. They are the works of the Holy Spirit (see 2 Timothy 3:16). If we trust God, we must also trust His Words and obey His commandments. Most of the time, we tend to pick God's Words for our own preference, such as love, compassion, gentleness, or peace. But we ignore the scriptures that warn us of serious consequences.

There are some Bible scriptures that really scare me. God is all-merciful and gracious, yet He is also righteous and just. He is always ready to pardon, yet He does not excuse the guilty. We have to believe every word in the Bible and not pick and choose. We cannot be the *"Salad-bar"* Christians. Some believers ended up in hell because they took God's Words lightly.

All Scripture is breathed out by God and profitable for teaching, for reproof, for correction, and for training in righteousness.

—2 Timothy 3:16 ESV

Mary K. Baxter revealed some Christians are in hell in her book *A Divine Revelation of Hell*. When I read the following scriptures, my heart trembles, I would rather fear God than take advantage of His kindness. I would rather tremble before Him than concentrate only on His mercy.

> *[Jesus said,] You can enter God's Kingdom only through the narrow gate. The highway to hell is broad, and its gate is wide for the many who choose that way. But the gateway to life is very narrow and the road is difficult, and only a few ever find it.*
>
> —Matthew 7:13–14 NLT

> *[Jesus said,] "Not everyone who says to Me, 'Lord, Lord', shall enter the kingdom of heaven, but he who does the will of My Father in heaven. Many will say to Me in that day, 'Lord, Lord, have we not prophesied in Your name, cast out demons in Your name, and done many wonders in Your name?' And then I will declare to them, 'I never knew you; depart from Me, you who practice lawlessness!'"*
>
> —Matthew 7:21–23

The above scriptures are serious warnings from Jesus to all Christians. The road to hell is wide open, but the road to heaven is narrow and difficult—only a few will ever find it.

There are 7.9 billion people on Planet Earth in 2022. How many are few? The definition of *"few"* is *"a small number"* or *"hardly any."* Many people declare they know the Lord, but they do not read the Bible, obey His commandments, or seek His Person. Even Christian ministers who prophesy in the name of Jesus, yet continue sinning. They still think they can go to heaven, but the above scriptures affirm otherwise. People think going to church once a week is good enough to go to heaven, but in reality, they never give their hearts to Jesus.

Our Performance Is Measured by Love

God gives us many commandments in the Bible. From the book of Genesis to Deuteronomy (the Old Testament), there are 613 laws. In the New Testament, there are 1,050 commandments given by God. Nevertheless, among all of the commandments, *love* is the greatest one.

> [A Pharisee lawyer asked Jesus,]
>
> "Teacher, which is the great commandment in the law?" Jesus said to him, "'You shall love the Lord your God with all your heart, with all your soul, and with all your mind.' This is the first and great commandment. And the second is like it: 'You shall love your neighbor as yourself.'"
>
> —Matthew 22:36–40

> [Jesus said,] Now I am giving you a new commandment: Love each other. Just as I have loved you, you should love each other. Your love for one another will prove to the world that you are my disciples.
>
> —John 13:34–35 NLT

During prophet Bob Jones's near-death experience in 1975, he found himself waiting in the line to heaven. He saw Jesus standing there as *The Gate* to heaven. There were three people in line ahead of him. The first person was a black woman who was surrounded by more than one hundred angels. She was a minister of a church. The second person was a young girl who was crippled. All her life was in a wheelchair. Even though her condition was not encouraging, she spent most of her time praying for other people. The third person was a ninety-three-year-old woman. Jesus asked each of them only one question: *"Did you learn to love?*" After each of them answered "yes," Jesus opened Himself like a double door, and they went into Him.

After the three people went into Jesus, it was Bob's turn. Jesus paused. He told Bob the enemy had killed him before his time. Jesus asked him to go back to the earth. But Bob did not want to come back, and protested the hardships and evilness on the earth. However, when Jesus pointed to the people who were in the line to hell (98 percent of the people were in that line), Bob agreed to come back and win souls for the Kingdom of God.[5]

Beloved readers, when we read the Bible, we have to believe God's Words like little children. Jesus meant what He said in John 14:6, *"I am the way, the truth, and the life. No one can come to the Father except through me"* (NLT). He also said, *"I am the door. If anyone enters by Me, he will be saved"* (John 10:9). Jesus Christ is literally the *Gateway* to Heaven.

At the Gateway of heaven, Jesus did not ask any other question, but *"Did you learn to love?"* We can speak in tongues, have faith to move mountains, and sacrifice ourselves as a burnt offering, but all these works are pointless if we do not have love (see 1 Corinthians 13:1). God requires us to love one another because love is His number one nature. He uses love to judge our performance.

> [Apostle Paul said,] If I speak in the tongues of men and of angels, but have not love, I am a noisy gong or a clanging cymbal. And if I have prophetic powers, and understand all mysteries and all knowledge, and if I have all faith, so as to remove mountains, but have not love, I am nothing. If I give away all I have, and if I deliver up my body to be burned, but have not love, I gain nothing.
>
> Love is patient and kind; love does not envy or boast; it is not arrogant or rude. It does not insist on its own way; it is not irritable or resentful; it does not rejoice at wrongdoing,

> but rejoices with the truth. Love bears all things, believes all things, hopes all things, endures all things.
>
> —1 Corinthians 13:1-7 ESV

The cross is the signature of God's love for mankind. It was His love that defeated Satan. Jesus disarmed the principalities and the powers of darkness with love. He laid down His life and made atonement for humanity with love. The cross is God's ultimate love to His sons and daughters on the earth.

The entire Bible is a love story from God to mankind. *"God is Love"* (1 John 4:8). Love is His greatest attribute. Even if we do not love God, He still loves us because He cannot deny Himself. God does not demand us to love Him—He gives us a choice. Besides, demanded love is not love at all. However, there will be a time that God demands obedience from the citizens of the earth; by then, to prove our allegiance and love to Him will be too late.

Walking in love is our daily calling. Love is the greatest weapon to destroy Satan's work. God's love cannot be measured—it is too awesome to comprehend. We can never truly understand *"how wide, how long, how high, and how deep his love is"* (Ephesians 3:18 NLT), but the cross said it all!

In author Rick Joyner's book, *The Final Quest*, he shared a touching story about how God rewarded a person who walked in love. He described a vision that he had during his visit to heaven.

Rick saw a homeless man named Angelo, who was treated like a king in heaven—countless angels surrounded him. But his life on the earth was not so good. He was born deaf. At age eight, he was harshly abused and kept in a cold attic until authorities found him. Eventually, he ended up on the street and became homeless.

Angelo lived on the street and collected cans and bottles in exchange for food. One day, the Holy Spirit opened his heart, and he gave his life to Jesus. Ever since, Angelo started using half of the money he made (selling bottles) on gospel tracts. Day after day, year after year, he stood on the street distributing the tracts. One day, to encourage his hard work and honor his faithfulness, God led him to save one soul—a dying alcoholic.

Rick was shocked. He reasoned that a homeless man, who won only one soul for the Kingdom of God, was being regarded as a king in heaven. He inquired the Lord, and Jesus told him that Angelo actually died as a *martyr*. On a frozen winter night, he gave his only cardboard box to an old man to keep him warm. As a result, he himself froze to death. Jesus emphasized that Angelo overcame the world by operating in love. He died not for doctrines or fame, but for loving his neighbors as himself. Jesus gave Angelo a small portion of God's love to help him overcome hardships. Yet, with the little love Angelo received, he mustered every bit of it.[6]

Beloved readers, many people work hard to live in luxurious homes, feast on the finest food, and indulge in material things, yet, they end up in hell. Others, such as Angelo, missionaries, or evangelists, give up their comfort to care for the poor. They lay down their lives as living sacrifices to God. These ones are God's heroes. One day, just like Angelo, they will be regarded as kings and queens in heaven.

God is just! He exams everyone on the earth (see Psalm 11:4). A homeless man is treated like a king in heaven, while a billionaire goes down to hell. God sees every action of love we give. As we love others, we love the Lord. Jesus said, *"Truly I tell you, whatever you did for one of the least of these brothers and sisters of mine, you did for me"* (Matthew 25:40 NIV). Therefore, we should care nothing of this world, only care about what matters for the Kingdom of God. Let us operate in love!

> *The Lord still rules from heaven. He watches everyone closely, examining every person on earth. The Lord examines both the righteous and the wicked.*
>
> —Psalm 11:4–5 NLT

I Will Vomit You out of My Mouth

Christians are not immune to the consequences of our actions. In fact, some Christians are in hell—including pastors and church leaders. *"If we deliberately continue sinning after we have received knowledge of the truth, there is no longer any sacrifice that will cover these sins. There is only the terrible expectation of God's judgment and the raging fire that will consume his enemies"* (Hebrews 10:26–27 NLT).

What does God require of us? He wants us to obey His commandments, walk in His ways, fear Him, serve Him wholeheartedly, pursue holiness, and love Him. However, some Christians take God's kindness for granted.

Let me explain: Most churches in America are restrained by the 501(c)(3) system, which means they fall under the category of nonprofit organizations—churches have been approved by the Internal Revenue Service (IRS) for tax exemption. It sounds like a good deal, but in reality, it prohibits churches from participating in political agendas or campaigns. This system silences the body of Christ (church) from functioning as it should.

Two thousand years ago, Jesus gave authority and dominion to the church to rule the earth. He said, *"I tell you that you are Peter, and on this rock I will build My church, and the gates of Hades will not prevail against it"* (Matthew 16:18 BSB). However, many churches are not taking this authority and duty seriously. Using the 2020 U.S. presidential election as an example, many churches approved the illegitimate Biden administration. They did not have the courage to speak up for the duly elected (legitimate) President, Donald J. Trump. These churches love money over justice.

Some prophets prophesied that 501(c)(3) is under God's judgment. This system is from the devil; just as Satan uses coronavirus to muzzle (masks) our voices, so he uses the 501(c)(3) to silence the churches.

Some Christian ministries are terrified to mention President Trump's name on TV or YouTube. Instead, they call him *the 45,* even though they know Mr. Trump is God's anointed president. These ministries are afraid of losing tax-exempt privilege or being censored, so they stay quiet. If we let Satan hush us because of money or censorship, aren't we in covenant with Satan instead of God? Jesus said, *"No one can serve two masters. Either you will hate the one and love the other, or you will be devoted to the one and despise the other. You cannot serve both God and money"* (Matthew 6:24 NIV).

Being lukewarm and loving money is not acceptable to God. Have we not been commissioned to do our Father's business? We are supposed to be bold and courageous to promote God's plans in all aspects. Supporting the right leader for a nation, such as Donald J. Trump, is *absolutely crucial* for accomplishing our Father's business. Thus, what will God do to the lukewarm churches or cowardly Christians? He states in the following scripture:

> [Jesus said to the church of Laodiceans,] "I know your works, that you are neither cold nor hot. I could wish you were cold or hot. So then, because you are lukewarm, and neither cold nor hot, I will vomit you out of My mouth. Because you say, 'I am rich, have become wealthy, and have need of nothing'—and do not know that you are wretched, miserable, poor, blind, and naked."
>
> —Revelation 3:15–17

God is not joking. He means what He says. Being *vomited out* (rejected with disgust) by God is a serious matter. He often shouts with the loudest voice to get our attention, yet we cannot even hear Him, because we are so preoccupied with worldly things. We are indifferent toward His Kingdom business.

Many people, who have been taken to heaven for visits, saw Jesus crying. He cries because we do not know how close we are to His second coming and *the great tribulation* (the last few years on the earth). Our Lord does not wish anyone to be left behind and go to hell. But when the day comes, He has no choice but to leave some behind because He cannot take sinners to His home—heaven.

Therefore, let us be zealous, not lukewarm. Let us serve Master Jesus, not money. Beloved readers, *He is coming soon!* Are you ready for His second coming? Are you prepared to face the King? If not, repent your sins now! Otherwise, it will be too late. As the Holy Spirit declared in the following scripture:

> *Listen to me, all you rebel kings and all you upstart judges of the earth. Learn your lesson while there's still time. Serve and worship the awe-inspiring God. Recognize his greatness and bow before him, trembling with reverence in his presence. Fall facedown before him and kiss the Son [Jesus] before his anger is roused against you. Remember that his wrath can be quickly kindled!*
>
> —Psalm 2:10–12 TPT

Christians Stab Other Christians

Sadly speaking, since the day I became a born-again Christian, the people who have discouraged me the most have been Christians. Self-righteousness, fault-finding, condemnation, jealousy, and religious spirits are the causes for Christians to act against other Christians. Even Jesus Himself, being God, was condemned and murdered by the most religious people—the Pharisees and the Sadducees.

I remember vividly, after two months of being a Christian, I encountered some great discouragement from a church member. One of the older sisters, who had been a Christian for more than fifty years, said to me, "How come the church made you the leader of the nursing home service? You are a baby Christian. I am a seasoned Christian. You need to buy a bottle of milk and suck on the nipple. You drink milk; I eat solid food." Week after week, she kept mocking me. I cried out to God. Eventually, I quit serving the nursing home.

I encountered many discouragements and condemnations from mature Christians during my baby-Christian stage. I felt devastated. Later, after reading Rick Joyner's book, *The Final Quest*, I learned that demons could use Christians to destroy other Christians. In his book, Rick described a horrible vision he saw—Christians were wounding other Christians:

> *The demonic army was so large that it stretched as far as I could see. It was separated into divisions, with each carrying a different banner. The most shocking part of this vision was that this horde was not riding on horses, but primarily on Christians! All of these captive Christians were wounded, and they were guarded by smaller demons of Fear.*
>
> *Surprisingly, these prisoners still had their swords and shields, but they did not use them. Sometimes the weaker prisoners would stumble and fall. As soon as they hit the ground, the other prisoners would begin stabbing them with their swords, scorning them for their weakness. The vultures would then come and begin devouring the fallen ones even before they were dead. The other Christian prisoners stood by and watched this approvingly, occasionally stabbing the fallen ones again with their swords.*[7]

Satan often quotes scriptures and uses God's laws to condemn us. He often uses Christians to quote scriptures to judge other Christians. He even quoted scriptures to Jesus during Jesus' forty days in the wilderness. The devil has never stopped speaking through the midst of the

Tree of the Knowledge of Good and Evil. Day and night, he compels us to eat the fruit from this tree, and causes us to be self-centered, self-righteous, self-promoting, and fault-finding. His purpose is to draw us away from Jesus (grace) and concentrate on ourselves.

As Christians, we should not run around judging and criticizing other people, let alone other Christians. Judging and discouraging other fellow believers are the worst things to do. It is contrary to what God commands us, for the Bible says:

> *Who are you to condemn someone else's servants? Their own master will judge whether they stand or fall. And with the Lord's help, they will stand and receive his approval.*
>
> —Romans 14:4 NLT

> *Why do you condemn another believer? Why do you look down on another believer? Remember, we will all stand before the judgment seat of God.*
>
> —Romans 14:10 NLT

> *[Jesus said,] Judge not, and you shall not be judged. Condemn not, and you shall not be condemned. Forgive, and you will be forgiven.*
>
> —Luke 6:37

> *[Jesus said,] Why do you look at the speck in your brother's eye, but fail to notice the beam in your own eye? How can you say to your brother, 'Let me take the speck out of your eye,' while there is still a beam in your own eye?*
>
> —Matthew 7:3–4 BSB

I must admit that I am guilty as well regarding judging others. I frequently use my own ruler to measure other people—especially my employees. I often fail to sympathize with people's weakness and have a habit of fault-finding. I am very sorry, and *I repent of my sin!*

Jesus Is My Cardiac Surgeon

*I*n the previous chapter, I have described how I had gone through months of inner healings and how demons were cast out of my body. Even though some of the wounds in my heart were dealt with at that time, many scars can be reopened through demonic attacks or people in my life. Soul-level healing can be lifelong—not just one time. As James Hanley (the Christian counselor) often tells me, "Go through these repentance materials frequently. Even the counselors in my ministry would go through them on a weekly basis because demons can come back anytime when there are sins or unhealed wounds still exist." I do know that many deep pockets of wounds in my soul are still hidden—yet to be discovered.

I once heard a sermon from a Christian minister. She had suffered some excruciating pains from childhood to adulthood. One day, she cried out to Jesus and asked Him to heal her broken heart. Jesus told her, "I cannot heal your broken heart now; if I do, you will break it again. I have to remove the things that injured your heart first."

On August 16, 2021, Lord Jesus showed me a gruesome picture of my heart. It was shattered (cut through) by many sharp glass-like objects. The heart was bleeding profusely (see Figure 12). He then gave me the following visions. In them, Jesus functioned as a Cardiac Surgeon on my injured heart. Almost all these injuries are caused by the spirit of *rejection*, which leads to fear, bitterness, anger, and unforgiveness. The events in these visions were my real-life experiences from childhood to adulthood. Jesus performed each surgery separately—event by event.

Figure 12: My broken heart.

Vision 1:

August 16, 2021, at 3:00 a.m., I lay on an operating table in *God's hospital*. Surgeon Jesus came in and asked me, "I want you to tell Me the very first time you felt rejected." I closed my eyes and saw none but my own mother, who abandoned me during the Chinese Cultural Revolution. Instantly, I covered my face with my hands and cried uncontrollably. Jesus remained silent.

    I saw myself (five-and-a-half or six years old) in the hospital bathroom with my mother. With her horrified voice, she whispered to me, "The Red Guards are here to arrest me. I want you to listen to the doctors in the hospital." She quickly handed me over to a woman who had just given birth to a baby. My mother begged her to take care of me. All these took place in a few minutes. Then the Red Guard gangs violently took my mother away. I cried to her helplessly as she disappeared from my sight.

I lay on the bed, not knowing what would happen to me. The kindhearted lady motioned me to come to her. She found a way to cheer me up by squeezing some of the milk from her nursing breasts on my face. It sprayed like a water gun. I laughed. The nurses and doctors thought I had cancer because they could not diagnose what was wrong with me. Eventually, the lady checked out, and I was alone for two months there.

One afternoon, Jesus walked into my room with an angel behind Him. They were in bright white garments and engulfed with brilliant white light. Jesus squatted down, and I ran to Him. He held me tightly in His arms with tears in His eyes. I cried—*a little child's pitiful cries!* The angel gave me an apple. I took it and had a bite, then went back to Jesus' arms and sobbed again; the apple dropped on the floor. Jesus said, "From now on, you are under My guardianship. I will be your Father and take care of you."

Jesus then told me, "At the time of the Red Guards taking away your mother, your little heart was injured and broken." He continued, "Now, tell me, who rejected you or abandoned you?" I said, "It was my mother. I knew she loved me very much, but I did not understand why she left me."

Then Jesus took me out of the hospital and brought me to a beautiful meadow with pure blue sky and lush greens grass (this place is celestial, not earthly). There were many Labrador puppies and other animals running around. They all came to me and wanted to play with me. I was *super excited*.

Jesus dressed me in a fluffy white dress and a pair of adorable white shoes. He put me down. I kissed His face, nose, and hair. His right hand held me, and His left hand hid behind His back. Then He surprised me with a chocolate bar. I said, "What is it?" He said, "It is chocolate, candy." I said, "I never had it before." In China, I had never seen chocolate until I was twenty years old. Jesus broke the chocolate, had one piece for Himself, and put a piece into my mouth. I smiled by the unique-sweet taste.

I then started running around with the puppies. They rolled on the grass with me. Jesus was so happy to see me like that. He said, "Now, I want you to tell me, who am I?" I said, "You are my Guardian and Father." He continued, "Now, I want you to forgive your mother, the Red Guard gangs, and the country of China." I did as He told me.

At that very moment, Jesus reached into my heart with His hand and took some sharp knife-like objects out. I literally saw those broken and bleeding gaps in my heart were closed. Nevertheless, many sharp objects still remained—waiting to be removed at later operations. Jesus performed His surgery on my heart event by event.

Since that afternoon to this day, I have continued seeing this little girl (me) playing on this green meadow with puppies and rolling on the grass with child innocent joy. This vision is in real-time, does not end, and remains there permanently. Even now, I can still see myself playing on that meadow.

Vision 2:

August 17, 2021, at 3:30 a.m., I lay on the same operating table again. Surgeon Jesus came in and asked, "Ying, I want you to tell Me the very second time you felt rejected." Instantly, I started crying because I saw myself (six years old) being stoned by many kids on the street. There were about twenty of them—chasing after me, cursing me, and throwing stones on my back while I was sending food to my mother. She was imprisoned by the militants of the Chinese Cultural Revolution.

Suddenly, Jesus appeared, standing between the kids and me. He blocked the stones from hitting me with His own body. The kids were scattered. Jesus picked me up and held me in His arms. An angel, who came with Jesus, took over the lunchbox from my hand. We were then on the way to the prison. From entering the jail door, handing food to my mother, and walking out of jail, Jesus was there with me.

While walking back home, to cheer me up, Jesus started swinging me by the arms in a circular motion. I was excited and giggling. My gorgeous little white dress and shining crystal shoes were dazzling in the air. These were not my clothes. Mine was broken with patches. These adorable, six-year-old fashions were from Jesus. He then placed a lovely crystal tiara on my head and said, "My child, you have done well in taking care of your parents. You have done well for the assignments that I gave you!"

I looked so different from that wretched child—Jesus made me look like a little princess. He held my hand and talked all the way (about two miles) to my home. He and the angel watched me entering the door, which was guarded by two military soldiers as though I, too, was a criminal. However, these soldiers could not see Jesus.

The next day, when I came out, Jesus was already there waiting for me. He did this every day. One day, He asked me, "Are you still afraid?" I said, "My Father, since You are with me, I am no longer afraid."

Jesus then asked me to forgive the militants who tortured my mother (she fainted many times from beating.), forgive the country, and forgive those kids for stoning me. He said, "Not only forgive them, but also bless them." So I did. I then saw Jesus reaching into my heart with His hand and taking some of the sharp glass-like objects out of my wounded little heart.

Vision 3:

August 20, 2021, at 3:30 a.m., I lay on the same surgical table again. Surgeon Jesus had me recall the next major rejection that I experienced in my life. Then this vision came into my mind: the music teacher (DaWei Yu) from my elementary school. This teacher favored me very much in the beginning. He even made me the lead dancer and singer among more than one hundred talented student entertainers. I was constantly in the spotlight. However, at a later time, somehow, Mr. Yu began to dislike me, so much so that he started mocking and humiliating me in front of other school kids.

One time, this teacher was doing makeups for all the school performers. When it came to my turn, he pushed me away and said, "I don't like to do your makeup. Your cheekbones are too high, and your forehead is too short. I will do your makeup the very last." I was humiliated and heartbroken by his comment. At that moment, all the curses and rejections that I had experienced from childhood resurfaced. I actually believed his word because the street kids who stoned me before often called me ugly.

My heart was crushed by this teacher. Jesus then showed me an image of my heart. I saw sharp knives pierced through my cardiac chambers, and the heart was bleeding profusely.

At this very moment, I saw Jesus sitting on the chair doing my makeup instead of Mr. Yu. Jesus was excellent—like a professional makeup artist. He made me look so gorgeous, much better looking than all the student performers. When I saw myself in such prettiness, I realized that I was not ugly after all.

Jesus then asked me to forgive that music teacher and bless him. I did. After that, Jesus removed the sharp knives from my heart with His hand—the surgery ended.

Subsequently, many surgeries have taken place. I cannot list them all in this book. Indeed, the wounds in my heart have been mended one by one, but more surgeries are needed because many knife-like objects are still there. My heart will continue bleeding until Surgeon Jesus remove them all.

Beloved readers, you may ask me how Jesus appeared in different time frames in my life. The truth is that God is outside our earthly time. He created time. He can show up at any time or any place as He wishes.

Women Are Special to God

Throughout history, women have played significant roles in God's Kingdom. Hence, He has a special love for women. Our God is faithful to His children. Therefore, it will please Him greatly if His children are also faithful to Him.

Jesus spent three years with His beloved disciples on the earth. Day and night, they fellowshipped together. These disciples indeed believed Jesus was the Messiah, yet they still forsook Him when He was taken away by the Roman soldiers— *"All his disciples deserted him and ran away"* (Mark 14:50 NLT).

However, it was a group of women who showed their loyalty to Jesus. When He was enduring the most painful death on the cross, women stood by Him at the crucifixion scene. *"Standing near the cross were Jesus' mother, and his mother's sister, . . . and Mary Magdalene"* (John 19:25 NLT).

These female followers were with Jesus at His crucifixion, burial, and resurrection while the men were hiding and moping. Among those women, Mary Magdalene was an exceptional admirer of Jesus. Her name is mentioned thirteen times in the New Testament—more than some of the male disciples.

> *After Jesus rose from the dead early on Sunday morning, the first person who saw him was Mary Magdalene.*
>
> —Mark 16:9 NLT

Jesus did not appear to His male disciples at the time of His resurrection. He appeared to His female follower. It was those faithful women who went to the tomb to anoint Jesus' body and discovered His resurrection. Women were the first to know this good news. Our Lord treasures women's fidelity dearly.

Ruth

Throughout history, women have demonstrated their loyalty, devotion, and faithfulness to the Lord. Take the characteristics of Ruth; she possessed meekness, gentleness, and fidelity toward God.

In the book of Ruth, we discover God's desire for His perfect bride. Ruth had all the qualifications that met His desire. She was submissive, loyal, faithful, obedient, humble, gentle, and sacrificial. Her inner beauty was precious to the Lord. As Apostle Peter said, *"Let your adorning be the hidden person of the heart with the imperishable beauty of a gentle and quiet spirit, which in God's sight is very precious"* (1 Peter 3:4 ESV).

The Samaritan Woman

I have mentioned the Samaritan woman in the previous chapter. In John 4:5, Jesus met this woman at the well of Jacob. He revealed Himself as the Messiah to her (a gentile) first before telling His Jewish disciples. This was a big deal in those days because the Jews had no business with the Samaritans. Even His disciples marveled that He actually talked to a gentile woman.

At the well, Jesus knew the woman was living a sexually immoral life, yet He did not judge her. He neither despised her nor condemned her. Instead, He treated her as a daughter and a friend.

Eventually, this woman became a Christ believer and an evangelist. She took the name Photini at her baptism, which means *"enlightened one."* She and her five sisters and sons traveled to many nations to preach the gospel. In Rome, at the time of Emperor Nero's reign, Photini gathered a large crowd and preached Jesus Christ and the gospel with great boldness. Later, she was imprisoned and severely tortured; yet her faith in Christ was steadfast. In the end, after her five sisters, two sons, and many other saints were beheaded, she surrendered her spirit into God's hands and died in prison.

Women were created by Jesus' own hands. Therefore, He treated women with tender love. We are created for a special purpose. We are His *loyal lovers!*

Deborah and Jael

Throughout history, God used women as His special force in battles. Psalm 68:11 says, *"The Lord gave the command; a great company of women brought the good news"* (CSB).

Deborah, a prophetess and a fearless warrior, was God's chosen female judge. She led ten thousand Israelites into battle against Sisera (the commander of Canaan) and defeated the enemies.

When Sisera was on the run, God used Jael, a housewife, to kill Sisera with a tent peg and a hammer. She became a heroine for Israel.

Our God is truly humorous. He *"chose the weak things of the world to shame the strong"* (1 Corinthians 1:27 NIV). By using women to defeat the mighty army and their commander, God delivered the message to the whole world that women were equally strong on the battlefield. Thus, our message to Satan is: *don't mess with God's women!*

Esther

The enemies of God have never stopped attacking His chosen nation—Israel. Anti-Semitism has been once again rising throughout many nations since WWII. Hostility and prejudice against the Jews can still be seen in Europe and many countries today.

The book of Esther reveals how God turned a devastating situation into a victory through a woman. While Haman (the prime minister for King Ahasuerus) plotted to annihilate the Jewish people, God created

Esther to save the Jews from being destroyed. She risked her own life by exposing Haman's evil scheme. The whole situation turned from sorrow to joy. To this day, the feast of Purim is to honor Esther's courageous act of defeating the enemies of the Jewish people.

Women are part of the Lord's end-time army. We are the company of interceders, seers, watchwomen, ministers, missionaries, and prophetesses. We are fearless and bold on the battlefield. We sacrifice our lives for the sake of God's Kingdom. We are highly favored by the Lord. We are the company of Esthers who are born for such a time as this!

I hope the story of Esther sends a strong warning to the people of Anti-Semitism. God made it crystal clear, *"I will bless those who bless you [Jews] and curse those who curse you"* (Genesis 12:3 BSB). In other words, anyone who curses the Jewish people or the nation of Israel will be cursed by God. Therefore, it is extremely dangerous for the former president of Iran, Mahmoud Ahmadinejad, to say "Israel must be wiped off the map."

I love the Iranian people. They are the kindest and most hospitable people I have ever seen. In fact, some of my best friends are Iranians. In recent years, millions of Iranians have accepted Christ. Christianity is the fastest-growing religion in Iran. Therefore, I don't wish that country to be cursed because of its leaders' foolishness.

Anna

God raised many prophetesses and female intercessors throughout history. Among them was Anna—a great prayer warrior. She became a widow at a very young age. Throughout her eighty-four years of life, Anna literally lived in the temple and interceded for Israel. She fasted and prayed day and night (see Luke 2:36). Sometimes she would fall asleep in the temple, but God would send His angels to wake her up and cause her to continue praying.

Anna bore witness to the Messiah when Mary and Joseph brought Jesus to the temple. He was only eight days old at that time.

> *There was one, Anna, a prophetess, . . . She was of a great age, . . . and this woman was a widow of about eighty-four years, who did not depart from the temple, but served God with fastings and prayers night and day.*
>
> —Luke 2:36–37

Many intercessors today are women. Lots of prayer groups are equipped with female prayer warriors. Based on my observation, most of them are baby boomers (birth range from 1946 to 1964). They are God's generals. Daily, they tear their hearts to ask God's mercy on behalf of the citizens of the earth. Our God treasures these individuals. Their prayers, like incense, ascend to the throne of God and are collected by the angels of heaven in bowls.

> *When He [Jesus] had taken the scroll, the four living creatures and the twenty-four elders fell down before the Lamb (Christ), each one holding a harp and golden bowls full of fragrant incense, which are the prayers of the saints (God's people).*
>
> —Revelation 5:8 AMP

One day, God will pour those incense onto Planet Earth, and the earth will never be the same. Do not think those grandmas, who have been in their prayer closets for most of their lives, have less value than combat soldiers. In the spirit realm, as soon as these intercessors start to pray, swords begin to form from their mouths. The angels will wait for them to finish praying; then, they will take the swords to slaughter the enemies.

These mighty women are special to God. They are His priceless treasures, dearest beloved, and faithful maidservants. They are

His courageous and fearsome commanding officers. They are His *darling daughters!*

It is these female intercessors who stand in the gap between heaven and hell, between mercy and judgment, and between life and death. They tear their hearts before God for those who do not deserve mercy. They weep for nations upon which judgment is due. Our God desires mercy over judgment. He does not wish to punish His children, but when the time comes, He has to because He is a righteous God. As He judges, He weeps. He cries for the impending judgment over His beloved creation. He is a tenderhearted Father who holds His anger and waits for someone to plead for His mercy.

God regards these intercessors as His superheroes. They are greatly rewarded in heaven. People, who have been to heaven, saw God building a special place in heaven just to honor these prayer generals.

Jesus often expresses His tender feelings toward women. He put a lot of hope in His daughters to do the end-time works. He chose daughters instead of sons because daughters are more loyal than sons.

Throughout history, God has raised many female generals, such as Maria Woodworth-Etter, Aimee Semple McPherson, Corrie ten Boom, Kathryn Kuhlman, Darlene Deibler Rose, Amy Wilson Carmichael, Evangeline Booth, Charlotte Digges Moon, Joan of Arc, and Heidi Baker, etc.

These mighty women are ministers, evangelists, prophetesses, revelators, intercessors, seers, and missionaries. They sacrifice their lives to win souls for the Kingdom of God. They have obeyed God's callings and operated as a special force for the Lord's army on the earth. Women are God's female navy seals—*His G.I. Janes!*

Part Five

Meeting My Heavenly Father

To His Throne Room

In early 2016, two years after becoming a Christ believer, the Holy Spirit introduced God the Father to me. Even though I knew Him through scriptures, I had never encountered Him in person. One day, during my devotion time, I saw a vision:

I saw myself as a four-year-old girl, wearing a beautiful white fluffy dress with red-flower embroideries at the bottom hemline. I had a pair of shiny red shoes on. Jesus was holding me in His arms and walking toward the throne of the Father.

The throne room was huge. Many people and angels were surrounding and worshiping Father God. About fifty feet from the bottom of the throne, Jesus put me down. I ran to the base of the throne and started climbing the stairs. There were at least sixty stairs. I was very small, and the stairs were too high for me, so I used my hands to climb. While I was climbing, the Father lifted me up in the air, and I landed in His arms.

"Are You really my Daddy?" I asked.

"Yes, I am," the Father said. He began to cry and said, "Oh, My beloved child, how I have missed You!"

I then held the Father tightly and cried in His bosom. "Daddy, Daddy, why did You send me away? Why didn't You look for me? Do You not want me anymore? Have You ever missed me?" I was choking—an innocent four-year-old's cry.

I felt the Father's tears dropping on my head. He was crying with bittersweet emotions. He could hardly control Himself. We both held each other closely and wept together—such emotional reunion . . . years of longing . . . mixed feelings. At that moment, heaven silenced. I could not hear any sound in the throne room, only the Father and the daughter's inaudible cry.

I could not see the Father's face clearly, but I did see His arms, legs, hands, and body. He was wearing a white garment. His voice was echoing-deep, yet Fatherly tender. He was huge, and I was tiny. I was literally buried in His bosom. I just held Him and kept crying. Neither one of us could even speak. Never had I imagined the Father could be this emotional and tenderhearted.

Beloved readers, I did not know why I became a little girl again when I met the Father. Just like when I first met Jesus in my three-year-old spiritual body, now, it happened again when I met the Father. I could not explain it; only the Holy Spirit could because He arranged all my encounters with Jesus and the Father. No one can approach God unless the Holy Spirit bids them, just as Jesus said, *"No one can come to me unless the Father who sent me draws them to me"* (John 6:44 NLT).

Daddy's Garden

A few days later, Jesus held me in His arms and walked into a gorgeous garden. I was still in my four-year-old spiritual body. The Father walked toward Jesus and took me into His arms; then Jesus left. I held the Father's neck and kissed His face with many kisses. I was not shy, and He kissed me back with a big smile on His face. He was *extremely excited* to see me again. Unlike in the throne room, I now could see the Father's face. I will describe His appearance in a later chapter.

Daddy's garden was stunningly beautiful—none like it on the earth. To a four-year-old girl, this place was a cartoon-like wonderland. There were lots of flowers, fruit trees, butterflies, peacocks, giraffes, etc. There was a round table and chairs next to the flowers. The Father bent down, and I jumped off of His arms. I said, "Daddy, do you want me to dance for you?" He said, "Yes, I want to see your dance."

I then started doing a tap dance (see Figure 13). Beloved readers, I never learned tap dance with my earthly body. I really did not know where this little girl learned tap dance. I believe it was given to me by the Holy Spirit at that moment.

Figure 13: Tap dancing for my Father.

I wore the same fluffy white dress as I did in the throne room. I could not believe my eyes—this little girl (I) danced perfectly. The red-shiny shoes moved so fast and precise. *Toe tap, shuffle, double tap, brush and drag, triple tap, ball change, step heel and heel step, single buffalo, heel drop, flap, hop and leap* . . . The choreography was seamless, and the little shoes made crisp and lovely noises.

While I was dancing, my eyes were checking on the Father's face. I tried very hard to please Him. "Do you like it, Daddy?" The Father cracked up and laughed so hard, "Ha, ha, ha, ha! Wow, ha, ha, ha!" He kept clapping His hands and said, "Oh, My daughter, you dance beautifully. I love it!" Then more clapping. He appeared so amused and thrilled. He then scooped me up into His arms and kissed me with excitement. I kissed Him back. It seemed as though I knew how to please the Father, even though we just met a few days ago in His throne room.

As He held me, He began walking toward a big tree. I leaned my head on His neck, enjoying His pampering love. There were many fruit trees in the garden, such as peach and apricot, which are my favorite fruits. But the Father stopped at one tree with big purple fruits on it. The size of the fruit was much bigger than a large apple. The Father picked one, handed it to me, and I ate. *Oh, My goodness!* It was so delicious—non like it compared with earthly fruits. It was impossible to describe its taste—extremely sweet and delightful. It also released a beautiful fragrance. *I loved it.*

I wrapped my little arms around Daddy's neck and kissed Him. I said, "Thank You, Daddy. It is so good, one more please!" He laughed and picked one more. I had not even finished eating it yet and asked Him again, "More Daddy!" He kept laughing and gave me a few more. I tried to hold them with my little hands (see Figure 14). When He put me down, they dropped all over the place. He said, "My child, next time, just one. If you need more, I will get you more."

Figure 14: Eating the fruit from my Father's tree.

From 2016 until now, I have visited Daddy in this garden whenever I want to; only a few times have I met Him in the throne room. No matter where we meet, He is always ready to receive me. It has become a routine. Every time I come to see Him, He always gives me the same purple fruit to eat. I am so *addicted* to it!

Later, I found a possible explanation about this fruit from Rick Joyner's book *The Final Quest*, where Jesus explained to Rick about the Tree of Life. The fruit that the Father has been feeding me is the *Father's Love*. No wonder it is so delicious and sweet!

Jesus said to Rick:

The greatest weapon you have been given is the Father's love. As long as you walk in My Father's love, you will never fail. The fruit of this tree is the Father's love, which is manifested in Me. This love, which is in Me, must be your daily bread.[1]

My relationship with the Father developed exactly like the stages of knowing Jesus—beginning with my four-year-old spiritual body. As our relationship grows, my age grows. Each visit, I was brought to the Father by Jesus. However, thinking back on it now, I am not sure it was Jesus or the Holy Spirit who brought me to the Father's garden. It was probably the Holy Spirit.

Father's Library

The Father used to read books in His library, which was also located in His colossal garden. He would let me go out to play with the animals, such as peacocks, butterflies, and giraffes. They called me "Miss Ying." The butterflies were in many different colors—pink, red, green, yellow, orange, or blue. They followed me everywhere and danced with me.

While Daddy was reading, I would pick some flowers and bring them back to Him. He loved it. Sometimes, I would hold His feet and lay my head on His feet while He was reading. Other times I sat on His lap and pretended that I was reading with Him. He enjoyed and indulged all my innocent child characters.

There were many bookshelves in this library, filled with all kinds of books. These books did not look brand new—somewhat aged. When the Father wanted to reach a book, He just simply pointed His figure to the book, and the book flew off the shelf and came to Him.

Since that experience, I have been asking the Father to let me borrow some of His books from that library. I often say, "Daddy, can

I borrow some of Your books? I promise I will return them to You as soon as I finish reading. Please let Your angels send them to me." Until now, I have not received any book yet. Still waiting.

He Rocked Me Like a Baby

By 2016, I had been on my own for six years after my divorce. I remembered how lonesome I was. One day, I felt such unbearable loneliness in my soul. I requested to see the Father. As I have said before, He is always ready to receive me whenever I ask to see Him.

So, I immediately saw myself in His garden. In my four-year-old spiritual body, I ran to Him with sad tears. He picked me up and gently put my head on His right shoulder and my little cheeks on His neck. He then started walking around the garden, softly rocked me like a baby, and patted my back with His big hand (see Figure 15).

I buried my head on His neck and heard an inner voice from the Father, "You are with Me now. Do not cry, My sweetest child. Do not cry."

Figure 15: The Father rocking me in His arms.

Another time, I felt excruciating pain in my soul. I cried out to the Father, "Daddy, I want to see you." Instantly, I saw myself in my four-year-old spiritual body in His garden. I ran to Daddy, grasped Him tightly, and wept with such sad tears. This time, He put me on His back and had my little hands hold His neck. He then started gently walking around the garden, humming softly, and bouncing me up and down like an earthly father or mother.

Beloved readers, our God indeed is the most sympathetic and tenderhearted Father. He cares about each of His children deeply. As I am writing this chapter, I am crying because He truly is a good Father! *Run to Him*, beloved child of God, and He will hold you in His arms too.

Daddy Carried Me on His Wings

*I*n July 2021, I was sick for a week—to the point I could hardly walk. I requested to see the Father. Immediately, I was in Daddy's garden. I saw myself in my four-year-old spiritual body, wearing an adorable floral dress and a pair of white shoes. The Father was so happy to see me and eagerly picked me up. I kissed His face all over and hugged His neck with over-excitement. He put me down, and I ran around the garden, picking flowers. I then jumped back into His arms and gave Him more kisses. He was thrilled with laughter.

He walked to my favorite fruit tree and had me pick one by myself—the same purple fruit that I loved. I ate with such delight. We then sat on a garden bench. I was hyperactive and could not stay still. I jumped out of His lap and began dancing for Him. In the middle of the dance, I started doing somersaults. I rolled over and over toward Him until I landed on His feet. We both laughed so hard.

I was being mischievous and super excited. The symptoms of sickness (with my earthy body) could not be found in this little girl at all. Through this experience, I realized that all illnesses could be healed in the presence of God.

I then came up with a more thrilling idea—asking the Father to take me to ride the dinosaurs. Instead, He got a better idea. He stretched out His enormous wings and put me on it (yes, the Father has wings). I held His neck when He took off. Daddy said to me, "You have been sick for a week, and I have been watching over you. I love you, My darling daughter." I said, "I love you, Daddy."

From the bird's view, I saw snow mountains, lush green meadows, endless forests, and beautiful flower fields. Passing through the fluffy clouds, I saw herds of unicorns, deer, giraffes, and many other animals running along the same direction where my Father flew. The mountains, meadows, forests, flowers, clouds, and animals sang worship songs to Him. They seemed more excited than I was.

Then, the Father took a sharp downward and plunged into the blue ocean. We swam with the dolphins for a while. He then took off; His gigantic wings hit the water with a mighty splash. We landed on a charming flowerbed and danced there. Later, we flew back to the garden. After hours of excitement, my little body was so relaxed and fell asleep in Daddy's arms.

Beloved readers, the Father is the best Doctor. He wanted me to forget about my sickness by giving me these extraordinary adventures. Seeing me sound asleep, Daddy hushed the animals in the garden not to make any noise. He wanted me to rest in His arms as long as possible.

While all these went on with my Father, I also saw myself dancing with the Holy Spirit. Since I was so small (still in my four-year-old body), I could only hold His leg and dance. He then picked me up—with one hand holding me to His chest and the other holding my hand in a dance position. He turned and moved as though dancing with an adult (He did this to cheer me up).

After a while, He put me down and ran ahead of me. I chased after Him. He then ran in a zigzag direction, and I ran after Him with giggling—we laughed and laughed. Beloved readers, if you want to know what the Holy Spirit looks like, I will tell you in a later chapter.

Meanwhile, I saw myself dancing with Jesus in another garden. We kissed and hugged romantically. I was in a fourteen-year-old spiritual body, dressed in a lovely white silk dress.

All these happened simultaneously (with the Father, Holy Spirit, and Jesus). They did these amusements to cheer me up. They wanted me to be healed from sickness and be happy. They truly are the most tender-loving Trinity—the best Physicians.

Dancing with Butterflies

A few months later, I turned into a fourteen-year-old teenager. At this age, I usually wore gorgeous dresses whenever I visited my Father. These dresses made me look like a royal princess. They were in many different colors—pink, blue, white, orange, green, yellow, red, or lavender. I really did not know where these dresses came from. I believe they were all arranged by the Holy Spirit.

I would usually kiss and hug the Father first; then, He would take me to walk around the garden. Lots of times, we danced. Other times, He would sit on a garden bench and ask me to dance for Him. When that happened, thousands of butterflies would come and dance with me.

Interestingly enough, if I wore a pink dress, mostly the pink butterflies would come, along with other colored butterflies (as complements). They came with their own color group. They were swirling around me like bands of multi-colored garlands—dazzling with spiral dance to harmonize my dance rhythm (see Figure 16). They spoke like little children's voices. The whole dancing scene was *remarkably beautiful*.

Figure 16: Dancing with the butterflies.

Swimming with Fish in My Father's Lake

The Father had a charming flower archway which was covered with light pink roses. They were incredibly fragrant. He would hold my hand and walk through this archway. At the end of this arbor, there was a green pasture. Far to the left, there was a lake. The Father usually sat on the green pasture with Jesus and the Holy Spirit while I went swimming in the lake. The fish in the lake were exceedingly colorful, more so than the tropical fish in Hawaii. They swam with me and allowed me to touch them. They even talked to me—everything in heaven talked and sang. I always had so much fun whenever we came here!

A few times, after swimming, I danced with the Holy Spirit on this beautiful green meadow while the Father and Jesus were talking. The Holy Spirit is a *brilliant Dancer*. He is part of the Trinity who created dance. All artistic talents, such as music, dance, literature, and drama come from the Holy Spirit.

While we were dancing, ribbons of dazzling lights encircled us. I could hear very soothing music in the background. I did not know where the music came from, but I do know that all things worship God in heaven. Grass and flowers sing. Maybe the music was coming from the green grass.

Father's Character and Appearance

When I saw the Father in the throne room for the first time, I did not see His face clearly. But, in His garden, I did see His face. He is very tall. I would say He is about eight feet tall. He can change His height or shape in any way He wishes. His facial features are more like the Europeans. His hair is pure white, with waves, down to His shoulders. He has a very pointed nose and a neatly trimmed beard, which are also pure white. His eyes are sapphire blue. He is about sixty years old. Most of the time, He wears a white garment, other times blue or dark red. Like Jesus, He sometimes wears sashes. But I have not seen Him wearing crowns.

His voice is very deep and Fatherly. He loves to hug me, and He loves to be hugged. He has genuinely enjoyed every moment of being with me. I have kissed His cheeks and His hands a lot. We have also hugged a lot. Our Father is actually *very handsome!* He always smiles and sometimes laughs. He is *a happy* and *adorable Father*.

God the Father is the Owner and Creator of the universe. Eternal life comes from Him. He is a consuming fire. Holiness is His nature. He holds the power to save or destroy every living soul. All dominions and kingdoms belong to Him. He is the boss within the Trinity (according to some prophets). All spirits come from the Father. Heaven calls Him: *The Ancient of Days, The Judge of all Creation, The King of all Ages,* and *The Most-High God Almighty.*

In spite of all His power and might, when it comes to His children, He is the most tender-loving and merciful Father. Each child is *unique* and *special* to Him. I do not remember Him ever being angry with me during all my visits. He has corrected me from time to time out of His love, but He has never condemned me or put me to shame.

I always feel very much at home whenever I am with Him. Sometimes, I am so relaxed and forget to fear Him. One time, I asked the Father, "Are You ticklish, Daddy?" He just laughed. Most of the time, when I visited the Father, I was in my four-year-old spirit body. That was why I often asked child-like questions.

The Father cares about every little thing in my life. He wants me to be happy and enjoy life to the fullest. From the day I became a Christian in 2014, I spent almost all my weekends with God—I hardly ever went out. One Friday evening, I was spending time with God in my prayer room. The Father said, "My daughter, what are you doing here? It is Friday. Go out and have dinner with friends, or watch a movie in the theater. Go and have fun." I was amazed. I thought He would like me to spend more time on devotion, but in reality, He wanted me to have fun too—as an ordinary child would.

Even though He is God Almighty, He is also a Father. He gives love, but He also wants to be loved. He longs for His children to surround Him, dance with Him, sing with Him, kiss Him, and hug Him. He longs for a family, and we are His family. His heart will not be complete without His children being reconciled to Him. That is why He sent His own Son, Jesus, to redeem us and bring us back to Himself.

On July 19, 2020, the Father said to me:

> "You have been on My heart every day. Sometimes, I miss you terribly. Therefore, spend more time with Me. I need you. I need your worship. I need your love. Believe Me, I, the God Almighty, need to be loved too. I give love, but I also yearn to be loved by my children. That is the reason I created you all. So, love Me more, My child!"

My earthly father died twenty-eight years ago. For a long time (before knowing my heavenly Father), I had been searching for a father to adopt me. My soul yearned intensely for a father's love, not mother; I did not know why. Many times, I almost posted an advertisement in newspapers to search for a father who would adopt me. I know it sounds bizarre, but that was how desperate I was. I now know why—the separation from my real Father in heaven caused my soul to search for Him, because I belonged to Him before I came to the earth.

Beloved readers, as soon as a child is born, the Father assigns one or two guardian angels to guard that child. He is truly a protective Father. Yet, what do we give Him? Our prayers are mostly: "Bless me, give me, favor me, love me, I want this, I want that." But we hardly ever consider what our Father wants.

The Bible says the Father is a longsuffering God and a jealous God. Yet, to whom is He suffering for? Or to whom is He jealous for? Is it not for us—His beloved children? We are made in His image and after His likeness. He does not have to suffer for us, but He chooses to. The depth of His love is unexplainable, immeasurable, unlimited, infinite, and absolute!

Jesus is everything to the Father, yet He graciously gave Jesus up for us. Minister Todd White usually says, "Heaven went bankrupt to save us." Our God is the most gracious and unselfish God. He is an extravagant and a lavish Giver.

Pastor Benny Hinn usually says, "It took God nothing to create the earth and humans, but it took Him everything to save even one soul." This saying is so true. It took God six days to create the earth and everything in it. God spoke and Jesus created it. But to save us, it took the very life of Jesus—He is *everything* to the Father. Sometimes, we humans do not truly comprehend our value and importance to God. We allow the devil to devalue us. God sent His only Son, Jesus, to die for us in order to redeem us. Yet, many humans still reject God's redemption and choose Satan as their master.

Every day, the Father watches people go to hell. They are His beloved sons and daughters. Have we ever thought about how much pain our Father has to endure daily because we reject Him? People end up in hell for not accepting Jesus Christ as their Lord and Savior. Seeing His children being tortured in hell breaks the Father's heart.

Father Cried

Whenever I spend time with the Father, He is always happy and upbeat. But one day, this was not so. On January 15, 2020, at 3:00 a.m., as usual, I went to my prayer room and started to worship God. Immediately, I sensed the Father's heart was exceedingly sorrowful, so heavy, it caused me to stop worshiping. Through my spiritual eyes, I saw the Father crying. I did not know what to do, so I just kept silent. I had seen the Father cry before, but I had never seen Him cry this hard. At that moment, I held the Father and cried with Him. I did not ask Him why He was crying. After a while, He spoke:

> "It breaks My heart to see My children go to hell and be tormented by My enemies. I have given My sons and daughters free will to choose, but they do not choose Me. By the time they end up in hell, it is too late. My heart grieves for them. Oh, My beloved children, how foolish! I have given them everything—My own Son died and paid for their

ransom; yet they still reject My Son, forsake Me, and curse Me to My face. *It breaks My heart!"*

Yahweh [God] saw how extremely wicked humanity had become, for they imagined only evil, for all they thought about was doing evil all the time. And Yahweh was saddened that he had made humanity, and his heart was filled with pain. So Yahweh decided, "I will do away with my ruined creation—human beings that I created—people and animals, creeping things and flying birds, for it breaks my heart that I made them!"

—Genesis 6:5–7 TPT

Beloved readers, is there anyone on Planet Earth whom the Father did not carry? No! Our spirits existed inside the Father before the cosmos was ever created. He carried us for eons and eons inside His being—like a pregnant Mother. We are His offspring. He is a jealous God, and He is jealous over us. Seeing His children, one by one, going to hell, truly breaks His heart.

I charge you, beloved readers, child of the Most High God: stop what you are doing right now, close your eyes, and imagine the face of the Father. Look at His face; He is crying for you. He is pleading with you, "Wake up my children, choose life and not death; choose Me and not the devil, for the devil's only purpose is to kill you and bring you to hell!"

On June 21, 2020 (Father's Day), I wrote the following poem to the Father.

My Father's Tears

Eons and eons ago,
When the heavens were created,
Angels were made,
Kingdoms were established,

My Father cried with tears of happiness.

Billions of years ago,
When the earth was formed,
Humans inhabited,
Dinosaurs settled,
My Father cried with tears of amusement.

Millions of years ago,
In the pre-Adamic Age,
Lucifer betrayed God.
God's wrath destroyed the earth that Lucifer defiled.
My Father cried with tears of a broken heart.

Millions of years after,
Adam and Eve were created.
The earth was replenished.
All living things were populated.
My Father cried with tears of joy.

Until one day,
The serpent deceived Eve—
Adam and Eve ate the forbidden fruit.
The fall of mankind started.
My Father cried with tears of sorrow.

At the time of Noah,
The Nephilim corrupted the earth.
God destroyed it with a flood.
All living creatures perished.
My Father cried with tears of sadness.

At the time of Moses,
God heard the cries of the Israelites.
He sent Moses to lead them out of Egypt.
Yet, they disobeyed God for forty years.

JESUS, MY FOREVER LOVE

My Father cried with tears of frustration.

For thousands of years,
The Father stretched out His arms to the children of Israel.
He showed them love,
But they worshiped the idols.
My Father cried with tears of disappointment.

In order to save the fallen mankind,
The Father sent His own Son, Jesus.
He died on a cross to redeem our sins.
He shed His blood to wash away our iniquities.
My Father cried with tears of gratitude for His Son.

Throughout history,
From Adam to his descendants today—
We, the citizen of the earth
Have never truly appreciated the Father's kindness.
We have never understood His suffering.

He is a longsuffering God.
He has suffered for us.
He cries for each of His children.
He yearns for each of His offspring,
With His tender mercy and longing tears.

My Father's heart is infinitely merciful.
His love is ocean deep.
His grace is everlasting.
His patience is never-ending.
He is a wonderful and amazing God.

My greatest desire is to understand His heart.
One day, I want to taste My Father's tears—
The tears of eons, billions, and millions of years.
They are shed for His beloved children.

They are the tears of the Father's love!

His precious tears were collected in bottles,
Documented in *The Book of Remembrance,*
Imprinted in the history of creation,
And poured into the hearts of His beloved children.
They are the tears of the Father's compassion.

One day, we will be back to heaven,
To be with our beloved Father.
We will sing and dance with Him.
We will shower Him with hugs and kisses.
Then, Father will have His final tears—the tears of celebration.

Oh, my wonderful Father,
My perfect Daddy,
The Creator of heavens and the earth,
How I love you with all my heart.
How I adore you with all my being.

On this Father's Day,
Let me kiss You with love.
Let me hug You with passion.
Let me dance with You with joy.
And let my tears join Your tears in celebration!

Happy Father's Day, my beloved Daddy!

Your little princess,

Ying

He Is a Longsuffering God

The fruit of the Spirit is love, joy, peace, longsuffering, kindness, goodness, faithfulness, gentleness, self-control.

—Galatians 5:22–23

What does the scripture mean by our God is a longsuffering God? I have been asking the Father to share this aspect of Him with me. From an online dictionary, I found *"suffering"* means to undergo pain, death, distress, injury, or loss. It implies enduring physical or mental anguish. It entails experiencing hardship, torment, misery, and affliction.

According to *Merriam-Webster Dictionary*, *"longsuffering"* means patiently enduring lasting offense or hardship. *Dictionary.com* says *"longsuffering"* means enduring injury, trouble, or provocation long and patiently.

Prophetess Wendy Alec once shared the following story in a church service. She carries a special anointing of revealing the Father's heart. All of her books have a common theme that discloses our heavenly Father's love. The story she shared concerning the *suffering* of our Father shocked me.

After more than twenty years of marriage, Wendy's husband left her. She was devastated and heartbroken. At her lowest moment, the Father told Wendy that what she experienced was only a *tiny* and *infinitesimal* amount of what He has gone through. The loneliness that the Father has undergone of being *alienated* from His own creation is *unbearable!*[2] Most of His children do not even know who He is. The Father openly revealed His sorrowful heart to Wendy. I cried when I heard this.

It is hard to believe that the Creator of the universe has been enduring such painful loneliness for eons. In order to truly understand my

Father's heart, I asked Him to reveal His suffering to me. On June 6, 2020, the Father allowed me to experience a tiny bit of what He has gone through.

One afternoon, I was out shopping. Suddenly, I felt extreme heartache and death in my soul. It hit me like a tidal wave. I did not know where it came from. I then rebuked the devil, yet it did not go away. I commanded the demons to leave me alone, yet it did not work. Immediately, I remembered my inquiry to the Father about experiencing His suffering.

The next morning, the Father spoke to me and said, "I allowed you to taste a fraction of what I have been experiencing every day. You suffered loneliness, rejection, abandonment, trauma, and pain from only a few events or people in your life. But I have been grieving for the *entire human race* (billions of people) for thousands of years. Many of My children do not even know that I am their Father. I have been rejected by billions of My offspring. I cry for each of them. Yet they do not know nor regard My tears. My heart breaks for My sons and daughters every hour, every minute, and every second." When I heard this, *I was speechless!*

He then continued: "Learn from Me, my child. The only way for Me to carry on each day is to *forgive*. Every morning, I renew My mercy toward those who hurt Me (see Lamentations 3:22). I choose to be joyful because there is *joy in forgiveness*—this is why forgiveness is very important. Be an overcomer, My child, for I am an Overcomer."

> *The faithful love of the Lord never ends! His mercies never cease. Great is his faithfulness; his mercies begin afresh each morning.*
>
> —Lamentations 3:22-23 NLT

Daddy Taught Me How to Overcome

I had suffered from rejection all my life—my childhood trauma and the two divorces. I became *absolutely terrified* of people *rejecting me*. Even a tiny rejection could literally *cripple me*. Whenever someone wanted to have a close relationship with me, I would push them away because I could not risk being rejected—*too painful!* Rejection would bring back the excruciating memories of my tragic childhood and heartbreaking divorces.

On many occasions in my life, when I meant to do good and help people, I often received unkind words, blames, or even offensiveness in return. These experiences caused me to continue believing: "Maybe it is true that I am an unlikeable person. Just like when I was six-year-old, people hated me, and no one wanted me. No wonder my husband left me. Even the fellow Christians despise me."

In October 2017, an older sister from my church invited me to her family's Thanksgiving dinner. I was so happy because my Thanksgiving would not be spent alone. For many years, after my second divorce, I would close all the curtains and windows on Thanksgiving night. Seeing neighbors gathered together with families and friends, carving turkeys, and sitting around tables made my loneliness even worse. Thus, I was excited to be invited by this sister.

However, a week before Thanksgiving, she called me and said, "Ying, the Holy Spirit just told me to stay away from you and not be friends with you for a while." She then uninvited me from attending her Thanksgiving dinner. This *crushed me to the core!* All my childhood memories of rejection and abandonment came back. It hit me like a tsunami. I could hardly get up, walk, or eat for more than a week. I had to stay in bed. My heart was broken and bleeding again. At this weakest time, the Father spoke to me:

"My precious child. I feel every pain and sorrow in your soul. I know rejection is painful to endure. Come to Me and let Me speak to you.

"You had a very painful childhood, Father understands. But My beloved child, I want you to learn from Me, for I too face rejections from My own children every single day.

"I offered My Son's life to save My children. I have loved them, but in the end, many do not choose Me. They have rejected Me and chosen Satan instead. Now they are in hell. I cry for them often because they are being tormented mercilessly by demons.

"Nevertheless, I cannot live with tears all the time. I have to forgive and move on. I choose to be cheerful every day. I do not let pain and sorrow dominate My life. I have to endure and overcome. Beloved child of My heart, learn from Me, forgive those who rejected you, and continue loving them and blessing them.

"Live a celebrated life and do not forget to have fun, for fun is a weapon too. Do not let the enemy steal your joy, but rather, rejoice in Me. I am rejected by millions every day; you are rejected by only a few throughout your life. Therefore, imitate Me and overcome your fear."

After the Father told me this, I realized how much He has endured for His lost children. I also learned that our God is truly an Overcomer and a forgiving God. He has every right to be angry with us, even destroy us, but He chooses to renew His mercy every morning. Time after time, He has restrained His anger and chosen mercy instead. This takes great patience, endurance, and strength. *Bless His heart!*

> *They [Israelites] would flatter him [God] with their mouths, lying to him with their tongues; their hearts were not loyal to him, they were not faithful to his covenant. Yet he was*

merciful; he forgave their iniquities and did not destroy them. Time after time he restrained his anger and did not stir up his full wrath. He remembered that they were but flesh.

—Psalm 78:36-39 NIV

The Lord's kindness never fails! If he had not been merciful, we would have been destroyed.

—Lamentations 3:22 CEV

The Lord God, merciful and gracious, longsuffering, and abounding in goodness and truth, keeping mercy for thousands, forgiving iniquity and transgression and sin.

—Exodus 34:6–7

One day, I went to Moriah Freedom Ministries for inner healing. The topic of that day was dealing with the spirit of rejection. I shared the story of what that church sister did to me. Then the Christian counselor asked me to forgive her and bless her. As soon as the counselor mentioned that sister's name, I instantly screamed at the top of my lungs (unconscious reaction). At that moment, I literally felt *a sharp knife* piercing through my stomach, and I burst into a loud cry. But the counselor kept saying, "Ying, bless her! Bless her now! Do it now!" I followed the instruction and blessed that sister, yet the pain was still there. Then the counselor said, "Ying, bless her again! Do it again!" I did it again—five times, ten times . . .

Beloved readers, the spirit of rejection is demonic. Demons use this spirit to paralyze God's children. What that church sister did was not hurtful to the point of paralyzing me, but it did trigger my past trauma and deep wounds in my soul. Rejection is a lethal weapon that the enemy uses to torment us, and *it is very effective*. I am living proof of it.

Upon the counselor's instruction, I continued forcing myself to forgive and bless that sister daily. I had to do it over and over again until the pain was totally powerless. Six months later, that sister called me and apologized for what she had done. At that moment, I realized that it was the devil who used her to hurt me, and she might not know the enemy's intention. The demons intended to open my past wounds and cause me to fall into their trap again.

Satan has no sympathy. He feeds on our pains, miseries, and sufferings. He is a cold-blooded, pitiless, cruel, and wicked foe. But My Father watches every movement of the devil. Daddy is always there to help me overcome hardships. He is my Refuge from every evil attack. He will not allow His enemy to snatch me out of His hand (see John 10:27). He guards me as the apple of His eyes. Whoever attacks me will be crushed by His mighty hand (see Zechariah 2:8). He will protect me at every turn of my life. He loves me so dearly and even engraves my name on the palms of His hands (see Isaiah 49:15). If God is for me, who can be against me?

> *[Jesus said,] My sheep [believers] hear My voice, and I know them, and they follow Me. And I give them eternal life, and they shall never perish; neither shall anyone snatch them out of My hand. My Father, who has given them to Me, is greater than all; and no one is able to snatch them out of My Father's hand.*
>
> *—John 10:27–29*

> *[The Lord said,] Whoever touches you touches the apple of his eye—I will surely raise my hand against them.*
>
> *—Zechariah 2:8–9* NIV

> *[The Lord said,] Can a mother forget the baby at her breast and have no compassion on the child she has borne?*

Though she may forget, I will not forget you! See, I have engraved you on the palms of my hands.

—Isaiah 49:15-16 NIV

God loves courageous children. He wants us to carry His might. What is courage? Courage is the demonstration of faith in God. Courage is the ability to do things even though we are afraid. Courage is when we face pain and danger, yet still push through with total endurance and resilience. God is teaching me to overcome rejection by His might and courage.

The heart of my Father is extremely tender and sympathetic. Seeing me alone and lying there crying on that Thanksgiving night, He could not bear to see me like that. Suddenly, my cell phone rang.

"Ying, are you home? Have you had dinner yet? If not, I will bring food to you. I cooked a lot for my guests, and I have plenty!" The call was from Michelle (a sister in Christ), a beautiful Korean girl whom I had not spoken to in many months. At that moment, I immediately knew it was from the Father.

"Michelle, I have not eaten yet. But I am okay; do not worry about me. Take care of your guest. Do not come!" I answered.

"Ying, I want to bring food to you. I am coming now!" She insisted.

My heart dropped. I lifted up my hands toward heaven and cried out to the Father, "Daddy, thank you so much for thinking of me. You truly are a loving Father. You could not bear to see me cry. Thank you so much for the Thanksgiving dinner!"

Since that night (every year), Michelle has been bringing Thanksgiving dinner to me. Her heart is beyond generous and benevolent. I am sure she will be rewarded by God, and her good deeds will be recorded by the angels in heaven.

To His Throne Room Again

*J*esus accompanied me to the Father's throne room again. This time, I was in my sixteen-year-old spiritual body, wearing a gorgeous peach-colored dress. I had long-silky-straight hair down to my waist. Jesus was holding my hand, walking toward the throne of God. There were millions of people and angels worshiping God. As Jesus and I walked closer to the throne, my heart started racing. About fifty feet from the bottom of the throne, Jesus released my hand and let me walk by myself. As I stepped on the stairs, instantaneously, I reached the Father.

I bowed down at the Father's feet; He took me into His arms. He was delighted to see me. My body was trembling as I hugged and kissed Him. "Daddy, my Daddy, I love You!" I could feel His all-consuming glory and tender love wrapped around me. I could do nothing but hug Him and cry. It was a very emotional moment. He continued holding me in His arms. His glory and brilliance were too intense to behold. At that point, I could not hear any music or worship sounds. It seemed as though heaven waited.

I have seen the Father so many times in His garden, but meeting Him in the throne room was a different experience—I did not know why. He sat me on His lap and started to talk:

> "My beloved child, I have a great plan for you. You will do mighty work for My Kingdom. There is no time to waste. Be diligent, consistent, and persistent. Do not be distracted. The enemy has been attacking you at your workplace and through different people in your life. But do not listen to the devil's voice. Stay close to Me!
>
> "Your problem is self-pity. You constantly look down on yourself. Self-criticism and self-condemnation are also sins. I do not view you as you view yourself. The lens you

use to view yourself is from the enemy and is deceiving you. Demons speak lies about you, and you often listen to their lies.

"The reality is where I am and who I am. The reason you feel lonely and self-pity is because you do not know the truth. The true reality is: you have been washed by My Son's blood; you are a new creation now. Your old self does not exist anymore. Nevertheless, your carnal nature (flesh) tries to pull your mind back to your old self and brings up all the painful memories.

"Your flesh (old self) cannot forgive nor can be redeemed. Therefore, the demons are using it to confuse your new identity. The enemy leads you to see yourself in a broken mirror, which gives you a distorted and false image. This image is the enemy's lies, deceptions, delusions, and confusions.

"Lean on Me, trust Me, and have total faith in Me! Your past pain, sorrow, trauma, and failure no longer represent who you are. Crucify your flesh on the cross, so that no longer you who live, but I live in You.

"You are not saved just so you can come to heaven, but you are called to be a soldier! I have excellent plans for you. Apply My Words to your daily life and practice what I have been teaching you—learning without practicing is useless. If Apostle Paul only spent time learning and praying at home, there would be no gentile churches today.

"Hell has unleashed an immense force to fight because they know that heaven is about to invade the earth. You will face more darkness and persecution than ever before. But remember, beloved child, My glory is so much greater."

 I do not remember how long I was with the Father at His throne because heaven does not measure by time. As I came down from the Father's throne, Jesus was there to receive me. At that time, I could hear the music again. We then danced with other worshipers for a while. After that, He took me to our secret garden. There was no more loud music, only quiet and romantic love between the two lovebirds.

A Taste of His Glory

I have always been curious about what God's glory looks like or feels like. On April 28, 2021, at 3:00 a.m., I asked the Father to show me His glory. About ten minutes later, it came. Waves of electric current hit my body. At that moment, I was in the middle of worship with my hands up toward heaven. When the glory hit me, I felt the presence of God surge through my being like an immense voltage. I could not worship anymore. My feet became feeble, and my arms were like spaghetti, as though I was drunk. My whole body melted like wax, and I was unable to stand.

I then managed to lie down and immersed myself in His glory. The feeling was incredibly peaceful. My entire body was tingling—hands, arms, legs, and feet felt pins-and-needles sensations. I could hardly breathe due to the intense electric current flowing through my body. For about two hours, the glory kept cascading on me. I just lay there and let the glory of God shower me.

The same phenomena can be found in 1 King 8:11 when Solomon dedicated the temple to God. During the ceremony, the priests could not continue ministering in the temple because the glory of the Lord God was so thick.

> *The priests could not stand [in their positions] to minister because of the cloud, for the glory and brilliance of the Lord had filled the Lord's house (temple).*
>
> —1 King 8:11 AMP

A Dozen Handkerchiefs

From February 2, 2014 (the day I became a Christian) until now, I have written letters or poems to the Father every holiday. I also buy cards and gifts for Him. Throughout these years (times spent with my Father), I noticed He often cries. He weeps for His beloved children on the earth. His heart is so *sensitive*, *tender*, and *affectionate*.

At Christmas of 2018, I bought a few gifts for the Father: a long-sleeve shirt and a dozen handkerchiefs. I said, "Daddy, I know you cry a lot. We often grieve Your heart and hurt Your feelings. So, I bought You twelve handkerchiefs. They are 100 percent cotton. They are for Your tears." He touchingly received my gifts.

Beloved readers, our Father is mighty and powerful—the supreme Owner of the cosmos. It is good that we worship Him corporately in church gatherings. However, deep in His heart, He seeks a child pursuing His Person. A dozen handkerchiefs are insignificant to an earthly father, yet to the heavenly Father, they are substantial.

My Poetry to the Father

In eight years of knowing my heavenly Father, I have written Him more than twenty poems and letters. This is my way of expressing love to Him. I am not a writer nor a poet. In fact, I had never written poetry before. But these rhymes keep flowing out of my sincere heart. Whatever my heart composes, I pour it out on paper. I desire to express my heart songs to the beloved *King of All Ages*—my Father. On November 23, 2017, Thanksgiving night, I wrote the following poem for the Father. This is the poem's background:

During the Chinese Cultural Revolution, my earthly father was imprisoned for ten years. By the time he was released, I was already sixteen years old. Thereafter, I went to an art school and lived in the dormitory. Unlike a normal child, I had never had a vacation with my father. At age twenty-six, I came to the United States of America. Throughout my whole life, I had been yearning for an intimate father-daughter relationship. I longed for a vacation with my father alone, but never had a chance to do so.

Now, my earthly father had passed away and left a great regret in my heart. So, this poem was written with the hope that my heavenly Father would take me on a vacation.

One day, I asked the Father, "Daddy, my biggest wish is to have a vacation with You—Just You and me. Would You take me?" He smiled and said, "Yes, My beloved child, I will."

Our First Vacation

Holding my Father's hand,
Walking on a celestial beach.
Silver sand and jade ocean,
Heart pounding and blood tossing,
My first vacation with the Father, how exciting!

Leaning on His arm and whispering into His ear,
"I have been longing for this day, Father.
I have been dreaming for this hour, Daddy."
The Father's hands started shaking.
From His brilliant countenance, tears were running.

The Father started telling me:
How much He had longed for me,
How much He had wept for me,
How much He had laughed for me,
And how much He had rejoiced for me.

He told me how mischievous I was
When I was inside of Him eons ago.
He told me how lovely I was
When I sang and danced with Him.
For before I came to the earth, I was with Him.

I started to weep and clung to His arms,
Burying my face in His embrace.
Streams of joy like the ocean waves,
I cried out, "Abba, Abba, oh, my dear Abba.
How I have yearned for You, my beloved Abba!"

He lifted His hands toward the ocean,
Drawing out fish of many kinds.
He smoked them with charcoals.
We had our first adventure meal.
We then cuddled with inexpressible bliss!

Night falling, moon dancing,
Ocean clapping, stars singing—
"Rejoice, blessed child.
Be glad, Father's princess,
Enjoy in His everlasting embrace!"

Daddy revealed His creation to me—
The wonders of His universe.
How things were created.
How He formed mankind and loved us,
For we are all His offspring.

The warm breeze was kissing our faces.
The stars were dazzling with glowing praises.
Father took the lead, and I followed.
We danced in this celestial place.
Our hearts refused to end the bliss!

Moonlight was rolling with joyful dancing.
Our shadows were jumping with jubilant rejoicing.
Our bodies were wrapped with aurora coloring.
Our eyes were twinkling with silent loving.
Father and daughter with inseparable bonding!

Joyful tears were dropping from the Father's face.
His heart was leaping and hands were shaking.
Eons and eons,
He has yearned for His children.
Without them, His wish can never be ending!

We turned and swayed.
We laughed and giggled.
We kissed and hugged.
Suddenly, the morning stars were rising.
Yet our hearts refused to be parting!

"Beloved child of My heart,
It's time for you to go back to the earth.
You have work to do for My Kingdom.
I will always dance with you in your heart.
For our love shall never be ceasing!"

Tears, tears, my silent tears,
More tears, and sad tears,
Mingled with my Father's tears.
"How can I let you go, my precious princess?
For your love to Me is fervent and pleasing!"

"Father, I will kiss You with my worship songs.
I will hug You with my musical notes.
I will touch Your heart with my passionate praises.
I will adore You with my ready fruit.
Dearest Daddy, I am Yours, and You are mine!"

> "Beloved Father of my heart,
> On this very Thanksgiving night,
> As we are vacationing on this beautiful beach,
> Allow me to hold You just a little tighter,
> Permit me to be with You just a little longer."

> Tears and tears,
> More silent tears.
> His tears,
> My tears,
> Our tears!

Happy Thanksgiving to My Beloved Father!

Your little princess,

Ying

On December 24, 2017 (Christmas Eve), I wrote the following poem to express my understanding about God's creation, about *the Word* (Jesus Christ), about how Lucifer fell, and how mankind was created in God's image.

Beloved readers, to refresh your memory, "Jesus" is His earthly name. His heavenly name is the "Word" (see John 1:1).

> *In the beginning [before all time] was the Word (Christ), and the Word was with God, and the Word was God Himself.*
>
> —John 1:1 AMP

Every day, I care about my Father's well-being—is He happy or sad? I always ask, "Daddy, are You happy today? Are You busy? Are You in meetings? Is there anything bothering You or causing You to be sad? Would You share Your heart with me?" I want to be a child who is after God's very heart.

God, Creation, Mankind

Eons Ago

All existence started with Your thoughts.
You painted marvelous paintings in Your heart.
Through Your wisdom, they were painted.
Through Your understanding, they were formed.

God, the Word (Jesus), and the Holy Spirit met,
Plans and strategies were outlined.
Because Your heart longed for a family,
You designed humans after Your own kind.

The Plan

The creation of souls was shaped;
The creation of angels was intended;
The creation of humans was fashioned;
The creation of heavens was scheduled.

While all wonders were planned,
All formations were enlisted,
You already foresaw the crucifixion of Your Son—
The sacrifice of Your only begotten Son.

The Word (Jesus)

In the beginning, the Word was with God (Father), *
And the Word Himself was God.
When the Father spoke,
The Word created all things—

Realms of heavens,
All types of angels,
Innumerable species of creatures,
Planets, galaxies, and cosmos.

Lucifer Fell (Pre-Adamic Age)

One of Your anointed cherubs (Lucifer) betrayed You,
You cast him out of heaven along with his angels.
Though You were furious, You held Your peace,
And endured pain from their betrayal!

Out of Your wrath,
Hell was created for them.
You sent a flood to destroy them,
All living creatures were extinguished by flood and Ice Age.

Mankind Fell

Eons later, human beings were formed,
In Your image, they were created.
Yet Satan deceived them.
So from Eden, You drove out Eve and Adam.

Then You sent the Word to rescue Adam's descendants.
He paid the ransom price on the cross.
Heaven suffered a great loss to save us,
Because nothing could stop You from rescuing us!

Longsuffering

For eons, You have carried us.
For ages, You have tolerated us.
For centuries, You have wept for us.
For many moons, You have grieved for us.

Yet still stretching Your arms to embrace us,
Keep renewing Your mercy every morning,
Always ready to pardon our sins,
And show Your unfailing love to us.

YING FLYNN

Infinite

Yahweh, the Lord— *
The God of mercy and grace,
Slow to anger,
Full of goodness and truth,

With infinite love,
Infinite mercy,
Infinite forgiveness,
And infinite grace.

Time

Now, the time has come to an end.
Your marvelous painting is almost finished.
Your plans, Your longings, and Your hopings,
Are about to be fulfilled.

The time to be with all Your children
Has never been this close.
The time to dance with all Your offspring
Is about to become a reality.

Wholeness

Your longsuffering will turn into joyful dancing.
Your heart song will reach its crescendo.
Your children will surround You.
And Your heart will be made whole.

The earth will be made whole.
The heavens will be made whole.
Our hearts will be made whole.
And all things will be made whole in You!

Forever Remember

While things are coming to an end,
We will never forget how it began.
How much Father invested in Your children;
How much You underwent painful expectations.

Your faithfulness,
Your compassion,
Your everlasting love,
Will forever be remembered in our hearts!

The Cross

The cross was the Father's grace to His children.
The cross was the Father's gift to His children.
The cross was Christ's sacrifice for mankind.
The cross was God's absolute love for His offspring!

On this very Christmas Eve,
With my thanksgiving heart,
I honor the cross,
And Your unfailing love for mankind.

My Christmas Wish

My Father, if You ask me,
"What is your Christmas wish?"
I will say, "My wish is to visit You,
To see You in heaven on this Christmas Eve."

Call me up, Father.
Call my name, Father.
Let me appear before Your throne, Father,
For my soul thirsts for You, dearest Father!

Merry Christmas to my beloved Father!

Hugs and kisses,

Your little princess,

Ying

* John 1:1; "Yahweh" means "God" in Hebrew.

On June 16, 2019 (Father's Day), I wrote a poem titled *"A Pink Butterfly"* to my heavenly Father. As I said in the previous chapter, the butterflies would dance with me every time I visited the Father in His garden.

Throughout the world, butterflies represent beauty, spiritual rebirth, endurance, change, resurrection, and life. In many cultures, butterflies symbolize strength and achieving goals through perseverance. It takes great power to transform a plain caterpillar into a beautiful butterfly. This process is called "metamorphosis," which means "change in shape" or "transformation."

A butterfly goes through four stages of transformation, and each stage has its own result. This mimics my life-changing journey. Even though some stages have been extremely painful, they have served God's purpose.

My life-changing events resemble the metamorphosis of a butterfly: from traumatized childhood to goal-achieving adulthood (I am a director in a Fortune 100 company), from a sinner to a born-again Christian, I have been transformed into a new person by the grace of God. Sometimes, when I am with the Holy Spirit, He literally transforms me into a pink butterfly. This will be described in a later chapter.

The following poem describes a little butterfly having a fantastic time inside the Father. The *"pink butterfly"* is me, the *"Word"* is Jesus, and the *"Daddy"* or *"Ancient of Days"* is God the Father. The *"paradise"* is inside the Father. As I mentioned in the previous chapter, there are no organs inside the Father, but an eternal world—mountains, trees, rivers, gemstones, etc. We humans cannot understand God fully—He is a Spirit. Therefore, we should not limit Him using our human intelligence.

A Pink Butterfly

I am a pink butterfly,
Living in an amazing paradise.
My wings dazzle with glittering lights.
I am pretty in color, lovely in splendor.

I land on the vibrant flowers.
They sing worship songs to the God Most High.
I land on the lavish meadows.
They dance to glorify the Ancient of Days.

I tap dance on the riverbed;
It flows with springs of living water.
I land on the stones of fire;
They are engraved with the Father's love.

I ballet dance on music notes,
And fly with garlands of rainbows.
I swim in the liquid sapphire,
And breathe air from the Holy Spirit.

It is here I fall in love with the Word.
He is the Lover of my soul.
He is the precious Son of God,

And my Savior and Redeemer.

It is here I become a friend of the Holy Spirit.
He is my dance Partner,
My best Friend,
And my divine Teacher.

Where is this paradise?
Why is it so breathtaking?
It is none but the inside of the Father—
The everlasting dreamland.

In here, the mountains cheer,
The flowers sing,
The rivers dance,
And all living creatures worship Him.

Every day,
I will kiss Daddy with my butterfly kisses.
He will kiss me back with His lovingkindness—
Like liquid love dripping on my wings.

Every morning,
I will say, "I love you, Daddy."
He will answer me back with the warmest embrace—
The embrace of the Fatherly affection.

Throughout the day,
I will ask Him hundreds of questions.
He will answer me with everlasting patience.
He delights to satisfy all my innocent inquiries.

Every so often,
He will put me on His hand and speak to me.
He even engraves my name on His palms
To express His never-ending love and compassion!

JESUS, MY FOREVER LOVE

Who is He?
He is the Creator of the universe.
He is the Father of all living beings.
He is God Almighty—my Daddy Yahweh.

My Father is a consuming fire—
The fire of love and holiness.
His love and mercy last forever.
His glory illuminates trillions of galaxies.

My Father is a jealous God.
He is jealous over me.
He protects me at all costs.
He even sent His Son to die for me!

Oh, my dearest Father,
On this very Father's Day,
Your little pink butterfly
Is here to give You butterfly kisses—

The kisses of longing,
The kisses of yearning,
The kisses of wanting,
For I long, yearn, and want You!

Happy Father's Day!

Your pink butterfly,

Ying

On November 21, 2021 (Thanksgiving), I wrote the following poem to my Father.

Beloved readers, I want you to know this truth. Rainbows are not generated by phenomena from the sky. They are originated from the heart of the Father.

Many people witnessed this truth when they visited heaven. They saw countless rainbows flowing out of the Father God. Sometimes, when He wants to see a certain child on the earth, He will release rainbows to fetch that child to Himself.

Rainbow

Once I was taking a shower in the afternoon,
When the sun glowed on the waters,
I discovered something spectacular.
I saw rainbows in each drop of the water.
I cheered with joy, "Daddy, daddy, You are in the water!"

Indeed, rainbows come from You, my Father,
The first-time humans ever saw rainbows
Was when You made a covenant with mankind after the flood.
You set rainbows in the sky as the sign of Your promise:
"Never again shall there be a flood to destroy the earth." *

Daily, rainbows are flowing out of Your being,
They are the living colors of Your heart—
The color of Your character,
The color of Your emotion,
And the color of Your desire.

Red represents Your love and compassion.
Orange signifies Your kindness, goodness, and holiness.
Yellow symbolizes Your joy and glory.
Green characterizes Your faithfulness and gentleness.
Blue embodies Your peacefulness and strength.

Indigo indicates Your wisdom, righteousness, and justice.
Violet epitomizes Your royalty, power, and majesty.
Wherever the rainbow is seen,
There Your presence is found.
What a colorful God You are!

JESUS, MY FOREVER LOVE

You are an omnipresent God,
You can be found in all creations—
In every cell, every atom, every living organism.
Rainbows can be seen wherever Your presence is—
In morning dews, summer rains, ocean sprays, and waterfalls.

Whenever people see rainbows,
They cheer with joy,
Because You are in the rainbows.
Your heart shines with seven beautiful colors—
The divine color pallet—the seven Spirit of God.

When I was inside of You before coming to the earth,
I ballet danced on Your rainbows.
I did somersaults on Your rainbows.
I was engulfed with the color of Your love.
I was the happiest child who once lived in Your heart!

On this thanksgiving night,
When my neighbors are feasting at their dinner tables,
And families are gathering at their fireplaces.
I am alone, waiting for Your rainbows to fetch me
To spend a night with You.

How joyful would it be to spend this night with You?
To deliver my thanksgiving kiss to You in person,
To embrace Daddy with my thankful heart,
To show gratitude for Your goodness and tender love,
To express my appreciation for Your mercy and grace.

Daddy, can You hear the melody of my heat?
Can You hear the harp of my soul?
Can You hear the heart-songs of my thanksgiving?
Can You see the color of my longing?
For I sing and long for You!

There are many things to thank You for:
Thank You for loving me while I was in my mother's womb.
Thank You for protecting me since the time of my birth,
Thank You for guiding me throughout my life journey.
Thank You for never leaving me nor forsaking me.

Thank You for companying me when I go out.
Thank You for staying with me when I come in.
Thank You for allowing me to visit You whenever I desire.
Thank You for holding me when I am in sorrow and tears.
Thank You for telling me that I am Your "sweetest."

Thank You for hearing every prayer that I made.
Thank You for receiving the lawsuits I filed against evil.
Thank You for defending our nation's liberty and freedom.
Thank You for assigning hosts of heaven to assist me,
Thank You for empowering me to fight the end-time battles.

Thank You for Your glory glowing on me constantly.
Thank You for Your light shining on me unceasingly.
Thank You for Your love showering me continually.
Thank You for Your presence surrounding me incessantly.
Thank You for calling me "The precious child of Your heart."

Oh, my dearest Father,
How I love You, my sweetest Daddy.
Please don't be too far,
Come closer to Your daughter at this night,
And let me kiss You with the warmest thanksgiving caress!

Happy Thanksgiving to my loving Father!

Your little daughter,

Ying

* Genesis 9:11.

Experiencing His Ocean of Love Tangibly

I have been longing to know how wide, how long, how high, and how deep is the love of God. Even though I feel His love every day, I know much more is yet to be discovered. So, as part of my daily prayer, I always ask the Father to show me His love in a deeper dimension.

To my surprise, on October 26, 2020, He allowed me to tangibly feel the magnitude of His love that I had never experienced before.

At that moment, my heart was filled with an explosion of love—like a nuclear fusion. I was utterly overwhelmed by this experience. I, therefore, wrote the following poem on Christmas Eve of 2020. The events in this poem *actually happened* during my encounter with God.

The Father's Heart

Ocean of Love

One day, I asked the Father to show me His love.
Instantly, I found myself in a vast blue ocean.
There, I breathed like a fish,
And danced with Jesus on the ocean floor.
My whole being was drenched with immense love.
I marveled, "where is this place?"
"It is the Father's heart—His ocean of love," Jesus said.

Endless Space

The next day, I found myself in an endless space.
I was flying with my White Eagle (Jesus).
He carried me on His outstretched wings.
We were soaring in this endless cosmos.
My whole body was filled with tremendous love.
I asked Jesus, "where is this place?"

"It is the Father's heart—His endless love," He replied.

Blue Fire

Days later, I found myself in a gigantic sphere of blue fire.
The blaze flowed like liquid sapphire.
Shock waves were issued from the blaze.
I was floating like an astronaut in a spaceship.
I felt an explosion of love in my veins.
I wondered, "where is this place?"
"It is the Father's heart—His fire of love," Jesus answered.

Beyond Measure

God is love!
Love is His nature.
His heart is filled with consuming love.
His love is beyond ocean deep—immeasurable.
His passion is flames of fire—all-consuming.
His holiness is endless space—unlimited.
His grace is lavish divine—abundant.

Please Let Me . . .

My beloved Father,
On this Christmas Eve,
Let me swim in Your ocean of love again,
Let me fly in Your space of love again,
Let me float in Your flames of love again.
For I long to experience—
The width, length, height, and depth of your love again.

Merry Christmas, my beloved Father.

Kisses and hugs,

Your daughter,

Ying

Dancing in the Heart of the Father

On December 20, 2021, the Father allowed me to experience His immense love again. Even though I have tasted His love daily, these unique encounters are worth recording and remembering.

In this vision, I saw myself (in my fourteen-year-old spiritual body) dancing in a vast fiery sphere. This place is different from the sun's interior, yet the color of the fire is the same. I wore a gorgeous red dress, and it was coated with blazing flares. The more I worshiped and danced for God, the brighter the fires became. The flames followed my dance moves and danced with me. This place is the *heart of the Father*. He then started to speak:

> "My sweetest child, do you know how much you mean to Me? Your worship always touches My heart. From now on, you can directly sing and dance in My heart—you have full access to it.

> "Do you know that I want all my children to have this access? Yet, many do not have the desire. Some of them worship Me in vain; hence, their worship cannot reach My heart. But you have gained the access. I am a loving Father, and My heart is the most beautiful place for My children to dwell."

I then said to Him, "Father, you know that I am *crazy* about You. You are a perfect Father, and You are the Love of my soul. I do not want anything else in this world but You."

The Father Came to My House

On December 24, 2020 (Christmas Eve), I discovered something unusual. As I mentioned before, I often see Jesus and the Holy Spirit in my house—meaning they come to my house physically during my devotion time. But I rarely see the Father in my house. However, on this Christmas Eve, He came.

As usual, I bought gifts for Jesus, the Father, and the Holy Spirit. I set up the table and chairs for each of Them with my Christmas gifts on the table. All three of Them came. With my spiritual eyes, I saw the Father sitting on the chair to receive His gifts. I was shocked. Ever since, I have arranged three chairs in my prayer room. Previously, I only had two chairs—one for Jesus and one for the Holy Spirit. After putting a chair for the Father, He has been coming to my prayer room. They delight to be worshiped and loved. They cannot wait for a child to intimately fellowship with Them. They long for a *Mishpachah* (family) with mankind.

My Christmas Gifts from God

On December 24, 2021 (Christmas Eve), as usual (each year), I decorated my dining room table with flower petals and green foliage. I used the red berries of heavenly bamboo from my backyard to form a "HAPPY BIRTHDAY JESUS" on white table linen (see Figure 17). At the end of the table, I placed a bouquet of red roses and a birthday cake for Jesus. On the cake, a red-colored "*Happy*

Birthday Jesus" was written against a white-icing background—very pretty. My Christmas gifts and cards (love letters inside) for the Father, the Son, and the Holy Spirit were placed on the nearby buffet table. The whole setting was extremely striking.

Figure 17: Christmas table setting for Jesus' Birthday.

At 7:30 p.m., I started to sing worship songs to celebrate Jesus' birthday. Immediately, The Trinity came. With my spiritual eyes, I saw the Father and the Holy Spirit sitting on the sofa and Jesus sitting on the French bergère chair. I was thrilled, kept singing Christmas songs, and threw kisses at them. At 8:30 p.m., we all sat down at the dining table. I started reading my cards, love letters, and opening my gifts for them.

I bought three beautiful winter sweaters with Christmas-knitting patterns on them. They are incredibly soft and double-layer knitted. Since the Father and the Holy Spirit are tall and big (seven to eight feet tall), I bought 3x for them. For Jesus, I purchased 2x. I also bought multipurpose tools for each of them. These tools are compact and versatile, with fourteen all-in-one gadgets. I am hoping one day they will use them for camping with me.

They came with Christmas gifts for me too. The gift from the Father was a gorgeous red dress (like a Cinderella dress). The red color was a bit dark, which resembled the color ruby. It made me look like a queen or royal princess. Gifts from Jesus were an exquisite red necklace with many deep blood-red rubies on it and a pair of striking red-crystal shoes (I suppose no one can fit them, but me—I am His Cinderella.). The gift from the Holy Spirit was a dazzling-diamond crown with many crystals around and a red gemstone in the center.

Beloved readers, when I put on all these gifts, I truly looked like a regal princess—majestic and splendid. Yet, deep inside, I knew the meaning of *red*. It signified the precious *blood* of Jesus. I was deeply touched by these gifts and kept thanking Them over and over again.

Not until after I received these gifts, I recalled . . . about two months prior, when I danced with the Father in His garden, I wore the same red dress, necklace, shoes, and crown. They already gave me my Christmas gifts before the holiday. They couldn't wait to see the beauty of Their child. By the way, these gifts cannot be seen with my physical eyes. They can only be seen with my spiritual eyes.

"This Thunder and Lightning Are for You!"

During the week of the "Feast of Trumpet" in 2021, I suffered severe tooth pain—to the point I couldn't even pray and worship God. As the feast was ending, my situation got a little better. After a week-long tooth pain, on September 9 at 11:00 p.m., I finally went to my prayer room to spend time with God. As soon as I started worshiping, God's presence came *instantaneously*, as though He couldn't wait to see me.

I sang songs like "Alpha and Omega," "Way Maker," and "God You Are So Good." Ten minutes into the worship, something spectacular happened. The sky blasted with rumbling thunders and bolt of lightning throughout the city I lived. They were so earsplitting and intense; I felt the windows and walls were shaking. I got scared and started screaming.

Eventually, I managed to resume the worship. As soon as I started singing, the Father said to me, "This thunder and lightning are for you, My child." I ignored this saying because no such thing had ever happened before—too extraordinary to believe! But God kept saying the same while I was singing. Finally, I recognized the voice was true, not my imagination. I then did something special. I invited the thunder and lightning to join me in worship, and they did—these resounding roars and flashy lights lasted about half an hour.

That night, the sky was filled with worshipping explosions. Afterward, I went outside and noticed that there was hardly any rain. The Holy Spirit said to me, "This phenomenon is not your imagination. These roaring booms and flashing lights are truly for you. The Father has missed you. He utters His love through rolling thunders to show His intense longing for you because you were sick for a week." I was *amazed* and *speechless!* I said to the Holy Spirit, "No one will ever believe me if I tell them about this." I then kept thanking God for this extraordinary marvel and love.

Beloved readers, I know why this wonder happened to me. When I worshiped God during sickness, it touched His heart deeply. He couldn't restrain Himself but manifested His excitement in such a marvelous way. He rumbled the entire city with piercing blasts and blazing lights. How remarkable is my Daddy! One such wonder can also be found in Exodus 19 when the Israelites met with God at Mount Sinai:

> *On the morning of the third day there was thunder and lightning, with a thick cloud over the mountain, and a very loud trumpet blast. Everyone in the camp trembled. Then Moses led the people out of the camp to meet with God, and they stood at the foot of the mountain. Mount Sinai was covered with smoke, because the Lord descended on*

it in fire. The smoke billowed up from it like smoke from a furnace, and the whole mountain trembled violently.

—Exodus 19:16–18 NIV

That night I was deeply touched by the Father's affection. How in the world would I ever expect that He sent thunders and lightning to cheer me up after a week-long tooth pain? He is indeed the most tender-loving Father in the whole universe!

Humility Is a Weapon

One of the greatest weapons in God's Kingdom is the "Mantle of Humility" because God's grace is in it. When Jesus walked on the earth, He wore the same mantle. As long as we are clothed in this mantle, we are safe from the enemy's detection.

Prophet Rick Joyner witnessed something astounding about the ranking system in heaven. In his book, *The Final Quest*, he mentioned that Jesus gave him a mantle to wear in the middle of an intense spiritual battle. This mantel was very plain, making him look like a homeless man instead of a mighty warrior. However, a great company of angels started to bow down to him. He asked the angels why they were doing so. They all pointed to the mantle he was wearing. The angels revealed to him that the "Mantle of Humility" represented the highest rank in the Kingdom of God.[3] Beloved readers, I have observed that many prideful people (myself included) are those who have suffered tremendous trauma in their childhood. During their adulthood, they often use pride to counterbalance their inner pain. Prideful people have a habit of boasting on the outside, but inwardly, they are weak and fearful. These people were rejected, abandoned, or abused when they were very young. When they grow up, they are inclined to be self-righteous, self-promoting, and arrogant. Pride is a demonic spirit. There are six things that God hates, and pride is the worst one:

> *These six things the Lord hates, yes, seven are an abomination to Him: A proud look, a lying tongue, hands that shed innocent blood, a heart that devises wicked plans, feet that are swift in running to evil, a false witness who speaks lies, and one who sows discord among brethren.*
>
> —Proverbs 6:16–19

I have been struggling with the spirit of pride my whole life. Deep inside, I loathe myself, yet at the same time, I hate to be criticized or put down by others. I talk a lot about myself and brag about how good I am. I compare, judge, and envy others. These characteristics are not from God but Satan.

Jesus revealed to a prophet that Lucifer fell because of his pride. He was the most beautiful and anointed cherub whom God created. But Lucifer started to admire himself instead of God. He began to take pride in his position, power, and splendor. Jesus addressed that as soon as God's glory was given to church ministers, in most cases, they would fall the same way as Lucifer did. All sins are abominable to God, but pride is the worst of all.

> *Everyone who is proud in heart is an abomination to the Lord; be assured, he will not go unpunished.*
>
> —Proverbs 16:5 NASB

Humility, on the other hand, reflects God's character. He loves those who are meek, lowly, obedient, and humble (see 1 Peter 5:5). He is closer to the homeless people than to kings and queens.

> *Clothe yourselves with humility toward one another, because, "God opposes the proud, but gives grace to the humble."*
>
> —1 Peter 5:5 BSB

Jesus demonstrated the power of humility by washing His disciples' feet. Heavens and earth were created through Him. All glories and dominions belong to Him. Yet, He is also the humblest Person we have ever seen. *"He humbled himself in obedience to God [the Father] and died a criminal's death on a cross"* (Philippians 2:8 NLT). Jesus used humility as a powerful weapon to defeat Satan on the cross. Today, He commands us to use the same weapon in combat.

I have experienced so many failures in my life because of pride. On October 8, 2019 (Yom Kippur), the Father said to me:

"My beloved child, I want you to walk in love and humility because pride is a deadly sin. It will kill you just as it killed Lucifer. Pride destined him to hell—he will soon be tormented in the lake of fire forever. Pride has also led many of my children to hell. Therefore, learn from Me, for I am lowly in heart. When you act humbly and stay low, you will be protected by My presence.

"I am purifying and beautifying you because I want you to be the best bride for My Son. The beauty that I speak of is humility.

"Pride is your main problem. As long as you are prideful, I cannot be close to you. Humility is the key to My Kingdom. Regarding Lucifer, I had to let him go because he was corrupted by his pride—to the point he could not be salvaged.

"I am greater than all, but I am also humbler than all. Humility is heaven culture, and I use it to govern My Kingdom. Glory can only be found in humility. Even within the Trinity, we are humble to one another. If you truly want to know My heart, you must first humble yourself. Always stay in the lowest position—that is the place of beauty; that is where you will encounter Me.

"Think of yourself as nothing; think of Me as everything. Without Me, you can do nothing. Lucifer couldn't understand this simple equation. He has no respect for his Creator. He is a rebellious spirit."

The Worst Enemy Is "Self"

In the spiritual realm, Satan is our number one enemy; but in the natural realm, "me," "self," and "I" are our number one enemy. Self-centeredness hinders us from being close to God. It is easy to deny Satan, but it is hard to deny "self." Hence, our worst enemy is not Satan, but "me," "self," and "I." Jesus repeatedly instructs us, *"If anyone desires to come after Me, let him deny himself, and take up his cross, and follow Me"* (Matthew 16:24).

What does the Lord mean by "take up His cross?" It means we must die to our fleshly desires. We must deny ourselves and crucify our carnal nature daily. As long as "self" exists in our thoughts, God cannot use us.

> *The mind set on the flesh is death, but the mind set on the Spirit is life and peace, because the mind set on the flesh is hostile toward God; for it does not subject itself to the law of God, for it is not even able to do so, and those who are in the flesh cannot please God.*
>
> —Romans 8:6–8 NASB

If we love God, we must actively crucify our flesh daily until there is no "me" left, but only "Christ in me" (see Galatians 2:20). How do we crucify ourselves? By meditating on God's Word, lying down at His feet, enduring persecutions, forgiving others, undergoing sufferings, humbling ourselves, and obeying the Holy Spirit. At what point do we know our flesh is dead? It is when we are able to love others more than loving ourselves, because flesh is extremely selfish—it cannot love anyone but itself.

> *I have been crucified with Christ; it is no longer I who live, but Christ lives in me; and the life which I now live in the flesh I live by faith in the Son of God, who loved me and gave Himself for me.*
>
> —Galatians 2:20

No More Drill Sergeant!

As I stated earlier, at age six, when the Chinese Cultural Revolution started, my mother told me, "If you do not bring food, your father and I will die in prison. Learn to cook simple food and bring it to us daily." Since that day, I was given heavy duties that a normal child could never bear. It was very difficult, yet I was able to do it with unexplainable strength. Mostly, I was afraid that my parents would die because their very lives depended on me.

Unfortunately, my childhood traumas have affected my adulthood greatly. I have been wired to be driven and forceful, with a mission-critical alert system built into my mind. I have lived in *"survival of the fittest"* mode all my adult life.

This characteristic has stayed with me wherever I go. Throughout my career, I have always been a leader. At my current job, I am a director in the computer software field. I have brought my childhood "survival" skills to the workplace. Over time, I have noticed that I can accomplish tasks faster than my peers, but my employees are burdened by my forcefulness and *"drill sergeant"* style. In my subconscious mind, if I do not get things done quickly and perfectly, something terrible will happen. This is my traumatic childhood syndrome—it is irrational.

During one of my annual reviews, my boss said, "Ying, I never have to worry about your ability to deliver—you are a *bulldog deliverer!* Yet, it would be better if you improve your way of doing things. Try to take a deep breath and relax!" When I heard this, I said in my heart, "How can I relax? I have been wired this way since when I was six years old." My leadership style fits better for the military than private sectors.

Throughout my life, I may have inadvertently hurt many people—my parents, friends, colleagues, employees, husbands, family members, and even God. But I do not know how to change myself. I have cried out to God many times and asked Him for help. Then, on February 18, 2020, the Father spoke to me:

> "My beloved child, you have been visiting Me for six years now. Have you ever seen Me panic, worry, or lose control? I am always peaceful, calm, gentle, and soft-spoken. I created the heavens and the earth. All things are in subjection under My feet. There is nothing that I cannot handle. Therefore, you will always see peace in My manner.
>
> "You are My daughter. When you are harsh toward employees and worry about things, it shows you do not know who I am. The truth is that nothing you do will fall apart because I am behind you.
>
> "You are My child; you need not run around pushing people. You need not shout or be impatient. You need not act like a *drill sergeant*. All your strength should come from Me, not yourself. You will always be small and weak, but I am strong. I am your source of strength. Therefore, do not be afraid. It is easier for the Holy Spirit to help you when you are weak. He lives inside of you; He is your Helper.
>
> "The beauty of a woman is gentle and submissive. She is a hidden person of the heart with a precious and quiet spirit. She finds peace in Me. That is the true beauty of a woman,

a leader, and a child of Mine. Be patient with yourself, be patient with others, and be patient with Me!"

Let your adorning be the hidden person of the heart with the imperishable beauty of a gentle and quiet spirit, which in God's sight is very precious.

—1 Peter 3:4 ESV

Part Six

Holy Spirit— My Dance Partner

Meeting the Holy Spirit in Person

Beloved readers, we read about the Holy Spirit in the Bible. We have heard about Him in sermons. We sing songs about Him, and most Christians are baptized in the Holy Spirit. But have you ever met the Holy Spirit in person? He is not a cloud in the sky, nor a vapor in the air. Although He can transform Himself into any shape or form that He wishes, He is a *real Person*. He is part of the Trinity. Like the Father and Jesus, He is God, and He has *a body* form.

One day, I asked the Holy Spirit, "Would you show Me Yourself? I have seen Jesus and the Father, but I have never seen You in person." Just a few minutes later, I saw a vision. I saw the Holy Spirit in the form of a Dove, and I saw myself in the form of a pink butterfly. We were flying in a vast galaxy. He circled around me at an extremely high speed to express His feelings toward me. I heard an inner voice saying, "Beloved child, I love you! I love you! I love you! My child, I love you!"

I was shocked and cried instantaneously. I had never felt such intense love before. It was not like any human love, but divine love— like fire, flood, and whirlwind. I do not know how to describe it to you, my beloved readers. It was *incredible!* I then cried with a loud voice, "Oh, my beloved Holy Spirit. I never knew that You loved me this much. Oh, Holy Spirit, I love You too." I was in shock. I was undone— *totally undone!*

A few days later, the Holy Spirit appeared to me in the shape of a Man. However, His body was translucent with blue light and flash. He looked like a computer-generated, state-of-the-art image. Waves of bluish-electric beams arced within His Being. There were no clothes, skins, or organs, just an iridescent blue light and luminous body. I could see His facial features. He was about eight feet tall and *extremely handsome!* I was fascinated by His remarkable beauty in this unique appearance.

My Interpretation of the Holy Spirit

This is how I interpret the triune God (Father, Son, Holy Spirit): The Father is like the movie producer, Jesus is like the protagonist (main star), and the Holy Spirit is like the screenplay writer and director.

It is the Holy Spirit who plans each scene, arranges all the characters, and directs their actions. This movie is not a movie that we see in the theater, but it is real-time. All creations and living beings are part of this movie. The Holy Spirit is the One who ordains all things.

This movie has a beginning and an end. It has good characters and bad characters. It has everlasting happiness (heaven) and eternal damnation (hell). The movie ends with Satan, his demons, and all unbelievers being cast into the lake of fire. But those who accept Jesus Christ as their Lord and Savior will go to heaven to be with God forever!

Another way to interpret the Trinity is: the Father is the Designer—all creations were His idea. Jesus is the Builder—with His own hands, all things were made. The Holy Spirit is the Life-Giver, who breathed the "breath of life" into all creatures. In other words, when the Father spoke what He wanted, Jesus constructed the universe based on the Father's utterance, and the Holy Spirit imparted life, intelligence, and wisdom into all living beings.

From the day I walked into Joan Hunter's healing service in 2014, met the Indonesian girl Melisa, received miracle healings, obtained deliverance (demons were cast out), and encountered Jesus and the

Father in heaven, the Holy Spirit carefully orchestrated all these movie scenes. Step by step, scene by scene, the Holy Spirit gingerly arranged everything. I did not understand then, but looking back on my life-changing events, I now know that all events occurred because of the Holy Spirit!

From February 2014 to June 2014, the Holy Spirit initiated my spiritual journey, and things happened rapidly:

- Accepted Jesus Christ as Lord and Savior
- Baptized in the Holy Spirit
- Healed of long-term depression
- Received the gift of speaking in tongues
- Opened my spiritual eyes by the Holy Spirit
- Encountered Jesus in heaven
- Delivered from eleven demons

All these miracles happened within the first four months of my spiritual journey. It seemed that the Holy Spirit was in a hurry to prepare me for God's assignments.

He Is My Mother, Father, Friend, and God

One day in 2016, I encountered some intense difficulties at work. I was under severe demonic attack through two of my bosses—to the point I could hardly get up and go to work. So, I took a day off. Heavy sadness troubled my soul, and I began sobbing uncontrollably.

Suddenly, Pastor Rudi from the Indonesian church texted me. I didn't even want to get up and reach the phone because I was in such deep sorrow. Reluctantly, I did.

"Ying, why are you crying?" he said.

"Pastor Rudi, how do you know I am crying?" I answered.

"The Holy Spirit just told me to call you. He asked me to comfort you," he replied.

Beloved readers, I was a baby Christian. I had very little understanding of the Holy Spirit at that time. Even though I read about Him and met Him a few times in person, I never really developed a personal relationship with Him. Thus, when the pastor texted me, I got goosebumps. I could feel the Holy Spirit standing next to me tangibly. When He saw me crying, He could not bear to see my tears, as if He felt my pain in Himself.

I dropped my phone on the kitchen floor and fell to my knees with a gut-wrenching cry, "Oh, Holy Spirit! I did not know you cared for me this much. I did not know you cared for me so personally. Oh, Holy Spirit, my dear Holy Spirit, I love You . . . I love You . . . I love You!"

Tears raced down my cheeks and dropped on the floor. I kept sobbing . . . more sobbing. I was deeply touched by the Holy Spirit's attention to detail. He cared about every drop of my tears. He felt all my pains and sorrows. When I mourn, *He cries too.* When my heart is broken, He feels the ache too. He is my Sympathizer, Helper, Teacher, and Physician. He is my Mother, Father, Friend, and God!

The Holy Spirit lives inside of me (see Romans 8:11). He sees everything I see. He feels everything I feel. Like a mother, He is always there to love, comfort, and care. Like a father, He is always there to listen, provide, and discipline. Although He is the most powerful One who raised Jesus from the dead, He is also the most tender-hearted Person who provides gentle love. He is a regal Gentleman, a kind Comforter, a patient Helper, and an awesome God!

> *The Spirit of God, who raised Jesus from the dead, lives in you. And just as God raised Christ Jesus from the dead, he will give life to your mortal bodies by this same Spirit living within you.*
>
> —Romans 8:11 NLT

> *[Jesus said,] I tell you the truth, it is to your advantage that I go away; for if I do not go away, the Helper (Comforter, Advocate, Intercessor—Counselor, Strengthener, Standby) will not come to you; but if I go, I will send Him (the Holy Spirit) to you [to be in close fellowship with you]. And He, when He comes, will convict the world about [the guilt of] sin [and the need for a Savior], and about righteousness, and about judgment:*
>
> —John 16:7–8 AMP

The Bible says that the Holy Spirit lives *in us,* He is *with us*, and comes *upon us*. What does it mean? It means that before we receive Jesus Christ as Lord and Savior, the Holy Spirit is working *in us* to convict our sins and lead us to Christ. Once we become the believers of Christ, the Holy Spirit will live *in us* to seal our redemption. He puts a stamp on us at the time of our rebirth—kind of like, "This one is Mine now! Sealed!"

He is *with us* means He was sent to the earth by the Father for both believers and unbelievers. Therefore, Christians should not think that the Holy Spirit is only with the believers.

When Bible ministers preach sermons or prophets release prophecies, the Holy Spirit will come *upon them* (see Acts 1:8). Once the sermon or prophecy is given, the Holy Spirit may not continually remain upon the preacher or prophet. In other words, when the Holy Spirit *comes up* someone, it is for ministry, prophecy, or preaching purposes only.

> *[Jesus said to His disciples,] You will receive power and ability when the Holy Spirit comes upon you; and you will be My witnesses [to tell people about Me] both in Jerusalem*

and in all Judea, and Samaria, and even to the ends of the earth.

—Acts 1:8 AMP

Our eternal death penalty was placed on us since Adam and Eve sinned in the Garden of Eden. The human race lost its divine nature as God originally intended. Therefore, by default, we will go to hell when we die. But Jesus paid our death penalty on the cross. He took our sins onto Himself and died in our place, so that we don't have to go to hell (see 2 Corinthians 5:21). As long as we receive Jesus Christ as our Lord and Savior, we will have everlasting life in heaven.

> God made Him [Christ] who knew no sin to be sin on our behalf, so that in Him we might become the righteousness of God.
>
> —2 Corinthians 5:21 BSB

The Holy Spirit was sent to *seal the redemption* that Jesus made on the cross. He is the *"guarantee,"* the *"first installment,"* and the *"down payment"* of what God has promised (eternal life) to humankind. God the Father put His stamp of ownership on us by giving us the Holy Spirit. In other words, the Holy Spirit is the *engagement ring* from God to the brides—the believers of Christ. The following scriptures describe precisely the purpose of the Holy Spirit for the believers.

> You were sealed with the Holy Spirit of promise, who is the guarantee of our inheritance.
>
> —Ephesians 1:13–14

> Do not grieve the Holy Spirit of God, by whom you were sealed for the day of redemption.
>
> —Ephesians 4:30

> *He [God] has identified us as his own by placing the Holy Spirit in our hearts as the first installment that guarantees everything he has promised us.*
>
> —2 Corinthians 1:22 NLT

There Is Only One Spirit in Us— the Holy Spirit

When we accept Jesus Christ as our Lord and Savior and are baptized in the Holy Spirit, our spirits join with the Holy Spirit—become *one spirit*. By this, we are confirmed by the Spirit that we are God's children—calling Him *"Abba, Father"* (see Romans 8:14).

> *Those who are led by the Spirit of God are the children of God. The Spirit you received does not make you slaves, so that you live in fear again; rather, the Spirit you received brought about your adoption to sonship. And by him we cry, "Abba, Father."*
>
> —Romans 8:14–15 NIV

Beloved readers, when I join with the Holy Spirit, there is only one spirit in me, not two spirits. In other words, at the time I was baptized in the Holy Spirit, my spirit joined with the Holy Spirit, became one spirit. Like I said in the previous chapter, the Holy Spirit is a layered Being—with unlimited layers. At the time of my rebirth, the Holy Spirit deposited a layer of Himself into me; then, our spirits become one. Likewise, first Corinthians 6:17 explains: *"Anyone joined to the Lord is one spirit with him"* (CSB).

Also, please understand this, the Holy Spirit is the Spirit of the Father and Jesus. Among the Trinity, there is only One Spirit, not three spirits.

"My Hidden Hero"— A Poem to the Holy Spirit

On December 24, 2017, I wrote the following poem to the Holy Spirit. I regard Him as a hidden Hero because the world sees Jesus, but not the Holy Spirit. He is invisible to our human eyes. However, He does mighty works behind the scenes. All things are ordained by the Holy Spirit. Without Him, no soul can live because our very breath comes from the Holy Spirit. If He stops breathing, *we will all die!*

My Hidden Hero

The Voice

When I was in the deepest darkness,
When I was in unbearable pain,
When I had no will to live,
I heard a voice.

A voice I had never heard before.
The voice stopped me from ending my life.
Whose voice was it?
Why did this voice care for me?

Lost

When I lost everything—marriage, job, and friends,
When I was in my innermost desolation,
When I lost all hope,

A mighty arm wrapped around me.

This arm I had never felt before.
It embraced me with gentle comfort.
Whose arm was it?
Why did this arm hug me?

Wandering

When I was wandering in the wildness,
When I was lost in the jungle,
When I was attacked by the wild beasts,
A sword came and protected me.

A blazing sword went before me in the jungle,
Piercing serpents and monsters.
Whose sword was it?
Why did this sword protect me?

Tears

When my face was drenched with tears,
When my soul was screaming for comfort,
When my heart was yearning for ease,
A tear dropped on my face.

Why did someone cry for me?
Why did someone grieve for me?
Whose tear was it?
Why did someone sympathize with my pain?

The Power

When I was chained by depression,
When I was tormented by demons,
When I was suffocated by death,
A power fell on me and healed me!

A power I had never felt before—
Mighty and remarkable.
Where did this power come from?
Why would someone free me from demonic slavery?

The Dance

When I closed my eyes—
Looking through the eyes of my heart,
I saw a dance taking place in heaven.
A magnificent Figure held me on the dance floor.

This kind of dance I had never seen before—
Splendid and magnificent!
Who was this noble and striking dance Partner?
Why did He dance with me?

It Was You

The voice, the arm, the sword,
The tear, the power, and the dance,
Were none but You, beloved Holy Spirit—
My Protector, my Comforter, and my Friend!

It was You all along,
Watching over me with tender loving care;
Defending me with Your mighty power;
And refusing to let the enemies snatch me away.

Why

Why did You voice over me?
Why did You wrap Your arms around me?
Why did You protect me with the sword?
Why did You shed tears for me?

JESUS, MY FOREVER LOVE

Why did You heal me?
Why did You dance with me?
Why did you pay attention to me?
It is because You created me!

Forever Yours

Ever since You came into my life,
I fell in love with You.
I long to have fellowship with You.
I yearn for Your love!

I become Your butterfly.
I become Your dance partner.
I become Your follower.
I am all Yours, forever Yours!

You Were with Him

When Jesus was on the earth,
You were with Him thirty-three years.
You were with Him in every step and turn.
You anointed Him to promote the Kingdom of God.

You were with Him when He was scourged.
You were with Him when He cried for help.
You were with Him when He was on the cross.
And You resurrected Him from the grave.

Hidden Hero

Spirit of the living God,
You have been the hidden Hero to mankind.
Even though the world cannot see You,
Nothing can be achieved without You!

You give colors to the flowers.
You give breath to all living souls.
You confirm the adoption of the Father's children.
You seal our eternal redemption!

My Wish

On this very Christmas night,
I long for Your presence.
I yearn to speak to Your heart.
I desire to see Your face!

Let my songs touch Your heart.
Let my praises kiss Your countenance.
Let my worships bring You joy.
Let me be ever close to You!

Please

I know You hold the key to heaven.
It is You who bring Father's children home.
Would You consider me tonight?
Would You bring me to heaven for a visit?

I yearn to see my Daddy.
I ache to see my Husband, Jesus.
I wish to see You, my beautiful Holy Spirit,
For I am in love with all of You!

Merry Christmas, beloved Holy Spirit!

Your little pink butterfly,

Ying

One thing I can tell you, beloved readers, the Holy Spirit is an *incredibly emotional* Person. Within the Trinity, He is the One who carries the artistic anointings. According to prophetess Kat Kerr, heaven calls Him the "Holy Spirit" or the "Drama King" because music, art, literature, dance, and acting were all created by Him. He is the source of all artistic talents.

The Holy Spirit Is Exceptionally Handsome

A few weeks after my first encounter with the Holy Spirit, He appeared to me in a human form. With my spiritual eyes, I could see Him clearly.

The Holy Spirit is about eight feet tall. He has curly brown hair down to His shoulders. He has a pointed nose and a neatly trimmed beard. He is about forty years old. The color of His eyes is a green-blue combination. He is *remarkably handsome* with an incredibly gentle manner. He has some of the Father and Jesus' character traits, yet He still possesses His own distinct charisma.

The Holy Spirit's power is beyond human comprehension, His patience and tenderness are *superb*, and His knowledge and wisdom are *immeasurable*. Even though He is the *mightiest* in the whole universe, His voice is exceptionally soft with a small whisper. Within the Godhead, Jesus is the Image of the invisible Father, and the Holy Spirit is the Manifester of God's power.

His Dance Is Better Than the Blackpool Champions

Most of the time, the Holy Spirit wears a white garment; sometimes, He wears blue. But when we dance, He often wears formal ballroom dance attire. During my worship time, I frequently see myself dancing with Him.

We have danced in various places, such as celestial planets, cosmic stars, or green meadows in heavenly places. The Holy Spirit has very long legs and moves with grace and elegance. He is the best Dancer—far better than the Blackpool Champions. Blackpool Dance Festival is the world's most famous ballroom dance competition. It occurs annually at the Winter Gardens, Blackpool, England. The dancers in this competition are the best of the best in the world, but the Holy Spirit's dance surpasses these fabulous champions.

I have had one-year ballroom dance lessons and have participated in dance competitions. Some of my dance teachers, such as Slawek Sochacki, are national champions. But I have never seen such an outstanding Dancer like the Holy Spirit. One may wonder why? It is because *He created dance*. All artistic geniuses are from Him.

As He leads, I submit myself into His arms and follow His hand signals. I usually wear long, striking dance dresses, and He wears classy dance attire. He is tall and masculine; I am petite and slender—what a contrast and perfect pair. His hands are firm, and directions are clear. There is no stepping on each other's toes. He always lifts His chin in a regal and noble position—a perfect ballroom dance posture. He is *exceptionally fabulous* and *remarkably splendid!*

Dancing with the Holy Spirit is like dazzling elegantly on the dance floor—graceful and stylish. Sometimes, our choreography is similar to Waltz, Foxtrot, Quickstep, and Tango; other times, our composition is freestyle. His dance moves are fluid and agile; they flow with syncopation and rhythmical patterns. The amazing thing is that I did not take many classical ballroom lessons. I learned primarily Latin dance, such as Rumba, Cha-Cha, Samba, Paso Doble, and Jive. However, when the Holy Spirit dances in classical ballroom dance, picking up the choreography is easy for me because He leads well. He truly is a *fantastic Dance Instructor.*

JESUS, MY FOREVER LOVE

Figure Skating with the Holy Spirit

*M*any times, the Holy Spirit and I have danced on ice—like figure skating in the Olympics. The strange thing is that I have never learned ice skating; how in the world do I know figure skating? It is all because of the Holy Spirit. When I am with Him, *all things are possible.* I am astonished to see myself doing all kinds of professional figure skaters' techniques, such as: axel jump, layback spin, rotational jump, camel spin, counter turn, death spiral, and pattern dance (see Figure 18).

Figure 18: Figure skating with the Holy Spirit.

During ice dance, the Holy Spirit seldom says anything. He expresses His feelings and love through steps and rhythms. While our hearts are silently merged, all I can hear is the sound of our skate blades on ice and His warm breath on my face. These are heartwarming and unforgettable moments. As His dance partner, I simply accept the flow of His love and enjoy the romantic moment. There is no greater joy than skating with the Holy Spirit!

Beloved readers, dancing with the Holy Spirit is not just for fun or excitement. It has profound spiritual meanings. It is about oneness, synchronization, and *personal intimacy* with God Almighty.

My affection for the Holy Spirit is a bit different than my affection toward the Father and Jesus. How can I describe it? It is the combination of a daughter's love for a Father and a lover's love for a Husband, because the Holy Spirit is the Spirit of the Father and Jesus.

My Poetry to the Holy Spirit

Being a Christian for eight years, I have written about thirty love letters and poems to express my special affections for the Holy Spirit. Here is one of the poems I wrote on November 25, 2021 (Thanksgiving). As I said before, whenever Holy Spirit and I danced, we spoke very few words—only silently exchanged love between us. The Holy Spirit can be very talkative, but He is also profound with pure inner beauty. Everything I have written, either poems or letters, comes from actual encounters with Him.

Silent Love

All that can be heard is the sound of skating blades,
Near the snow mountains.
He holds my hand,
We are figure skating in silent love.

All that can be heard is the sound of flapping wings,
In the dazzling cosmos.
A white Dove and a pink butterfly,
Encircling each other in silent love.

JESUS, MY FOREVER LOVE

All that can be heard is the sound of dancing shoes,
On a floor of glittering stars.
He holds me in His arms—Tango, Foxtrot, and Waltz,
Immersing our hearts in silent love.

All that can be heard is the sound of brushing grass,
On a lush green meadow.
He embraces me passionately,
We are dancing in silent love.

We have danced on snow mountains,
We have danced in fluffy clouds.
We have danced on spectacular rainbows.
We have exchanged our silent love in many galaxies.

Our love is sweet and heart-melting—
Fervent, flaming, and profound!
Causing stars to sing,
And cosmos to clap hands.

There is a romance between us—
Like lovers' attraction.
There is a profound love between us—
Like Father and daughter's affection.

I am in love with Him—
The Spirit of the living God.
I adore and worship Him—
The Lover of my soul!

There are times He is a Gentleman,
Whispering in His children's ears,
Gently teaching and guiding,
Showing motherly tenderness to His created beings.

Yet, there are times He is a Drill Sergeant,
Training His earthly armies,
Equipping His people for fierce battles,
Fighting with demons and the devil.

There are times He is a College Professor,
Teaching wisdom, knowledge, and understanding.
Preparing His children for the eternal Kingdom,
And get ready to serve the everlasting King Jesus.

There are times He appears as a Destroyer,
Vanquishing His enemies with might and power,
Blowing them like tumbleweeds,
And melting them like wax.

Yet, there are times He is a Beautician,
Preparing the brides for the Bridegroom-King,
Teaching us how to please Him,
And beautify us to fulfill King Jesus' desire.

There are times He is in the whirlwind.
There are times He is in the fire.
There are times He is in the storm.
Yet, there are times He is in the gentle wind.

He is everywhere.
He is all-knowing and all-powerful.
He is my Father, Mother, Friend, and Teacher.
He is my hidden Hero!

On this Thanksgiving night,
On behalf of the entire human race,
We thank You, beloved Holy Spirit
For all Your marvelous works and mighty wonders!

I thank You for being my best Friend,
My dance Partner,
My wonderful Teacher,
And My great God!

Happy Thanksgiving, my beloved Holy Spirit!

Your pink butterfly,

Ying

On November 22, 2018 (Thanksgiving), I wrote the following poem to the Holy Spirit. Like Jesus, the Holy Spirit is a very romantic Person who holds remarkable artistic talent and ingenious creativity. I am always thankful for the artistic gifts He gave me—music, singing, dance, acting, painting, design, etc.

Beloved readers, have you noticed that all the figures, including the cover page painting in this book, were done by myself? Thanks to the Holy Spirit who gives me this artistic talent.

Autumn Dance

Walking in a deep forest with You,
Beholding sun rays through the leaves—
Red, yellow, and orange,
Vibrant autumn beauty!

Taking a deep breath—
Inhaling Your *breath of life*.

YING FLYNN

Love flows in my veins,
Soaking in Your presence.

As the leaves fall,
Forming a colorful dance floor.
You draw me gently into Your arms,
With divine love on Your countenance.

My left hand softly touches Your right shoulder.
My right hand surrenders to Your left hand.
Promenade walk, outside swivel, rock turns,
We are dancing on the carpet of autumn leaves.

As we twist and turn,
Sun rays are dazzling on our faces.
Birds are singing; leaves are clapping,
They are cheering for our intimate loving.

You hold my hand firmly;
Then You let it go gently.
You lift me up in the air;
Then You put me down gracefully.

Leaves are falling—
Red, yellow, and orange.
Forest is echoing—
Fabulous, marvelous dancing.

Oh, Spirit of the living God,
My hidden Hero,
My Father and my Teacher,
My Friend and my dance Partner,

Keep dancing,
Do not stop.
Let us dance deep into the forest.

JESUS, MY FOREVER LOVE

Let us dazzle with the autumn coloring.

Oh, how brilliant is the color of our faces;
How beautiful is the color of our hearts;
How pleasing is the color of our love;
All blend perfectly in this autumn painting.

My beloved Holy Spirit,
My fabulous dance Partner,
My best Friend,
And the Love of my soul,

My spiritual journey has just begun.
And the road is bumpy.
Please hold me through every step.
And guide me toward everlasting light!

Let our dance never stop.
Let our love never cease.
Let our friendship never end.
And let our hearts never separate.

On this Thanksgiving Day,
I am clinging to You.
Refusing to end our dance,
On this colorful and loving road!

Happy Thanksgiving, my beloved Holy Spirit,

Hugs and Kisses,

Your little dance partner,

Ying

Takes Two to Dance, Takes Two to Play Piano Duet

Throughout eight years of Bible study, I have learned that without the Holy Spirit, I can accomplish *nothing*. Even when Jesus was on the earth, He had to depend on the Holy Spirit. It was the Holy Spirit who anointed Jesus for His ministry. It was the Holy Spirit who gave Jesus the power to heal the sick, cleanse the lepers, and cast out demons. It was the Holy Spirit who raised Jesus from the dead. The Holy Spirit is *Jesus unlimited*. If Jesus, being God, needed the Holy Spirit, how much more do we need the Holy Spirit.

With our fallen nature, we will always seek pleasures of fleshly desire. However, the Bible says: *"Let the Holy Spirit guide your lives. Then you won't be doing what your sinful nature craves"* (Galatians 5:16 NLT). Most of the time, our sinful nature desires to do evil, but the Spirit wants us to do good. What the Holy Spirit desires are just the opposite of our carnal desires. These two are constantly fighting against each other. Just as Galatians 5:17 says, *"The flesh lusts against the Spirit, and the Spirit against the flesh; and these are contrary to one another."*

I am a strong-willed child. One of my biggest problems is letting my flesh dominate my life and not surrendering to the Holy Spirit. The Father and Jesus have repeatedly instructed me: "You *must* walk with the Holy Spirit. He will teach you all things. Do precisely what He tells you. Obey His voice at all times. He will guide you to all truth."

Walking with the Holy Spirit is like ballroom dancing. It takes two participants—the male leads and the female follows. The Holy Spirit leads, and I ought to follow.

Walking with the Holy Spirit is also like playing the piano. It takes two hands to play harmony. The right hand plays the melody and the left plays the chords. The right hand controls the central theme and the left acts as the complement. The Holy Spirit must be the right hand, and

I must be the left. He plays the melody, and I play the chords. He must be the central theme, and I must be the complement.

Nevertheless, this is not so in my case. All my life, I have been striving for success with my own strength. I have been like a wild horse, untamed and untrained. Even after becoming a believer, I still tend to run ahead of the Holy Spirit and do things my way. But frequently, I end up exhausted and unsuccessful. With my strong-minded and unyielding will, I can hardly hear the voice of the Holy Spirit—not to mention walking in harmony with Him.

Thinking back on my ballroom dance class, the teacher had an issue with me. He told me frequently, "Ying, you have a bad habit. You always try to lead. In ballroom dancing, the man must lead, and the woman must follow. It is very hard to teach you when you keep leading. So let me be the lead!"

To correct my bad habit, I forced myself to work with the Holy Spirit by initiating a daily conversation with Him (although I missed it many times). Routinely, I will sing a few songs to the Holy Spirit, such as "Come Holy Spirit, I Need You" or "Holy Spirit Thou Art Welcome in This Place." As soon as I start singing, almost 100 percent of the time, He will come immediately.

Through my spiritual eyes, I can see Him physically sitting next to me and ready to help. Other times, He speaks to me in a small voice. Once I present my questions to Him, I just keep quiet and listen to His voice. As soon as He speaks, I will quickly type His response on my laptop. It is always a two-way conversation, just like talking to an earthly father. There is no repetitive prayer language or buzzwords, just down-to-earth dialogue. The Holy Spirit loves to help His children; it was for this reason that He was sent to the earth by the Father.

On October 26, 2020, there was a massive wildfire near my house. Ninety thousand people were evacuated from their homes, and some firefighters were critically injured. Almost all my neighbors were gone. They urged me to leave the house. At that critical and frightening moment, I cried out to the Holy Spirit, "What should I do, Holy Spirit? Please tell me!" He immediately answered, "This fire will not come to your house. Do not panic!" Thus, I stayed in the house during the two days of evacuation—not to prove that I disbelieved the authority, but rather, I trusted the Supreme Authority.

Every so often, my heart is hardened with anger, hurt, and bitterness. Yet, after talking with the Holy Spirit, my heart becomes soft. The Holy Spirit can turn anger into happiness, pain into forgiveness, and bitterness into sweetness. He truly is a good Comforter, an excellent Teacher, and a mighty God.

The Holy Spirit Is Hilarious!

The Holy Spirit is a humorous Person. He tells jokes to me all the time. For example, I once said, "Holy Spirit, I am a little bit grumpy today." He then said with humor, "Really, just today?" And I said, "Oh, come on, Holy Spirit, give me a little credit. I am not grumpy all the time." We both laughed.

Other times I said, "Holy Spirit, I was too rough on my friend today. I should have been gentler with him." He noted with teasing, "Since when do you know gentleness?" With my naughty face, I said, "Oh, come on, Holy Spirit, please be nice!" We both chuckled.

Sometimes I say to Him, "Holy Spirit, where are your jokes today?" He will say, "I am running out of jokes." I laugh and laugh.

There are times when I cook something delicious, such as chicken stir-fry, Chinese dumplings, or spinach cheese ravioli, the Holy Spirit will say, "Wow, that looks so good," as though He wants to try some.

I laugh a lot in my house. I am sure my neighbors would wonder, "Why is she laughing by herself?" I have been the only one in my house for twelve years. No one can ever imagine that I am laughing with the

Holy Spirit. I can't stop giggling when He speaks because He truly is a *hilarious Person*.

Beloved readers, even though our God is high and enthroned in heaven, He is the most approachable Person. Unlike some religious leaders on the earth (Popes, for example—making themselves unapproachable and prestigious), our God is extremely humble. He is the Owner of the universe, yet, He is also the most down-to-earth God.

> *[Jesus said,] Whoever wants to be a leader among you must be your servant, and whoever wants to be first among you must become your slave.*
>
> —Matthew 20:26–27 NLT

I believe wholeheartedly that the culture within the Godhead (Trinity) is *servant heart, sacrificial love,* and *yielding as a slave* to one another. The Trinity will not teach us anything that They Themselves do not practice.

"I Like Your Hair Down"

The Holy Spirit is a very personal God, and He observes each little detail about His sons and daughters. One day, as I was driving, out of the blue, He said, "I like your hair down. It looks better this way. Very pretty!" I said, "Really? Holy Spirit, that's very sweet of You." Habitually, I like to tie my hair up and hardly ever put them down. Obviously, the Holy Spirit has His own preference for my hair. He knows exactly how many hairs are on my head (see Luke 12:6). He cares about all the tiny details and idiosyncrasies of His beloved child.

> *[Jesus said,] What is the price of five sparrows—two copper coins? Yet God does not forget a single one of them. And the very hairs on your head are all numbered. So don't be*

afraid; you are more valuable to God than a whole flock of sparrows.

—Luke 12:6–7 NLT

It is hard to believe that the Holy Spirit has trillions of angels, billions of humans, and innumerable living creatures to care for, yet still pays detailed attention to each of us. From the grand scale of the cosmos, I am smaller than a single particle of dust. But the Holy Spirit makes me feel like I am the most important child in the world. He is such an affectionate, tender, and caring God.

Every day, the Holy Spirit searches to-and-fro throughout the earth, seeking whom He can count on, whom He can dance with, and whom He can play the piano duet. He gave Planet Earth for humans to manage. He needs us to act on His behalf and do His biddings. If we do not know how to cooperate with the Holy Spirit, it is very hard for Him to use us. This is why Jesus said, *"Many are called, but few are chosen"* (Matthew 22:14). This scripture means: many people are called by the Holy Spirit to do God's will on the earth, but only a few have responded to His calling.

He Talks to Me in Subtle Voice or Dreams

Most of the time, the Holy Spirit communicates with me by putting things in my head or speaking to me in a very subtle voice. He talks to me throughout the day, such as telling me to watch a certain prophet on YouTube, go to a particular Christian conference, or watch a specific sermon. Other times, He talks to me through dreams.

Oftentimes, when the Holy Spirit tells me something through dreams, if I do not take action right away, He will repeat the same dream until I repent and act. For example, every time I lost focus, got distracted, or went in the wrong direction, He would repeatedly give me warnings through a series of similar dreams.

Dream 1: Lost in the College Campus

One time, after I finished a class, I could not find my way back to the dormitory. I had been walking the same way for many months, but this time, for some reason, I was totally lost. I walked in circles around the campus and completely lost my memory of where I lived.

Dream 2: Lost on the Highway

I was driving . . . suddenly realized I could not find the most familiar highway needed to get back home. Instead, I ended up in a totally strange place, which I had never been before. When I asked the people around, no one knew the city where I lived. I drove for hours on the road and could not find my way home.

Dream 3: Lost at a Shopping Mall

In this dream, I took a bus to a shopping mall, where I had been hundreds of times. But this time, when I was ready to go home, I could not remember which bus to take, nor did I remember where I lived. I was completely lost and running around aimlessly.

When these dreams are given to me, I know the Holy Spirit is trying to tell me that I am off the track. He is calling me to get back on the right road with Him.

Beloved readers, we walk on a very thin line every day. If we are not careful, we will walk into hell. Jesus said:

You can enter God's Kingdom only through the narrow gate. The highway to hell is broad, and its gate is wide for the many who choose that way. But the gateway to life [heaven] is very narrow and the road is difficult, and only a few ever find it.

—Matthew 7:13–14 NLT

Jesus also said in prophet Rick Joyner's book *The Call*:

The whole world still lies in the power of the evil one, and you walk on the edge of hell every day. Through the midst of it there is a path of life. There are deep ditches on either side of the path of life, so you must not deviate from the narrow way.

No one can find his own way out of those ditches. Following your own way is how you fall into them, and your own way will never lead you out. I am the only way out. When you fall, do not waste your time trying to figure everything out, for you will only sink deeper into the mire. Just ask for help. I am your Shepherd, and I will always help you when you call on Me. [1]

Parrot Birds on My Front Yard's Tree

*F*requently, during my prayer time, I have been saying, "Father, please don't take me home yet, for I cannot face You at this time. Other people have many fruits (spiritual accomplishments) to offer when they go home (heaven), but I have nothing to offer, for I have not produced any spiritual fruit yet. On the judgment day, You may say, 'You lazy and wicked servant.'" Every time I say this, I can sense God is not pleased with me.

In late January 2022, I noticed a problem that bothered me for a while. Every day, when I opened my front door, I saw many berries on my porch from the tree in front of my house. I supposed it might have been the ravens who did it. Ravens are considered bad luck in some countries. These berries were black and released rich oil that stained the stairs of my front entrance. I was annoyed by the mess they made.

Strangely, however, the same kind of tree in front of my neighbors' doors was not eaten by the ravens, even though their trees looked bigger and yielded more berries. Day after day, I went out to clean up the mess on my porch. I kept uttering with frustration, yet amusingly, "This is the devil's crime against me."

One day, my best friend Shirin (also my neighbor) sent me a video. She captured the truth of what was messing up my front porch. In the video, I saw a group of parrots eating these berries. Their feathers were greenish with a red spot on the head area—quite beautiful. I was stunned. Parrots did not usually come to the area where I lived—it was a dense-residential community. These birds typically resided in non-residential areas. Instantly, I realized the meaning behind this phenomenon.

God tried to tell me, "You do bear spiritual fruits. Do not speak down on yourself. I send my angels (parrots) to eat the fruits from your tree to show you that you do have many fruits to offer for My Kingdom." I was amazed by God's humor. He used parrots to rebuke me.

Parrot birds are viewed as divine creatures by some Asian nations. They represent longevity, freedom, liberty, and beauty. Spiritually speaking, parrots symbolize the power of our mouth—voice, communication, etc. They also signify elevation, advancement, and wisdom. Some paintings from the Middle-Age era epitomized parrot as the virgin birth of Jesus Christ. These birds appeared as the eye-witnesses of the fallen mankind who rejected God.

This incident also told me that the Holy Spirit tried to encourage me to continue praying, "Do not give up, pray unceasingly, like the parrots. While nations and people are masked (silenced) by the enemy (manufactured Coronavirus), speak the truth loudly like the parrots."

As I mentioned before, God commissioned me to quit my job in October 2020. The sole purpose was for me to pray for the presidential election, to drain the swamps worldwide, and to uproot evils on the earth. The more I prayed—the greater evil I discovered, the less strength I had, because the level of wicked things done by Satan's followers was overwhelming. I was just about to give up praying; God sent parrots to tell me not to do so. The Holy Spirit is exceptionally humorous.

Vengeance Is Mine, I Will Repay

The Bible says: *"Beloved, never avenge yourselves, but leave it to the wrath of God, for it is written, 'Vengeance is mine, I will repay, says the Lord'"* (Romans 12:19 ESV). I had meditated on this verse many times, but had never experienced it in real life, until . . .

After coming back from Heidi Baker's missionary school and evangelical outreach in Brazil, I desperately needed a job. Eventually, I found one in a different city, which was about eight hours away from where I lived. I had to move to that city and rent an apartment. However, two months into the job, I got fired because one of my employees reported me to HR for sharing Jesus Christ at the workplace.

Getting fired was difficult, but a sequence of problems that followed made the situation even worse. I had signed a thirteen-month lease for the apartment and took a $5,000 relocation fee from the company. If I departed from the job within a year, I would have to pay back all the relocation fees. I would also pay $3,500 for the early termination of the apartment. In addition, I had to hire a moving company to move all my furniture back, which would cost me another $2,500.

I was devastated and did not know how to cope with the situation. I cried out to God, but I did not hear any word from Him—maybe I was too emotional to listen to His voice. But in the middle of the devastation, a series of miracles happened.

First, the company decided not to collect the relocation fees. I was shocked. Then the apartment manager said, "You can leave the apartment now. We will send you the bill in about a week." However, after two weeks, I called the apartment more than ten times about the $3,500 bill. Each time, they told me that they could not find my record in their system. They did not know what to do. I was puzzled. How could it be? How could they lose my record? It should be in their computer system. I even requested to speak to their manager. To my astonishment, the manager said, "Since we cannot find your record, you do not need to pay the fine." *How strange!* I was perplexed.

When I contacted the moving company, they were surprised that I wanted to move back so soon. I told them what had happened. Their manager showed deep sympathy for my situation. He decided to charge me only the minimum price, and I was relieved by his kindness.

Better still, after two months of leaving the company, I received a $2,000 check. There was no letter of explanation in the envelope, just the check. I was perplexed even more.

By then, I suddenly realized that the Holy Spirit had been working behind the scenes for these miracles. He showed me the true meaning of *"Vengeance is Mine; I will repay!"*

Beloved readers, the company was not wrong. They did have a policy prohibiting religious discussions and sharing personal beliefs at the workplace. I indeed shared Jesus Christ and the gospel with many of my employees and peers. And I indeed violated their policies, but I followed God's policies!

I was so eager to share the gospel. I totally lost my mind because I was in love with Jesus. I wanted everyone to be saved. I risked my job to save souls. When HR questioned me, the lady grilled me about speaking in tongues. There was such a strange look on her face as if I was an eccentric creature. She investigated all my employees and peers—almost like I was a criminal.

No wonder the scripture says, *"All who desire to live a godly life in Christ Jesus will be persecuted"* (2 Timothy 3:12 ESV). Jesus said, *"You will be hated by all for My name's sake. But he who endures to the end will be saved"* (Matthew 10:22).

Even though I lost my job and was attacked by the enemy, God defended me. He slapped the devil's face by rewarding me with many blessings. What an awesome God I serve!

From 2014 until now, I have always prayed salvation for all my employees, peers, and bosses wherever I worked. I have declared Christ's redemption to every leader—from CEOs to lower-level managers. The company I have worked for has 125,000 employees. Thus, the list of leaders is in thousands, but I have declared that they will all receive Jesus Christ as Lord and Savior.

I frequently put their names in my prayer so that the angels can go after them. One day, if they indeed accept Jesus Christ as Lord and Savior, they will see me in heaven and thank me for praying for their salvation.

The Holy Spirit Takes Ownership of a Human Body

> *[Jesus said,] I will ask the Father and he will give you another Savior, the Holy Spirit of Truth, who will be to you a friend just like me—and he will never leave you. The world won't receive him because they can't see him or know him. But you know him intimately because he remains with you and will live inside you.*
>
> —John 14:16–17 TPT

Beloved readers, what does it mean that the *Holy Spirit lives inside me*? It means that at the time of my rebirth into Christ and being baptized in the Holy Spirit, my body was no longer mine, but God's. Jesus purchased it with His blood. My old body had been co-crucified with Jesus Christ and died (see Galatians 2:20). The new body I live in now does not belong to me anymore; rather, God lives through me.

> *[Apostle Paul said,] I have been crucified with Christ [that is, in Him I have shared His crucifixion]; it is no longer I who live, but Christ lives in me. The life I now live in the body I live by faith [by adhering to, relying on, and completely trusting] in the Son of God, who loved me and gave Himself up for me.*
>
> —Galatians 2:20 AMP

Ideally, upon my consent, the Holy Spirit would take over the ownership of my rebirthed body and perform His will through it. I should only be a shell, but He is the core and makes all the decisions. As Apostle Paul said:

> *Do you not know that your body is a temple of the Holy Spirit who is within you, whom you have [received as a gift] from God, and that you are not your own [property]? You were bought with a price [you were actually purchased with the precious blood of Jesus and made His own]. So then, honor and glorify God with your body.*
>
> —1 Corinthians 6:19–20 AMP

Nevertheless, if the Holy Spirit dwells in me, how come I am still struggling with pride, selfishness, bitterness, unforgiveness, jealousy, impurity, etc. This is because my old self (the fallen nature) does not want to give up and surrender to the Holy Spirit. It fights with Him constantly (see Romans 8:6).

> *The mind of the flesh is death [both now and forever—because it pursues sin]; but the mind of the Spirit is life and peace [the spiritual well-being that comes from walking with God—both now and forever]; the mind of the flesh [with its sinful pursuits] is actively hostile to God. It does not submit itself to God's law, since it cannot, and those who are in the flesh [living a life that caters to sinful appetites and impulses] cannot please God.*
>
> —Romans 8:6–8 AMP

The Bible keeps telling us, *"Do not grieve the Holy Spirit of God"* (Ephesians 4:30). This is because our flesh is continually fighting with the Spirit of God. Many Christians, myself included, are unwilling to fully submit to the Holy Spirit after being born again. We still stubbornly harbor the old carnal nature. Although the Holy Spirit lives in us, our old self is relentlessly in conflict with His will, which grieves Him tremendously.

On the cross, our sins are indeed forgiven through the blood of Jesus Christ, but our fleshly nature (lustful, sensual desires) still exists. It is not our sin that the Holy Spirit is after, but our carnal nature—*self*.

Is it possible for one to give up self and let the Holy Spirit take over completely? It is absolutely possible—Jesus is the perfect example. He *"was in all points tempted as we are, yet without sin"* (Hebrews 4:15). Nonetheless, it is not easy to give up self entirely and surrender to the Holy Spirit. Throughout history, only a few believers actually reached the point as Jesus did, while the majority of Christ believers are still struggling with carnality and sensuality.

In October 2020, God told me to resign from work and pray for the 2020 U.S. presidential election and spiritual battles in the unseen realms. At that time, more than 80 percent of U.S. voters supported President Trump. I thought it was a done deal. God's chosen one (Donald J. Trump) would be reelected. Hence, I wondered why God asked me to even leave my job and pray. Not until later do we learn the truth—the election was violently stolen by the deep state and wicked cabals (I call them satanic agents).

The election result infuriated me. I could not understand why God allowed this crime happened to America. Nevertheless, to obey God, I did manage to pray for more than a year and engage in spiritual battles daily. By December 2021, I finally wanted to give up. Out of my frustration, I said to God, "I give up! I don't want to pray anymore! You have told many prophets that President Donald J. Trump will be restored soon. But for more than a year now, I have not seen anything happening. I quit!" God did not say anything at that moment, but simply asked me to trust Him.

Interestingly enough, three days later, I received a package—a book titled *Intercessor* by Norman Grubb. It is the story of Rees Howells, a devoted missionary and a mighty intercessor of God. I finished the book in two days. By then realized that the book was sent to me by the Holy Spirit through a beloved Christian sister, Rebecca.

In preparing Rees Howells to be an intercessor and missionary, the Holy Spirit purged all the fallen natures (self) out of Rees. His testimony cut to my heart. At that point, I realized that the Holy Spirit—through the story of Rees—wanted to deal with my "I quit" syndrome. He used this book to convict my lack of faith, trust, patience, and endurance. He meant to tell me that my flesh was too strong. It needed to be toned down and yield to Him. The Holy Spirit intended to purge "self" out of me, and let Him have total possession of my being, so that He could use it for the Kingdom's purposes.

Through the book, I have truly understood the meaning—the Holy Spirit takes ownership of a human body:

- The Holy Spirit will never take possession of one's body without permission.
- Once permission is given, the Holy Spirit takes full control of the person's body, and the person is no longer allowed to have his or her own desire.
- As soon as the Holy Spirit comes in, that person *must go out!*
- The Holy Spirit comes in as God. Therefore, He will not tolerate human carnality and ambition—they must be purged.
- The Holy Spirit will not share His will with that person's will—no co-existence.
- Every bit of fleshly desire must be crucified. Every stronghold that conflicts with the law of God must go to the cross—such as pride, self-righteousness, selfishness, self-ambition, etc., until there is no *"self"* left.

Beloved readers, very few Christians have given the Holy Spirit full possession of their bodies (temples). Most of us only give Him some room to operate through our bodies. We are still indulging the lusts of our flesh and grieving the Spirit. However, people like Apostle Paul, Rees Howells, etc., have truly surrendered their temples to the Holy Spirit.

Jesus said, *"Many are called (invited, summoned), but few are chosen"* (Matthew 22:14 AMP). For a long time, I have been pondering the meaning of this scripture. Not until now have I come to realize its meaning. All human beings are called and ordained by God to do His Kingdom business on the earth. But only a few people have ever devoted themselves to God's calling and allowed the Holy Spirit to fully operate through their bodies.

After reading the book, the *"I quit"* tantrum was gone. I realized how stubborn my flesh was. I knelt down before God and asked Him for forgiveness. I now am eager to crucify my flesh and ready for the purging process. I know it will be painful, but I have made my choice. I no longer desire the ownership of my body. I want the Holy Spirit to take over completely. Everything I say, do, or act must come from Him, not me!

My Mishpachah

The definition of *"Mishpachah"* in Yiddish means *"Jewish family"* by blood or by marriage. I do not have a family in America. My parents passed away a long time ago, and my sister and brothers are all in China. So, when I married my husband in America, his parents had become my parents, and I loved them like my own. However, after the divorce, they faded away from my life.

For twelve years, I have not had a single person living with me. However, during this long and lonely time, I have found my heavenly *family*—God (Father), Jesus (Husband), and Holy Spirit (Friend). They are my true blood-related *Mishpachah*. I talk to them all the time—while cooking, driving, showering, or in the bathroom (which I should not do). They are more real than humans to me.

Almost always, when I close my eyes, waiting on Them in my prayer room, I can see all three of Them. In some cases, I see Them all together in the Father's garden. Other times, I see myself walking with the Father in His garden, hugging Jesus in a different place, and dancing with the Holy Spirit in another place—*all simultaneously*. Occasionally, we dance together, doing circle dance. Other times, when my worship reaches its crescendo, my body will join with all three of Them into One, just as Jesus said, *"I am in My Father, and you in Me, and I in you"* (John 14:20). I once saw the following vision:

All four of us (Father, Jesus, Holy Spirit, and I) flew in the cosmic galaxies. We were all in the form of eagles. As we soared and cruised in the vast celestial space, we suddenly merged and became a swirling cylinder—made of glowing lights and blazing twirls. Then this glittering cylinder split into four brilliant spheres—each entwined with vortex flames and luminous rings.

Then, with a booming sound, we divided into billions of multicolored particles, which illuminated the space with glowing lights. Then with another booming sound, these colored particles turned into four colored strings (red, green, blue, yellow). Slowly, each string came toward one another and interweaved into one thick cord.

This phenomenon tells me that God can manifest *oneness* with His children in any shape or form. He showed me the spectacular beauty of *togetherness* with His glorious Beings. Once His glory is in me, it does not leave me, because I was created to be the container and the living display of His glory.

Part Seven

My Four Babies in Heaven

Jesus Kept My Babies

*B*eloved readers, as I am writing this chapter, my feelings are bittersweet. Bitter because I aborted four babies in my early life; sweet because they are with Jesus now. All babies, either aborted or miscarried, are in heaven now—none get lost; Jesus keeps them all. Many prophets, who have been to heaven, say that there are nurseries in heaven, filled with infants and toddlers. These babies are kept in one of the most beautiful places in heaven.

When Jesus talks about these babies, He cries with sorrowful and heart-rending tears because *God hates abortion!* As soon as these babies are aborted, Jesus keeps them in the heavenly nurseries. If their parents come to heaven, He will return the babies to them. If not, other people will adopt these babies. As I said before, the only way to heaven is by accepting Jesus Christ as Lord and Savior—*all others go to hell.*

The aborted babies actually know they are unwanted by their parents. Jesus has a tender heart toward these little souls. He arranges angels to take care of them. The angels rock them in their arms. Jesus provides the most charming nurseries (cartoon-like fairyland) for these precious ones.

On earth, we bathe babies with water, but in heaven, they are bathed by the warm glory of God. The flowers sing to them, the animals play with them, and Jesus Himself frequently visits them. He teaches these little wounded hearts to forgive their mothers for aborting them.

Knowing my four aborted babies are living in this wonderful place, my heart is comforted. I am happy for them. I am also thankful to God because my children are under such tender loving care from Jesus Himself. One day, when I get to heaven, Jesus will give them back to me. I often imagine their faces. I yearn to see what they look like. I am sure they are waiting for me too!

Naming My Babies

Through some prophets, I learned that I could actually give names to my babies. Once I do so, the angels will bring each of them to the throne room of God, and the Father Himself will announce the baby's name. Then all the angels will clap their hands to congratulate them. Hearing this news made me excited to name my babies. But before I did so, the Holy Spirit gave me a dream. In the dream, I saw a few boys and a girl. Just in case there was more than one girl, I presented four sets of names for each gender to God.

For Boys:

- Boy 1: Christopher—Christ-bearer
- Boy 2: Luka—bringer of light
- Boy 3: Justin—just, fair, righteous
- Boy 4: Sean—God is gracious

For Girls:

- Girl 1: Sonia—wisdom
- Girl 2: Camilla—young servant for the temple
- Girl 3: Nora—light, honor, compassion
- Girl 4: Emma—my God has answered, whole

On the night of January 28, 2015, after worshiping God, I presented these names to the Father. Since that day, I truly believed that all my babies received their names, and they were cheered by the angels in God's throne room. They were kissed and hugged by the Father Himself during the naming ceremony.

For a long time, I have been blaming myself for killing four babies. But after repenting my sins and being washed by the blood of the Lamb (Jesus Christ), I know my sins have been forgiven. I am forever grateful for God's mercy and love. He is exceedingly gracious, absolutely good, and infinitely merciful!

Part Eight

Spiritual Hygiene

Soul Cleansing

Beloved readers, our souls are like a computer database that stores data from birth until we die. Everything we hear, say, see, touch, act, and experience are instantly deposited into our souls. Throughout our lifespans, millions of junk data, as well as clean data, are stored in our souls. However, if we do not delete the junk data, our souls can be congested and contaminated. In order to unveil the condition of my soul, the Holy Spirit gave me the following dreams.

Dream 1: Cesspool

On my kitchen floor, there was a cesspool about one foot high. It was so stinky and disgusting; I just wanted to vomit. I was standing in the middle of this cesspool and did not know what to do with it. I then had a supernatural urge to clean it up. I started scooping out the waste one container at a time. It was awfully tough to endure the odor, but I just kept cleaning. It took me hours to get the kitchen totally clean and smelling fresh.

Through this dream, the Holy Spirit intended to tell me that my soul was filled with disgusting junk. It was flooded with filth, waste, and stench. He wanted me to clean it up. Therefore, I took a complete inventory of my life from childhood to adulthood. I listed all the people who had hurt me and needed to be forgiven. I wrote down every sexual immoral act I had committed and every evil thing I had said or done.

I threw away all the ungodly books, movies, magazines, music CDs, photos, and paintings.

Jesus said, *"Whatever you bind on earth will be bound in heaven, and whatever you loose on earth will be loosed in heaven"* (Matthew 18:18). The word "loose" means "to release" or "let go." Based on this principle, I started soul cleansing by reciting the following prayer:

"Father, in Jesus' name, I declare a decree. As an act of my will, I want to purge all followings:

- I choose to loose all ungodly things from my soul.
- I choose to loose pride, self-righteousness from my soul.
- I choose to loose adultery, sexual lust from my soul.
- I choose to loose unforgiveness, bitterness from my soul.
- I choose to loose jealousy, envy, anger from my soul.
- I choose to loose shame, guilt, self-pity from my soul.
- I choose to loose all unholy soul ties from my soul—either with other humans or my ancestors.
- I choose to loose fear, pain, trauma from my soul.
- I choose to loose rejection, abandonment from my soul.
- I choose to loose idolatry, witchcraft from my soul.
- I choose to loose gossip, judgmental from my soul.
- I choose to loose lies, doubts, deceptions from my soul.
- I choose to loose all lacking—lack of faith, love, patience, endurance, and fear of God from my soul.

I now plead the blood of Jesus to wash me clean, and wash clean of my ancestry bloodlines—all the way back to Adam and Eve."

Then I waited for a few minutes. I could feel my soul was being cleansed at that moment. I then continued:

"Father, in Jesus' name, I now ask and receive:

- The nine fruits of the Holy Spirit: *"love, joy, peace, longsuffering, kindness, goodness, faithfulness, gentleness, and self-control"* (Galatians 5:22–23).

- Your wisdom, knowledge, and understanding.
- Your grace, holiness, and glory.

I choose to bind them into my soul, in Jesus' name. Amen!"

I said the "loosing" and "binding" prayers daily for a week. In the prayer, I mentioned the names of every individual that I needed to forgive and every evil deed that I had ever done. On the first day, I literally saw *thick-black liquid* coming out of my belly area (the location of my soul). A few days later, I saw yellow liquid coming out. Near the end of the week, I only saw a few drops of light-yellow liquid coming out. By the end of the week, I did not see any liquid coming out.

The soul-cleansing technique was from God the Father. He taught prophetess Kat Kerr this method during her visit in heaven. We need to cleanse our souls frequently because things we see, hear, and say daily are instantly deposited into our souls. Just as Proverbs 4:23 says, *"Above all else, guard your heart, for everything you do flows from it"* (NIV). The Bible usually refers to "heart" as "soul." Our souls can be contaminated or in good health. It is our responsibility to take care of it daily.

Sometimes, the Holy Spirit reminds me that my soul needs to be cleansed by giving me the following kind of dream.

Dream 2: Dirty House

I live in a very large house. Strangely enough, every part of the house, such as the kitchen countertop, bedsheet, dining room table, or sofa, shows spots of black dirt here and there. These spots are noticeable and annoying.

The walls in this house are as thin as paper. I can easily poke a hole with my finger. There is a hummingbird in the house. I try to chase it outside, but the bird says, "Please let me stay. I don't want to go out. This is my house."

Through this dream, the Holy Spirit tells me that my soul is getting dirty again and needs to be cleansed. He also reveals that my knowledge of God's Word is shallow—meaning my house (spiritual life) is built with nondurable materials. It can be destroyed with the touch of a finger. He tries to tell me that I need to go deeper into God's Words by spending more time and meditating on them.

The hummingbird is the Holy Spirit who lives in my house (my body) to teach and guide me. The Bible says that my body is the temple of the Holy Spirit:

> *Don't you realize that your body is the temple of the Holy Spirit, who lives in you and was given to you by God? You do not belong to yourself, for God bought you with a high price. So you must honor God with your body.*
>
> —1 Corinthians 6:19–20 NLT

Spiritual hygiene is vitally important. If our souls are polluted, we will be the perfect targets for demons to aim toward. Unfortunately, we live in a wicked world where Satan is still the ruler. The Bible says, "*We know that we are children of God and that the world around us is under the control of the evil one*" (1 John 5:19 NLT).

Every day, we are surrounded by lying media, corrupted politicians, traitors, terrorists, satanic societies, criminals, witches, idolaters, and demonic bombardments. Therefore, we must be cautious about things that enter into our souls. Just like brushing teeth or taking showers daily, our souls also need to be *cleansed daily*.

Removing Satanic Slimes with Blood and Fire

Beloved readers, when we go to public places, such as restaurants or stores, be cautious of things we touch or sit on; they could be contaminated by satanic slimes, vomits, or urine. It sounds disgusting or bizarre, but it is real. With our natural eyes, we cannot see them. Yet many seers, whose spiritual eyes are opened, can see them.

In prophet Rick Joyner's book, *The Final Quest*, he revealed that many Christians had become prisoners of satanic armies. The demons would vomit repulsive slimes and urinate on these Christians. These disgusting vomits, urine, and slimes have names, such as "Condemnation," "Pride," "Self- Ambition," etc.[1]

We are living in this fallen world, and its ruler is still Satan. How do we get rid of these demonic slimes? As the scripture says, *"Almost everything is purified with blood"* (Hebrews 9:22 ESV). The blood here refers to the blood of Jesus. No matter how filthy the slimes are, the blood of Jesus can cleanse them all.

In addition, at the time of accepting Jesus Christ as our Lord and Savior, God imparts His fire and light in us. We can use this anointing to cleanse the satanic filths. This is what I do: before sitting on the chair of a restaurant or opening a DVD from Redbox, I put my hands on the object and say, "I cleanse this with the blood of Jesus and fire." At that very moment (in the spirit realm), fire will issue out of my hands and burn the demonic slimes on the object. I have been doing this to my clothes, bed, furniture, doorknobs, shopping cart, credit card machine, and even to my trees and flowers.

As a matter of fact, I have a myrtle tree in the backyard. It used to bloom gorgeous pink flowers. But for many years, it stopped blooming because it was infected by the white-powdery-mildew disease. Myrtle tree is known for this kind of disease. This year (2021), I have been washing it with the blood of Jesus and fire—the same way I did to other objects. Amazingly, the mildew is *completely* disappeared.

To my understanding, there are five kingdoms in both spiritual and natural realms: God's Kingdom (in heaven), mankind kingdom, animal kingdom, plant kingdom, and satanic kingdom. However, all kingdoms must bow down to the King of kings—Jesus Christ (see Philippians 2:10). Therefore, the blood of Jesus has the power to cleanse all filths no matter which kingdom they are from.

> *The authority of the name of Jesus causes every knee to bow in reverence! Everything and everyone will one day submit to this name—in the heavenly realm, in the earthly realm, and in the demonic realm. And every tongue will proclaim in every language: "Jesus Christ is Lord Yahweh."*
>
> —Philippians 2:10–11 TPT

Evicting Demons from My House

I once invited Maria, a church elder, to my house. She is a seer and a mighty woman of God. I asked her to identify any demonic spirits or objects in my house. As she walked upstairs, she heard loud screaming from the upper cabinet in the study room. After she left, I searched the cabinet and found a picture of a family relative—this person was a Freemason. Many people believe that the Freemasons, the Illuminati, and the Skull and Bones are the world's most dangerous secret societies. They are satanic organizations.

Maria also sensed the house was unusually cold even though it was summertime. I then searched and found demonic images on my living-room paintings. One is titled "Amor and Psyche." This painting portrays a fallen angel touching a naked earthly woman. The book of Genesis tells us that these fallen angels followed Lucifer and did abominable things—having sexual intercourse with women on the earth. The other painting is titled "Diana and Cupid." I discovered that Diana was the same goddess as Ishtar, Ashteroth, Inanna, Astarte, and Artemis—all were different versions of the same demon. Diana was worshiped by the Babylonians, Sumerians, Phoenicians, Canaanites, Greeks, and Romans.

I then removed the photo from the cabinet and the paintings from my living room. Amazingly, the next time Maria came to my house, she said, "The screaming from the cabinet is gone, and the house is warm now."

Another example: I once put my house on the market for sale. The real estate agent brought a family to my house, and I was at work during that time. When I came back home in the evening, as soon as I opened the door, I sensed some evil spirits in the house. I instantly realized that these spirits came in through that family. They were from another country. The majority of the country's population worships idols and demonic deities. I then opened my door and said, "I command all demonic spirits, who have intruded my house, to get out of my property now, in Jesus' name! You are not allowed to come back. This house belongs to Jesus Christ!" Amazingly, they were gone at that very moment.

Ever since, evicting demonic spirits from my house has become a daily routine, especially after someone visiting my house or I come back from outside.

Part Nine

Persecution Is Coming, Be Prepared!

God Is Preparing an Army of Martyrs

Satan, the enemy of God and humanity, will never cease his diabolical onslaughts on the citizen of the earth until he perishes in the lake of fire (hell). The most recent crime that he committed was the U.S. 2020 election. His foreign and domestic agents in America and other nations conducted the most violent voter fraud in history by stealing votes from God's chosen and anointed President Donald J. Trump.

Whenever I ask God to reveal current situations on the earth, His first word is always, "Persecution is coming. My children are not prepared." No wonder God gives prophet Sadhu Sundar Selvaraj a commission to form an army of Christian martyrs in seven nations—the United States of America is one of them.

From the first to the twenty-first century, millions of Christians were murdered for bearing witness and testimony of Jesus Christ. Apostle Paul said, *"For Christ's sake we face death all day long; we are considered as sheep to be slaughtered"* (Romans 8:36 NIV, author's paraphrase). In the last few decades, half a billion people have been persecuted for their religious beliefs worldwide. Out of which, 65 percent were Christians.

Throughout history, we have learned that Christians are the most persecuted people in the world. The Center for the Study of Global Christianity (CSGC) did in-depth historical and contemporary research on Christian martyrdom. They estimated that more than nine hundred thousand Christians were martyred per decade worldwide, equivalent to ninety thousand Christians were killed per year.[1]

The Bible clearly tells us that if we accept Jesus Christ as Lord and Savior, we will (not maybe) suffer persecution. *"In fact, everyone who wants to live a godly life in Christ Jesus will be persecuted"* (2 Timothy 3:12 NIV). Indeed, Jesus Himself warned us that persecution is unavoidable for Christians:

> [Jesus said,] I send you out as sheep in the midst of wolves. Therefore be wise as serpents and harmless as doves. But beware of men, for they will deliver you up to councils and scourge you in their synagogues.
>
> Brother will deliver up brother to death, and a father his child; and children will rise up against parents and cause them to be put to death. And You will be hated by all for My name's sake. But he who endures to the end will be saved.
>
> —Matthew 10:16–17, 21–22

People may ask, "Why should we believe Jesus if we will be persecuted?" Then I will say to you, "Your destiny will be hell if you don't believe Him." Jesus did not just ask His followers to endure persecutions; He promised a great reward—eternal life in heaven.

> [Jesus said,] Blessed are you when people insult you, persecute you and falsely say all kinds of evil against you because of me. Rejoice and be glad, because great is your reward in heaven.
>
> —Matthew 5:11–12 NIV

God is a Rewarder. He will never ask His children to suffer for His Kingdom without compensation. The New Living Translation Bible mentions *"reward"* 107 times. Most of them refer to God's reward. If an earthly father knows how to reward his children, how much more does our heavenly Father reward us? To simplify: the ultimate reward for Christ believers is eternal life in *heaven*, and the ultimate reward for the unbelievers is eternal punishment in *hell*.

Why does God need us to be martyrs in this end-time? The following scripture explains:

> [Jesus said,] I assure you and most solemnly say to you, unless a grain of wheat falls into the earth and dies, it remains alone [just one grain, never more]. But if it dies, it produces much grain and yields a harvest. The one who loves his life [eventually] loses it [through death], but the one who hates his life in this world [and is concerned with pleasing God] will keep it for life eternal.
>
> —John 12:24–25 AMP

John 12:24 tells us that in order to yield more seeds and receive a fruitful harvest, a grain of wheat must die and fall into the ground. God is calling His believers to be the seeds (martyrs), so that great harvests will follow (souls be saved). Jesus, Himself was a Seed, who died on the cross, was buried in the tomb, and resurrected into heaven. As a result, billions of human souls have been redeemed.

As a martyr, one must be willing to die as Jesus did to produce a greater soul harvest. We must consider that being a martyr for Christ is the *highest honor*. A martyr has no fear of being killed because the devil can only destroy the person's body, not the soul and spirit:

> [Jesus said,] Don't be in fear of those who can kill only the body but not your soul. Fear only God, who is able to destroy both soul and body in hell.
>
> —Matthew 10:28 TPT

We need to prepare ourselves *now* so that when the persecution comes—when the Antichrist forces us to take the *"mark of the beast"* (see Revelation 14:9), when we are imprisoned and tortured, and when we are forced to renounce Jesus Christ—we will be ready to withstand evil.

In fact, Satan and his earthly agents have already conducted a dry run for the future *"mark of the beast"* by forcing the mandatory Covid-19 vaccines. Countries like Sweden have already implemented microchip-implant into people's hands as their Covid-19 vaccine passports. This tells us that Satan is eagerly pushing the coming Antichrist. He can't wait to slaughter the citizens of the earth. The following scripture clearly tells us that whoever takes the *"mark of the beast"* will be tormented in hell forever.

> *Then another angel, . . . saying with a loud voice, "Whoever worships the beast and his image and receives the mark [of the beast] on his forehead or on his hand, he too will [have to] drink of the wine of the wrath of God, . . . and he will be tormented with fire and brimstone (flaming sulfur) . . . And the smoke of their torment ascends forever and ever; and they have no rest day and night."*
>
> —Revelation 14:9–11 AMP

When persecution or slaughter comes, we should never forsake Jesus. He laid down His life for us; shouldn't we do the same and lay down our lives for Him? Jesus said, *"Those who declare publicly that they belong to me, I will do the same for them before my Father in heaven. But those who reject me publicly, I will reject before my Father in heaven"* (Matthew 10:32–33 GNT). Let us glorify God by partaking in Christ's suffering. For it is written, *"If anyone suffers as a Christian, let him not be ashamed, but let him glorify God in this matter"* (1 Peter 4:16).

Definition of Martyr or Martyrdom

A martyr is a person who endures persecution or death willingly instead of renouncing his or her religious beliefs. The word *martyr* in Greek means *"witness"* or *"testimony."*

A Christian martyr is a person who bears witness to biblical truth. He or she refuses to forsake God and chooses to suffer death for the cause of Jesus Christ.

Martyrdom is the actual death of a martyr who has endured great persecution and suffering for the sake of the Word of God and the testimony of Jesus Christ.

Who are the persecutors? They are those who reject Jesus Christ and His salvation; those who act as agents for Satan and conduct his biddings in governments and societies; those apostasies and false prophets who forsake Christ and follow the teaching of demons; those religious leaders who carry the spirit of Antichrist. They persecute Christians in the name of their religions. They are legalistic and reject God's grace. The ultimate persecutor is Satan himself. Jesus said, *"The thief [Satan] does not come except to steal, and to kill, and to destroy"* (John 10:10).

The Martyrs Who Have Gone Before Us

Throughout human history, there have been innumerable martyrs for Jesus Christ. They lived by faith in God. They had iron spines and refused to renounce the truth. They were crucified, beaten, stoned, imprisoned, tortured, burned on stakes, sawed in half, skinned alive, stretched on wheels, torn to pieces, fed to lions, and roasted in ovens. Yet, their faith in Christ empowered them to endure these indescribable brutalities.

Others were tortured, refusing to turn from God in order to be set free. They placed their hope in a better life after the resurrection. Some were jeered at, and their backs were cut open with whips. Others were chained in prisons. Some died by stoning, some were sawed in half, and others were killed with the sword. Some went about wearing skins of sheep and goats, destitute and oppressed and mistreated. They were too good for this world, wandering over deserts and mountains, hiding in caves and holes in the ground. All these people earned a good reputation because of their faith.

—Hebrews 11:35–39 NLT

These martyrs are true heroes. Many were women and children; some were well-known, yet many were unknown. They laid down their lives for the gospel of truth and the sake of Jesus Christ. They lived in hope without receiving the fullness of what was promised to them. They are admired for their faithfulness and loyalty to the Lord.

Some Courageous Martyrs in the Bible

- Prophet Isaiah was sawed in half by order of King Manasseh for exposing the king's evil deeds and prophesying the coming of the Messiah (Christ).[2]
- Apostle James was beheaded by order of King Herod Agrippa during the intense persecution of Christian leaders.
- Bishop Antipas was martyred by roasting slowly inside a brazen bull-shaped oven at Roman Emperor Nero's order.
- Saint Matthew was slain with a halberd (a large ax-like weapon) by order of Hirtacus, King of Ethiopia.[3]
- Apostle Andrew was crucified on an X-shaped cross, known as "St. Andrew's Cross" in Greece. This type of cross causes slow death—more agonizing.[4]

- Evangelist Mark was martyred in Alexandria, Egypt. He was tied with a rope and dragged on the street to pieces. His body was cut open and shredded by the sharp stones.[5]
- Apostle Peter was crucified during the reign of Emperor Nero. He requested to be crucified upside down on the cross because he did not think that he was worthy to die in the same position as Jesus did.[6]
- Apostle Paul was beheaded in Rome. He is one of the most important disciples of Jesus Christ in the apostolic age. More than half of the New Testament was written by Paul.
- Apostle Bartholomew was executed in Armenia at the order of King Polymius's brother—Astyages. He was severely beaten and nailed to a cross upside down. His entire body was flayed—skinned alive.[7]

Beloved readers, how many human beings can endure such painful brutality? These martyrs suffered indescribable torture, yet still held on to their faith in God. They beheld a little glimpse of the glory of God and remained steadfast for Christ in times of darkness. They were indeed remarkable role models for modern-day Christians. Even the mighty angels in heaven marvel at these heroes.

Apostle Paul said:

If we live, we live for the Lord; and if we die, we die for the Lord. So, whether we live or die, we belong to the Lord.

—Romans 14:8 NIV

To me, living means living for Christ, and dying is even better.

—Philippians 1:21 NLT

I am persuaded that neither death nor life, nor angels nor principalities nor powers, nor things present nor things to come, nor height nor depth, nor any other created thing,

> *shall be able to separate us from the love of God which in Christ Jesus our Lord.*
>
> —Romans 8:38–39

Female Martyrs

Throughout history, millions of courageous martyrs have been women. They are loyal, obedient, and faithful to Jesus Christ. Here are just a few:

Agatha of Sicily—Tortured to Death

Agatha—a young virgin martyr and a Christian—was remarkable in beauty and faith in God. She was born in Catania of Sicily in AD 231. At age fifteen, she made a vow of virginity (as a bride for Jesus Christ) and refused a marriage proposal from Quintianus—the governor of Sicily. This governor thought he could force her to renounce her vow to Christ and marry him instead. Yet, his tenacious attempts were repeatedly declined.

Quintianus then changed his lust into resentment. He had Agatha arrested, raped, scourged, stretched on a rack, torn with sharp hooks, burned with red-hot irons, and rolled naked on hot coals. Despite all these hellish tortures, he could not bend her will.

Then he commanded her breasts to be brutalized and then cut off with pincers. With painful tears, the fifteen-year-old Agatha prayed to her eternal Husband (Jesus Christ), "Lord, my Creator, you have ever protected me from the cradle; you have taken me from the love of the world, and give me patience to suffer: receive now my soul." She was eventually martyred in AD 251.[8, 9]

Anne Askew—Burned on a Stake

Anne Askew was born in 1521 in Lincolnshire, England. She was a sincere follower of Jesus Christ with an iron will and tremendous courage. In May 1546, Anne was condemned for heresy during the reign of King Henry VIII of England.

She was arrested, interrogated, and forced to confess the names of her fellow Protestants, but she refused. Then she was tortured on a punishing rack—a device so inhuman that most victims would confess immediately, yet Anne did not betray her fellow Christians.

Soon her body was torn apart. Her shoulders and hips were pulled from their sockets, and her elbows and knees were dislocated. She fainted from agony. Even the tormentors refused to carry on torturing her. After she regained consciousness, she kept preaching to the tormentors about Jesus Christ.

Due to days of tremendous torture, Anne was incapable of walking at her execution. Thus, she was placed in a chair, which was fastened to a stake, and burned to death on July 16, 1546, at age twenty-five.

Just before her execution, the king offered her a pardon if she would forsake her belief. Anne refused and declared that she came not to deny her Lord and Master (Jesus Christ). While she was burning in flames, she prayed for her murderers and asked God to forgive these heartless executors.[10, 11]

Beloved readers, millions upon millions of martyrs have died for the sake of Jesus Christ and the testimony of the gospel of truth. Their dedication and love for the Lord are phenomenal.

As I am writing this chapter, I cry, because I am deeply touched by these courageous men and women who endured tremendous physical torture and mental anguish, yet still held to their faith in God. They are heroes and heroines.

Jesus never promised us that His ways would be easy, but He did assure us that following Him would be worth it. He said in Revelation 2:10, *"Be faithful until death, and I will give you the crown of life"* (Revelation 2:10 NASB).

For those who are not believers of Jesus Christ, I say to you plainly: martyrs of God will end up in heaven even though they have suffered hellish tortures, but a person who lives a happy life without accepting Jesus Christ as Lord will go to hell.

> *[Jesus said,] But cowards, unbelievers, the corrupt, murderers, the immoral, those who practice witchcraft, idol worshipers, and all liars—their fate is in the fiery lake of burning sulfur [hell].*
>
> —Revelation 21:8 NLT

My Allegiance to Be His Martyr

Once, a church elder told me, "Do not say that you will die for Jesus Christ. The enemy is listening and may take it literally." I know the demons are listening. But, if I cannot declare my allegiance to Christ publicly now, how can I be His martyr when the time comes?

In Apostle Paul's letter to the Philippians, he publicly declared, *"Christ will be magnified in my body, whether by life or by death. For to me, to live is Christ, and to die is gain"* (Philippians 1:20–21).

My heart was deeply touched by the following scripture. It painted a profound picture of a devoted bride to her Bridegroom-King:

The Shulamite:

I've made up my mind. Until the darkness disappears and the dawn has fully come, in spite of shadows and fears, I will go to the mountaintop with you—the mountain of suffering love and the hill of burning incense. Yes, I will be your bride.

—Song of Songs 4:6 TPT

"*The mountain of suffering*" refers to "Golgotha," where Jesus was crucified. As the bride of Jesus Christ, "*If I am to share his glory, I must also share his suffering*" (Romans 8:17 NLT, author's paraphrase) in order to understand His suffering love.

Philippians 3:10 also voices my heart toward the Lord, "*I want to know Christ . . . I want to suffer with him, sharing in his death*" (NLT). After reading hundreds of martyrs' stories for Christ, I wrote the following poem on November 28, 2019 (Thanksgiving) to pledge my allegiance to be God's martyr.

The Martyrs' Joy

For Christ's sake,
Many took delight in dying for Him.
With pure joy,
To partake in His suffering.
With a thankful heart,
To pour out their blood like a drink offering.

For God's Kingdom's sake,
Isaiah was sawed in half;
Antipas was roasted in an oven;
Steven was stoned to death;
Matthew was slain with a halberd;
And Philip was crucified.

For the gospel's sake,
Believers endured martyrdom.
James died by beheading;
Luke died by hanging;
Mark was dragged into pieces;
Peter was crucified upside down.

They laid down their lives for Christ,
And rejoiced in suffering.
Paul was beheaded;
Bartholomew was skinned alive;
Andrew was crucified, then sawed in half;
Matthias was stoned and beheaded.

Throughout history,
For the testimony of Jesus Christ,
Many died by burning on sticks;
Some died by merciless tortures;
Others died by stretching on racks;
Yet, still rejoicing and persevering.

Many men, women, and children
Were eaten alive by lions.
They were burned like torches as streetlights,
Imprisoned and brutalized,
Yet they did not renounce Jesus Christ,
And did not forsake their faith.

Many were killed daily.
They were considered as sheep to be slaughtered.
Were these martyrs made of steel?
Were they not afraid of being killed?
What made them retain such iron will?
What sustained them to suffer such extremes?

Because of Jesus, our Lord and Savior.
He, Himself, was scourged for our healings;
He was pierced for our transgressions;
He was crushed for our iniquities;
He was chastised for our peace;
And He was crucified for our redemption.

Jesus, our Hero,
Set the highest expectation of sacrifice.
Christ, our Warrior,
Commanded the highest calling for martyrs.
Now, it is our honor and duty,
To carry the cross and follow Him!

On this Thanksgiving night,
My greatest gift to God is my allegiance—
To be part of His army of martyrs,
To be a seed for greater soul-harvesting.
To lay down my body on His altar as a burnt offering—
A sweet-smelling aroma to God!

Happy Thanksgiving to my beloved King, Jesus,

Your little Soldier,

Ying

Stay in My Goshen

God leased Planet Earth to Adam for six thousand years. After Adam fell, Satan took over the legal right of ruling the earth from Adam. According to the Jewish calendar, we are now at 5782 years. We are living at the end of the age!

Before Jesus ascended to heaven, He revealed the signs of the end time (apocalypse) to His disciples. This end-time prophecy was documented in the Gospel of Matthew 24, Mark 13, and Luke 21. Christians also call this prophecy the *Olivet Discourse* because Jesus gave this apocalyptic revelation on the Mount of Olives.

Jesus prophesied that the human race will face great tribulations which no one has ever seen since the beginning of the world. Many will be killed. Satan will be in great wrath and persecute the citizens of the earth, for he knows his days are numbered. His eternal destiny will be the lake of fire in hell. He intends to kill as many humans as possible before he is forever doomed. He does this to hurt the heart of the Father.

During the great tribulation period (the last three and half years of earth's time), the citizens of the earth will face the utmost suffering. No man can escape from this horrible time. Christ believers will face tremendous onslaughts like never before. Prelude to the great tribulation, death will come to one-fourth of the earth—just as Apostle John described in the book of Revelation:

> *I looked up and saw a horse whose color was pale green. Its rider was named Death, and his companion was the Grave. These two were given authority over one-fourth of the earth, to kill with the sword and famine and disease and wild animals.*
>
> —Revelation 6:8 NLT

Many Christians believe that Jesus will take all the believers out of the earth (called *the rapture*, see 1 Thessalonians 4:16) before the great tribulation. This is not so. The Lord told some trusted prophets, such as Sadhu Sundar Selvaraj, that we will have to go through the great tribulation. Regardless of when the rapture occurs, the earth (now) is more dangerous than ever before. However, there is only one place where we can find refuge: *God's Goshen!*

> *The Lord Himself will come down from heaven with a shout of command, with the voice of the archangel and with the [blast of the] trumpet of God, and the dead in Christ will rise first. Then we who are alive and remain [on the earth] will simultaneously be caught up (raptured) together with them [the resurrected ones] in the clouds to meet the Lord in the air, and so we will always be with the Lord!*
>
> —1 Thessalonians 4:16-17 AMP

The Bible tells us that God always protects His own people during perilous times. In the book of Exodus, God put ten horrific plagues on Pharaoh and the Egyptians. These plagues caused great anguish and death because Pharaoh refused to let the children of Israel go. But none of the Israelites, who lived in the land of Goshen, were touched by these ten plagues (see Exodus 9:24). The Bible says, *"Goshen is the best of the land of Egypt"* (Genesis 45:18, author's paraphrase). Goshen is also our *spiritual sanctuary* in this end time.

> *There was hail, and fire mingled with the hail, so very heavy that there was none like it in all the land of Egypt since it became a nation. And the hail struck throughout the whole land of Egypt, all that was in the field, both man and beast; and the hail struck every herb of the field and broke every tree of the field. Only in the land of Goshen, where the children of Israel were, there was no hail.*
>
> —Exodus 9:24–26

Jesus has been expressing His concerns regarding church people's lukewarmness and complacency. He has been warning us that no one is immune from the impending judgment and tribulation—earthquakes, famines, natural disasters, pandemics, and wars. These calamities are happening throughout the world where God has been rejected and blasphemed. He wants the Christians to know that we will face the same judgment coming to the wicked people if we do not stay in His Goshen.

Jesus is calling us to surrender to Him *completely* and *obey* His commandments faithfully! Otherwise, He cannot protect us during times of distress. The Goshen Jesus refers to is the spiritual safe haven—it is God's presence and glory. He is urging us to hide in His presence. As long as we are in His shield of glory, no viruses, plagues, catastrophes, and demonic attacks can touch us—just as King David said in the following scripture:

> Even though I walk through the valley of the shadow of death, I will fear no evil, for you [the Lord] are with me.
>
> —Psalm 23:4 ESV

Presently, the whole earth is experiencing great upheaval and wickedness—socialism, globalism, cabals, secret societies, and demonic attacks. Our planet is drenched with innocent blood—child sacrifice, abortion, pedophilia, sex trafficking, organ harvesting, spirit cooking, man-made pandemics, and biochemical weapons.

The very air we breathe is polluted by lies and curses from the wicked media, witches, and politicians. Many people reject Jesus and worship Satan. These people are heading for hell without realization. *"A shepherd called 'Death' [Satan] herds them, leading them straight to hell like mindless sheep"* (Psalm 49:14 TPT).

Injustice, corruption, idolatry, and murder are everywhere as if hell breaks loose. Yet, this is just the beginning of the birth pains. In fact, Jesus had already warned us about these end-time calamities:

> [Jesus said,] Nations will go to war against nations and kingdoms against kingdoms. And there will be terrible earthquakes, horrible epidemics, and famines in place after place. This is how the birth pains of the new age will begin!
>
> —Matthew 24:7–8 TPT

Beloved readers, remember Goshen! History will repeat itself. As long as we live in God's Goshen and stay under the shadow of the Almighty, we will be safe. He is a faithful God and He will protect us—just as Jesus said to the church of Philadelphia:

> *Because you have kept the word of My endurance [My command to persevere], I will keep you [safe] from the hour of trial, that hour which is about to come on the whole [inhabited] world, to test those who live on the earth.*
>
> —Revelation 3:10 AMP

How do we stay in God's Goshen? What does He require of us? The following scripture provides the key instruction:

> *What does the Lord your God require of you? He requires only that you fear the Lord your God, and live in a way that pleases him, and love him and serve him with all your heart and soul.*
>
> —Deuteronomy 10:12 NLT

Therefore, we must stay in God's Goshen by:

- Intimately fellowship with Him.
- Diligently wait on Him in the secret place.
- Repent of our sins and forgive others.
- Love Him with all our hearts, souls, and minds.
- Fear Him for His awesomeness as well as His severity.
- Walk in all His ways.
- Obey His commandments and perform them.
- Serve Him wholeheartedly as bondservants.
- Be innocent, pure-heart, humble, and holy.
- Preach the gospel, heal the sick, and cast out demons.
- Endure trials and tribulations patiently.
- Above all, show love—the greatest commandment.

Beloved children of God, our Father in heaven is waiting for us to humble ourselves and repent, just like He sent the prophet Jonah to prophesy the destruction of Nineveh (present-day northern Iraq) in 760 BC. When God's judgment was announced to the citizens of Nineveh, from the great king to the ordinary people, all repented. Only then, God spared the lives of 120,000 people. Our God always chooses mercy over judgment—as He said in the following scripture:

> *If My people who are called by My name will humble themselves, and pray and seek My face, and turn from their wicked ways, then I will hear from heaven, and will forgive their sin and heal their land.*
>
> —2 Chronicles 7:14

Message from Jesus to the Readers

Beloved readers, on January 31, 2020, the Lord gave me the following message. I think He wants me to share it at the end of this book. Whatever He says, He says from His sincere heart and urgent warning.

Jesus said:

> "Tell My children that My hands are not too short to help them. I am reaching out to those who are depressed, oppressed, worried, and fearful. Just as I delivered My servant Ying, I will do the same for you. Listen to Ying's testimony, and you will find hope, *for I am your hope!* Call upon My name, and I will come by your side and deliver you.
>
> "I will not tolerate the enemy any longer. Watch what My Spirit will do. Be encouraged and do not give up. Be an overcomer! Your reward is with Me for all who do not give up and overcome during this season of fierce darkness. My light is much greater, so seek My light, and you will be safe.
>
> "My heart is for all those who are lost. My blood was shed for all My children. Accept My salvation, and do not miss the chance. *I am coming soon!*"

Behold, I (Jesus) am coming quickly, and My reward is with Me, to give to each one according to the merit of his deeds (earthly works, faithfulness). I am the Alpha and the Omega, the First and the Last, the Beginning and the End [the Eternal One].

—Revelation 22:12–13 AMP

Beloved readers, I implore you—children of God, to *run to Jesus now!* Receive Him as your Lord and Savior, acknowledge Him as your eternal God, forsake all idols and unbelief, then you will have everlasting life in heaven when you depart from the earth!

Acceptance Prayer

If you are ready to receive Jesus Christ as your Lord and Savior, please recite the following prayer out loud:

Dear Heavenly Father:

Today, I come before you, in Jesus' name. I acknowledge that I am a sinner, and I am sorry for my sins. I ask You to forgive all sins, transgressions, and iniquities I have ever committed.

I believe Jesus Christ is the Son of God, who came in the flesh, shed His blood, and died on the cross to redeem my sins. After three days, He rose from the grave and is now seated at the right hand of the Father in heaven.

Right now, I renounce Satan and all his works in my life. I invite Jesus to be my Lord, Savior, and God, now and forever.

I ask Lord Jesus to baptize me with the Holy Spirit, so that He can dwell in me and guide me into all truth.

Amen!

Thank You, Father.

Afterword

My beloved readers:

I am an eight-year-old baby Christian. My knowledge of God and His Words (Bible) is still at the infancy stage. Nevertheless, I consider myself a blessed child because the Holy Spirit has allowed me to access God's heart at the beginning of my spiritual journey. Encountering the Father, Jesus, and the Holy Spirit has initiated a unique path for me as a baby Christian.

I have never written a book before, and English is my second language. So, please pardon my linguistic limitation. My purpose is not about writing perfect literature or polished vocabularies. It is about sharing my heartfelt stories.

My hope is that even if one reader receives God's grace by making Jesus Christ as Lord and Savior after reading this book, my work is worthwhile. I am sending God's love to your heart and hoping you too will fall in love with Jesus Christ.

The End

NOTES

Part One: Tragic Childhood and Rebellious Adulthood

1. Wikipedia, "Cultural Revolution," The Free Encyclopedia, February 3, 2022, https://en.wikipedia.org/wiki/Cultural_Revolution#:~:text=The%20Cultural%20Revolution%20was%20characterized,in%20China%20by%20death%20toll (accessed February 5, 2022).

Part Two: Spiritual Exploration

1. Centers for Disease Control and Prevention, "Suicide is a large and growing public health problem," CDC, August 30, 2021, https://www.cdc.gov/suicide/facts/ (accessed February 4, 2022).

Part Three: The Enemy of God

1. Karl Hille, "Hubble Reveals Observable Universe Contains 10 Times More Galaxies Than Previously Thought," National Aeronautics and Space Administration (NASA), August 6, 2017, https://www.nasa.gov/feature/goddard/2016/hubble-reveals-observable-universe-contains-10-times-more-galaxies-than-previously-thought (accessed February 5, 2022).

2. Wikipedia, "Observable universe," February 5, 2022, https://en.wikipedia.org/wiki/Observable_universe#:~:text=The%20observable%20universe%20is%20thus,8.8%C3%971026%20m (accessed February 5, 2022).

3. NASA Goddard Space Flight Center, "The Earth: Distance Information," National Aeronautics and Space Administration (NASA), October 22, 2020, https://imagine.gsfc.nasa.gov/features/cosmic/earth_info.html#:~:text=The%20diameter%20of%20the%20Earth,is%2012%2C756%20kilometers%20(km) (accessed February 5, 2022).

4. Brian Jackson, "How many stars are there in space?" The Conversation, September 20, 2021, https://theconversation.com/how-many-stars-are-there-in-space-165370#:~:text=An%20incredible%20number&text=Now%20the%20next%20step.,trillion%20stars%20in%20the%20universe (accessed February 5, 2022).

5. Joseph B. Lumpkin, *The Books of Enoch* (Blountsville, AL: Fifth Estate, 2011), 39.

6. Maurice Sklar, "Jeffrey Epstein in Hell," Facebook, August 11, 2019, https://www.facebook.com/mauricesklar/posts/10221060037474881 (accessed February 4, 2022).

7. The Gathering Place, "Maurice Sklar: The Message–The Gathering Place–Burbank," YouTube, March 3, 2019, https://www.youtube.com/watch?v=O0iuPgdKxKk (accessed February 4, 2022).

8. Rick Joyner, *The Final Quest* (Fort Mill, SC: MorningStar Publications, 1996), 21, 25–27.

9. Charles H. Kraft, *Deep Wounds Deep Healing* (Bloomington,

MN: Chosen, 1993), 212.

10. Theglorychannel, "Bob Jones died—God sent him back from heaven's door–1," YouTube, https://www.youtube.com/watch?v=3MRJ3wA5neU&t=413s (accessed February 4, 2022).

11. CDC, "Featured Topic: World Health Organization's (WHO) Report on Preventing Suicide," August 15, 2016, https://www.cdc.gov/violenceprevention/suicide/WHO-report.html (accessed February 4, 2022).

12. Sklar, "A Vision of the Courtroom of Heaven," Maurice Sklar Ministries, January 16, 2019, https://sklarministries.com/teaching/f/a-vision-of-the-courtroom-of-heaven---maurice-sklar (accessed February 4, 2022).

13. PragerU, "The Candace Owens Show: Tim Ballard," YouTube, February 2, 2020, https://www.youtube.com/watch?v=OhjkqLhbgu8 (accessed February 4, 2022).

14. International Labour Organization, "ILO says forced labour generates annual profits of US$ 150 billion," ILO, May 20, 2014, https://www.ilo.org/global/about-the-ilo/newsroom/news/WCMS_243201/lang--en/index.htm (accessed February 4, 2022).

15. Wikipedia, "Virginia Hall," The Free Encyclopedia, December 23, 2021, https://en.wikipedia.org/wiki/Virginia_Hall (accessed February 4, 2022).

16. Sadhu Sundar Selvaraj, "First Information Prophecy I Europe I Rise of the Beast," YouTube, January 1, 2019,

https://www.youtube.com/watch?v=6VM8pCo_u80 (accessed February 4, 2022).

Part Four: Unique Journey with Jesus Christ

1. Joyner, *The Call* (Fort Mill, SC: MorningStar Publications, 2015), 27–28.

2. James Strong, "Worship—Proskuneō," King James Bible Dictionary, 1890, https://kingjamesbibledictionary.com/StrongsNo/G4352/worship (accessed February 4, 2022).

3. Jonathan Cahn, "How to worship God with authentic praise, KISSING GOD, The Book of Mysteries," YouTube, July 27, 2019, https://www.youtube.com/watch?v=M7BVEiEEO3E (accessed February 4, 2022).

4. Brian Simmons, *The Book of Genesis* (Savage, MN: BroadStreet Publishing Group, LLC, 2019), 12.

5. Theglorychannel, "Bob Jones died," YouTube.

6. Joyner, *The Final Quest*, 181–184.

7. Joyner, *The Final Quest*, 21, 23, 25–26.

Part Five: Meeting My Heavenly Father

1. Joyner, *The Final Quest*, 49–50.

2. Justin Paul Abraham, "Wendy Alec + Justin Paul Abraham, Love Wins," YouTube, November 15, 2017, https://www.youtube.com/watch?v=7Q756_oEaUg (accessed February 4, 2022).

3. Joyner, *The Final Quest*, 67–68.

Part Six: Holy Spirit—My Dance Partner

1. Joyner, *The Call*, 27–28.

Part Eight: Spiritual Hygiene

1. Joyner, *The Final Quest*, 26–27.

Part Nine: Persecution Is Coming, Be Prepared!

1. Samuel Smith, "Over 900,000 Christians Martyred for Their Faith in Last 10 Years: Report," The Christian Post, January 16, 2017, https://www.christianpost.com/news/over-900000-christians-martyred-for-their-faith-in-last-10-years-report-173045/ (accessed February 4, 2022).

2. R. H. Charles, "The Apocrypha and Pseudepigrapha of the Old Testament—The Martyrdom of Isaiah," Oxford: Clarendon Press, 1913, https://www.ccel.org/c/charles/otpseudepig/martisah.htm (accessed February 4, 2022).

3. John Foxe, "The Project Gutenberg EBook of Fox's Book of Martyrs, Chapter I:IV—Matthew," www.gutenberg.org, August 25, 2007, https://www.gutenberg.org/files/22400/22400-h/22400-h.htm (accessed February 4, 2022).

4. Mark Water, *The New Encyclopedia of Christian Martyrs* (Grand Rapids, MI: Baker Books, 2001), 24.

5. "Miracle surrounding the death of St Mark," BibleProbe,

http://www.bibleprobe.com/stmark.htm (accessed February 4, 2022).

6. Water, *The New Encyclopedia of Christian Martyrs*, 31.

7. Dc Talk and The Voice of the Martyrs, *Jesus Freaks* (Bloomington, MN: Bethany House Publishers, 1999), 205.

8. Water, *The New Encyclopedia of Christian Martyrs*, 203.

9. Wikipedia, "Agatha of Sicily," November 1, 2021, https://en.wikipedia.org/wiki/Agatha_of_Sicily (accessed February 4, 2022).

10. Dc Talk, *Jesus Freaks*, 83.

11. Wikipedia, "Anne Askew," November 10, 2021, https://en.wikipedia.org/wiki/Anne_Askew (accessed February 4, 2022).